Microsoft® Office Live For Dummies®

D0351615

Picking an Office Live Flavor

Product Comparison	Basics	Essentials	Premium
E-Mail			
User e-mail accounts	25 accounts	50 accounts	50 accounts
E-mail storage space per account	2GB	2GB	2GB
Web Site Features			
Domain-name registration	Yes	Yes	Yes
Web-site storage space	500MB	1GB	2GB
Bandwidth	10GB	15GB	20GB
Web Site Designer software	Yes	Yes	Yes
Upload existing Web site	No	Yes	Yes
Use HTML/Web-design software	No	Yes	Yes
Advanced Web site reports	Yes	Yes	Yes
adManager	Yes	Yes	Yes
Basic Applications			
Office Live Mail	Yes	Yes	Yes
E-Mail Address Book	Yes	Yes	Yes
Personal Calendar	Yes	Yes	Yes
Business Applications			
Business Contact Manager	No	Yes	Yes
Workspaces	No	Yes	Yes
Time Manager	No	No	Yes
Project Manager	No	No	Yes
Document Manager	No	No	Yes
Sales	No	No	Yes

(continued)

Microsoft® Office Live
For Dummies®

(continued)

Product Comparison	Basics	Essentials	Premium
Company Administration	No	No	Yes
Application storage space	N/A	500MB	1GB
Users of business applications or workspaces	N/A	10	20
Software Integration			
Office Accounting Express 2007	Yes	Yes	Yes
Outlook	No	Yes	Yes
Support Options			
Online Help	Yes	Yes	Yes
E-mail	Yes	Yes	Yes
Toll-free phone	No	Yes	Yes
Monthly fee	FREE	$19.95	$39.95

Adding Options to Your Flavor

Option	Increment
Domain names	As many as you need
E-mail accounts	Bundles of five
Web site storage	100MB increments
Shared sites and business applications storage	100MB increments
Shared site users	Bundles of five
Bandwidth	24GB increments

*Check the Office Live Web site (*www.officelive.com*) for details about pricing.*

For Dummies: Bestselling Book Series for Beginners

Microsoft® Office Live

FOR

DUMMIES®

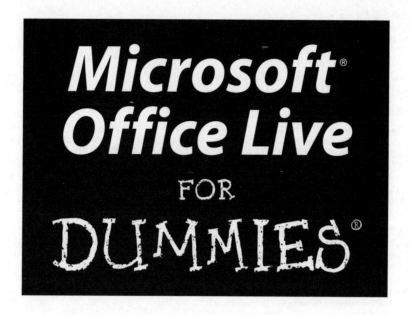

Microsoft® Office Live

FOR

DUMMIES®

by Karen S. Fredricks

BICENTENNIAL
1807
WILEY
2007
BICENTENNIAL

Wiley Publishing, Inc.

Microsoft® Office Live For Dummies®

Published by
Wiley Publishing, Inc.
111 River Street
Hoboken, NJ 07030-5774

www.wiley.com

Copyright © 2007 by Wiley Publishing, Inc., Indianapolis, Indiana

Published by Wiley Publishing, Inc., Indianapolis, Indiana

Published simultaneously in Canada

For general information on our other products and services, please contact our Customer Care Department within the U.S. at 800-762-2974, outside the U.S. at 317-572-3993, or fax 317-572-4002.

For technical support, please visit www.wiley.com/techsupport.

Wiley also publishes its books in a variety of electronic formats. Some content that appears in print may not be available in electronic books.

Library of Congress Control Number: 2007926377

ISBN: 978-0-470-11658-6

Manufactured in the United States of America

10 9 8 7 6 5 4 3 2 1

WILEY

About the Author

Karen S. Fredricks began her life rather non-technically growing up in Kenya. She attended high school in Beirut, Lebanon, where she developed her sense of humor while dodging bombs. After traveling all over the world, Karen ended up at the University of Florida and has been an ardent Gator fan ever since. In addition to undergraduate studies in English, Theater and Accounting, Karen has a Master's degree in Psycholinguistics. Beginning her career teaching high school English and theatre, Karen switched to working with the PC during its inception in the early '80s and has worked as a full-time computer consultant and trainer ever since.

Karen is an ACT! Certified Consultant, an ACT! Premier Trainer, a Microsoft Office User Specialist, and a QuickBooks Pro Certified Advisor. She is the author of four *For Dummies* books on ACT! In addition, she has co-written *Outlook 2007 Business Contact Manager For Dummies* and *Outlook 2007 All-in-One Desk Reference For Dummies*. A true fan of the Dummies series, she helped organize The Authors Unconference, the first ever gathering of *For Dummies* authors.

Karen resides in Boca Raton, Florida. Her company, Tech Benders, specializes in contact management and CRM software, and provides computer consulting, support, and training services. She is also a regular guest on several syndicated computer radio talk shows. In her spare time, Karen loves to spend time with family and friends, play tennis, workout, road bike, and write schlocky poetry.

Karen loves to hear from her readers. Feel free to send her your comments about the book to www.dummies@techbenders.com or visit her Web site www.techbenders.com to learn more about the products listed in this book.

Dedication

I dedicate this book to Gary Kahn. As the person in my life who put up with me as I wrote four books in less than a year he deserves a dedication, combat pay, and the Medal of Honor!

Author's Acknowledgments

This is my seventh book for Wiley Publishing and as usual they have made writing this book a pleasure! Thanks go out to Greg Croy, my Acquisitions Editor and Rebecca Senninger, my Project Editor. This is the third book I've worked on with each of them; as usual, they were great to work with! Barry Childs-Helton, the Copy Editor, had the unenviable task of making me look good; his edits were always right on! Technical Editor Kim Winton's sharp eye helped to spot all the changes between the Beta and final versions of Office Live.

Rich Tennant is the coolest cartoonist ever. I am astounded by the thought, research and time that he devotes to every one of his cartoons. I'm not sure which is funnier — his cartoons — or his stories about creating his cartoons!

The most important acknowledgment of all goes out to all of the readers of the *For Dummies* series, and more specifically the readers of this book. I hope you'll enjoy *reading* this book as much as I enjoyed *writing* it!

Publisher's Acknowledgments

We're proud of this book; please send us your comments through our online registration form located at www.dummies.com/register/.

Some of the people who helped bring this book to market include the following:

Acquisitions, Editorial, and Media Development

Project Editor: Rebecca Senninger

Executive Editor: Greg Croy

Senior Copy Editor: Barry Childs-Helton

Technical Editor: Kim Winton

Editorial Manager: Leah Cameron

Editorial Assistant: Amanda Foxworth

Sr. Editorial Assistant: Cherie Case

Cartoons: Rich Tennant
   (www.the5thwave.com)

Composition Services

Project Coordinator: Heather Kolter

Layout and Graphics: Stacie Brooks, Carl Byers, Joyce Haughey, Barbara Moore, Laura Pence, Heather Ryan, Alicia B. South

Proofreaders: Aptara, Jessica Kramer

Indexer: Aptara

Anniversary Logo Design: Richard Pacifico

Publishing and Editorial for Technology Dummies

   Richard Swadley, Vice President and Executive Group Publisher

   Andy Cummings, Vice President and Publisher

 Mary Bednarek, Executive Acquisitions Director

   Mary C. Corder, Editorial Director

Publishing for Consumer Dummies

   Diane Graves Steele, Vice President and Publisher

   Joyce Pepple, Acquisitions Director

Composition Services

   Gerry Fahey, Vice President of Production Services

   Debbie Stailey, Director of Composition Services

Contents at a Glance

Table of Contents

Introduction

• •

*O*ffice Live is Microsoft's first true foray into Software as a Service (SaaS). And who knows what features are going to be added or modified over the course of the next several years? The cool thing is that you'll be able to grow right along with Office Live because you'll be receiving those changes immediately — without having to invest more money in upgrading. And because Microsoft is banking that many people are willing to give Office Live a try, you get a deal that you basically can't refuse.

The other exciting facet of Office Live is the capability to share your data online without having to fork over thousands of dollars for hardware, software, and IT consultants. Just sign on the dotted line, and your employees and customers have immediate online access to the information you want them to have. For many businesses, having the company data online represents a whole new way of doing business. Remote workers can access information from a variety of locations rather than having to waste time driving to the office. Road warriors find traveling a bit easier, knowing that they can get to the needed data anywhere, at any time.

There's another reason for excitement as well. The Office Live feature set is designed to save you time and help make you more efficient in the bargain. Accomplishing more in less time is an exciting thought — it allows you to quit work earlier. With Office Live it's easy to get up and running in a very short time. You'll be amazed not only at how easily you can set up a business but also at how quickly you can get back to work rather than spending time tinkering on your computer.

About This Book

Office Live For Dummies is a reference book. As such, you can read each chapter independently and in the order you want. Each chapter focuses on a specific topic, so you can dive right in, heading straight for the chapter that interests you most. Having said that, however, I've put the chapters in a logical sequence; if you're new to Office Live, you can just follow from chapter to chapter. If you're more experienced with Office Live, use the Table of Contents and the index to navigate from topic to topic as needed.

Essentially, this book is a nuts-and-bolts how-to guide for accomplishing various tasks. However, I also draw on many of my own experiences as a full-time consultant — and provide include specific situations that should give you a feeling for the full power of Office Live.

Conventions Used in This Book

As with most Windows-based software programs, you often have several different ways to accomplish a task in Office Live.

For the most part, I show you ways to perform a function by using the Office Live menus. When an instruction reads Choose File⇨Open, you access the File menu (located at the top of the Office Live screen) by clicking it with the left mouse button and then choosing the Open option from the subsequent menu that appears. In most cases, you can access these commands from anywhere within Office Live, although I generally advise new users to always start a task from the home page, which is the first page you see when Office Live opens. If you must be in a particular area to complete a task, I tell you where you need to go.

I also present you with keyboard shortcuts here and there. Generally, Office Live shortcuts are triggered by simultaneously pressing the Alt key and another key on the keyboard.

When you need to access a hidden menu, click an appropriate area of the screen with the right mouse button and then choose from the contextual menu that appears. In these instances, I'll simply say *right-click* when you need to right-click.

What You Should Read

Of course, I *hope* you're going to sit down and read this entire book from cover to cover. But then again, this book isn't The Great American Novel. And, come to think of it, the whole reason why you bought this book in the first place is to get organized as quickly as possible because you're probably finding yourself with too much to do and too little time in which to do it.

For the time being, I'm going to let you get away with reading just the parts that interest you most. I'll let you read the last chapter first and the first chapter last if you like because this book is designed to allow you to read each chapter independently. However, when you find yourself floating in a swimming pool, soaking up the sun, and wondering what to do with all your spare time, you might want to go back and read some of those chapters you skipped. You just might discover something!

What You Don't Have to Read

This book is intended for both new and existing computer users. Most of the instructions apply to both groups of readers. Once in a while, I include some information that might be of special interest to more advanced readers. Newbies, feel free to skip these sections! Also, any information tagged with a Technical Stuff icon is there for the truly technically inclined; everyone else can just skip that info.

Foolish Assumptions

One of our least favorite words in the English language is the word *assume*, but I've got to admit that I've made a few foolish — albeit necessary — assumptions when writing this book. First of all, I assume you own a Windows-based computer — and that Internet Explorer is installed on it. Secondly, I assume you have a basic knowledge of how to use your computer, keyboard, and mouse, and that Office Live isn't the very first application you're trying to master.

I'm also going to assume that you have a high-speed Internet connection; you won't be able to use Office Live without Internet connectivity. And, although you can probably get away with using a dial-up connection, its speed will probably be too slow to be practical.

I assume you have a genuine desire to organize your personal life or business, and are intrigued by all that Office Live has to offer.

Finally (and I feel quite comfortable with this assumption), I assume you'll grow to love the whole concept of Office Live as much as I do!

How This Book Is Organized

I organized this book in five parts. Here's a brief description of each part, with chapter references directing you where to go for particular information:

Part I: Discovering This Thing Called Office Live

In Part I, you get an introduction to the concept SaaS (Software as a Service) and why Office Live is such a popular choice for computer users (Chapter 1). In this part, you also read about the three flavors of Office Live (Chapter 2) and how to sign up and start using the service (Chapter 3).

Part II: Getting Down to Basics with Office Live Basics

As its name implies, Part II focuses on the basics — including using e-mail (Chapter 4) and creating a Web site (Chapters 5). I even show you how to gauge the success of your site by using Site Reports (Chapter 6).

You also find out how to organize your day through the use of the Office Live calendar (Chapter 7).

Part III: Adding a Few Essentials

When you add Essentials into the mix, you get an online version of Business Contact Manager (Chapter 8) to help you keep track of your contacts. You also add the ability to set up Shared Sites that can be accessed by your employees and/or your customers (Chapter 9). If you travel a lot, check this out: You can synch Office Live to Outlook or your PDA (Chapter 10).

If you have a new business — or have been trying to conduct your business without the assistance of accounting software — you discover how to use Office Accounting Express 2007 with Office Live (Chapter 11).

Part IV: Getting Premium Service

A product name like "Premium" leads you to expect a lot — and Office Live doesn't disappoint. Chapter 12 shows you how to work with the different business applications that come with Office Live. You can keep a company calendar and schedule resources with Time Manager (Chapter 13). You can manage major projects and share the data with both your employees and customers (Chapter 14). You find out how Office Live takes you through every step of the sales process — from designing a marketing campaign and distributing collateral to creating estimates and taking orders (Chapter 15). You have a whole arsenal of human-resources tools at your disposal (Chapter 16) and have a bird's eye view of the state of your entire business (Chapter 17).

Part V: The Part of Tens

With apologies to David Letterman, Part V gives you three of my Top Ten Office Live lists. If you have a business — or are considering starting one — I list some ways that using Office Live can help grow your business (Chapter 18). I move on to a list of the types of people I think can most benefit from Office Live (Chapter 19). Finally, I give you a closer look at the whole idea behind Office Live: Software as a Service (Chapter 20).

Icons Used in This Book

A Tip icon indicates a special time-saving tip or a related thought that might help you use Office Live to its full advantage. Try it — you might like it!

This icon alerts you to the danger of proceeding without caution. *Do not* attempt to try doing anything that you are warned not to do!

These icons alert you to important pieces of information that you don't want to forget.

A Technical Stuff icon indicates tidbits of advanced knowledge that might be of interest to IT specialists but might just bore the heck out of the average reader. Skip these at will.

Where to Go from Here

If you've already dabbled a bit in Office Live, you might want to at least skim the entire contents of this book before hunkering down to read the sections that seem the most relevant to you. Office Live has a lot to offer — and you might have missed some of its functionality along the way!

For the Office Live newbie, I recommend heading straight for Part I, where you can acquaint yourself with Office Live before moving on to other parts of the book and the Office Live program.

Part I
Discovering this Thing Called Office Live

The 5th Wave   By Rich Tennant

©RICHTENNANT

"Well, the first level of Office Live security seems good—I can't get the shrink-wrapping off."

In this part . . .

I know you're excited about all the possibilities that Office Live has to offer, and want to dive into the program as soon as possible. Here's where you find an overview of some of the cool features you find in Office Live. You become familiar with the concept of Software as a Service. Then, like a little kid in the ice cream shop, you get to pick your favorite flavor of Office Live. After you have those basic concepts down, you go on a whirlwind tour designed to getting you up and running on Office Live in a jiffy.

Chapter 1

Who Moved My Shrinkwrap?

*P*robably the most confusing thing about Office Live is the whole concept of what Office Live is — and isn't. You probably have a lot of questions, not only about how to use the software, but also what exactly the software does.

Office Live is both brand new software and a brand new technology. In this chapter, you find out about *Software as a Service* (SaaS) technology, who's paying for it, and how secure the system really is. You also find out a bit about a few of the underlying concepts of Office Live. Finally, you discover where to turn for help should the need arise.

Getting SaaSy with SaaS

It's important to know the correct terminology for discussing software — especially when attending cocktail parties and other social gatherings. If you look for Office Live at your local computer store you won't find it. That's because Office Live is not *software* in the traditional sense; there's no shrinkwrap to wrestle with and no CD to install. Office Live is a *service* — hence the name *Software as a Service.*

I can hear some of you saying, "Ah, got it. This is like AOL." The answer to that is a definitive "kind of." Services such as AOL allow you to connect to the Internet, surf the Web, and send some e-mail. Office Live on the other hand includes real live *applications* that you can use to increase your productivity in both your home and office life.

The other huge benefit of SaaS is that you can share your data with other people in other locations. For example, a Little League coach can share the team's schedule and roster with the rest of the team, or a project manager can assign tasks to other members of the company's project team.

A Rose Is a Rose Is an Office Live

If you have children, you know that one of the hardest things to do is to give them names. You can take the road frequently traveled and call them *Jennifer* and *Jason*. You can take the road less frequently traveled and call them *Apple* or *Dweezil*. You can even name a son — or in George Foreman's case *five* sons — after his father.

Apparently Microsoft had a similar struggle with naming its new baby. Office Live must have seemed like a great idea at the time but unfortunately it sounds alarmingly close to several other popular Microsoft products.

Do not confuse Office Live with the following:

- ✔ **Microsoft Office:** Office is a suite of software that contains goodies such as Word, Excel, and Outlook. Office Live is most definitely *not* an online version of Office.

- ✔ **Microsoft's Live Search engine:** Microsoft recently launched a new search engine found at `www.live.com`. Live has nothing to do with Office Live (other than the fact that they sound so darn similar!).

- ✔ **Office Online:** Microsoft has a Web site that allows you to find out all kinds of neat information about the Microsoft Office products. And to make matters even more confusing, it has a direct link to Office Live.

You'll probably never know for sure whether this naming overlap was intentional or simply an oversight by some befuddled project manager who will spend the rest of his days exiled in Siberia. However, don't be surprised if you frequently land in the wrong portion of cyberspace!

So what exactly is Microsoft Office Live?

Probably the hardest thing you'll have to do with Office Live is to explain exactly what it is. Microsoft Office Live provides your company with a free domain name, Web site, and e-mail accounts. Additionally, Office Live offers several business-management applications — for example, tools for managing customers, projects, and documents. Office Live throws in the capability to create an *intranet* where you and your closest friends or enemies can work together and share information online.

Office Live comes in three sizes — small, medium, and large — although Microsoft calls them Basics, Essentials, and Premium. The bigger the size, the more features you'll have.

Personally, I suggest you begin by explaining Office Live using very politically correct terminology. The following is an example:

- ✔ You might consider Office Live to be a *contact manager* because it allows you to keep track of all of your contacts.
- ✔ Office Live is a *scheduler* because it allows multiple people to access the same calendar.
- ✔ Office Live is a *service* because you can only use it while connected to the Internet.
- ✔ Office Live is an *application suite* because it includes several applications or programs that help you organize your business.
- ✔ Office Live is an *application developer* because it helps you develop and maintain a Web site.
- ✔ Office Live is a *hosting service* because it not only hosts your Web site, it also hosts documents and other information that can be shared by your multiple partners-in-crime.

If your friends continue to look at you rather blankly, at least you have established that your knowledge of computing is equal to — if not greater than — theirs. At that point, you may wish to start listing some of the wonderful features of Office Live.

What does Office Live do?

Although Office Live does not offer the Microsoft Office suite as a part of this online offering, it does offer many of the tools that a business needs — at a fraction of the price you'd usually pay for them. Besides allowing you to have more free time — which means you have more play time — Office Live delivers a nice little shopping list of features you might want to show your friends as you sit poolside sipping your margarita:

- ✔ A company domain name, hosts it for free, and helps you to market it.
- ✔ At least twenty-five company e-mail addresses so you can say good-bye to your unprofessional Hotmail, Google, Yahoo!, and AOL monikers.
- ✔ A password protected private Web site (an *intranet*) for sharing information with key contacts, and over 20 Internet-based applications that can help you automate common business tasks such as contacts, projects, and document management.

- ✔ Integrates with popular Microsoft products like Microsoft Office Outlook, Excel, and Word.

- ✔ Links to a free version of Office Accounting 2007, which allows you to set up an online shopping cart.

- ✔ Stores complete contact, account, and opportunity information including name, company, phone numbers, addresses, and e-mail addresses.

- ✔ Allows you to record histories about your contacts, accounts, and opportunities. This is particularly useful for those of us who suffer from Senior Moment Syndrome.

- ✔ Provides a calendar that you can view in a daily, weekly, or monthly format. You can view a personal or company calendar. You can customize it. And, most importantly, you can share it with your friends.

- ✔ Prints your information if you still rely on paper and pencil.

- ✔ Allows you to accomplish more in less time — which explains why I am able to find the time to sit around sipping margaritas!

Who Can Join the Party — and What Can They Take With Them?

Wrestling your best pair of shoes out of the mouth of a Doberman is nothing compared to wrestling company data from the hands of a CEO. Most successful companies have spent years building their contact list; the thought of losing it is not a very enticing one. One of the biggest hurdles Microsoft undoubtedly faces is the fact that confidential company information is now hanging out in the Internet for all the world to see. The CEO, CFO, or someone else with a lot of Cs in their title will worry that their information is subject to pilfering by their competitors. They'll worry about whether their data is being safely backed up. They'll worry that their employees will stumble into the areas that they shouldn't be accessing — such as the salaries of all their coworkers.

Microsoft has taken a lot of steps to ensure the privacy of your data — and to make sure that the CEOs sleep well at night.

Exactly how secure is secure?

Microsoft follows the Security Development Lifecycle (SDL) when developing software. This means that during each phase of Office Live's development process the SDL team sets about trying to break into the service from every possible angle. Then, before Office Live was released to the public at large, an independent development team analyzed it. The thinking is that software that has undergone the SDL process is decidedly more secure than the software developed by the high school kid down the street.

Once the software is tested — and retested — your next concern might be about how easy it is to hack into your individual site. The data you store on Office Live is stored in computer systems located in controlled facilities. Additionally, Microsoft created an army of MPs, called the Microsoft Security Response Center (MSRC). MSRC's sole purpose in life is to protect Microsoft customers from vulnerabilities in Microsoft software. The MSRC don dark glasses and trench coats and snoop around looking for security leaks in Microsoft software. If the MSRC finds something that is suspect, they get all hot and bothered and moves in quickly to arrest all the bad guys. Okay, the bad guys aren't always arrested — but Microsoft is constantly searching for security leaks in much the same way that your antivirus software looks for new viruses.

Crash — am I dead yet?

Want to see a CEO change colors? Tell him that the server just crashed and watch him go from red to white in sixty seconds; you might even see a few lovely shades of purple along the way. Microsoft uses *redundant* hardware and software systems to protect against system failures. Redundancy means that Microsoft uses more than one server on a Web site to perform the same party tricks. If one of the servers crashes, another server takes its place without missing a beat. Redundancy ensures that your Web site continues to function and your data continues to be safe and sound.

What happens if I hit the Delete button?

Accidents happen. Suppose you're showing your boss all the neat sites you've created in Office Live to house every last piece of critical company information. And that the boss decides he'd like to play with all that neat, critical, important information you've just spent days putting into Office Live. And *then* suppose that the boss wonders what will happen when he hits that pretty button with the red X that says *Delete*. When the message shown in Figure 1-1 appears, he gets bored, doesn't bother to read it, and clicks OK.

Figure 1-1:
Will this really delete my database?

Not to worry. Microsoft maintains a backup copy of every Web site, all business applications and each and every shared site. It creates a daily backup copy of your data — so your backup data is one day old at most. A person with Administrator permission can restore the Web site or the business applications' data from the backup at any time, saving his or her delicate derrière.

Mama taught me to share

Just so you know: If you use Office Live in a standalone environment, you'll be the only one able to access your data. But getting your data to where it needs to go might make you so mobile that you'll seem like three people in one body as you scurry from one place to the next with your PDA in one hand and your laptop bag clenched in the other.

You'll probably find that because of the way Office Live allows you to run your business like a well-designed piece of machinery, you'll soon need to hire a couple of employees. My mother taught me that sharing is a good thing; obviously Office Live's mommy felt the same way, because you can share any information you want with the other people in your organization — or with your customers, for that matter. Of course, as your company expands, you might have some remote workers that you'd like to keep in touch with. Although smoke signals are kind of fun, you might prefer to have everybody (near or far) access your information online so the whole operation has the most up-to-date information.

Come on in, the water's fine

Whether you are expanding, or you already have a whole army of workers, you can share your information so everyone in your organization can view the same data. And you won't have to buy a fancy-schmancy server to do so.

Access to Office Live can — and should be — controlled by the administrator of the site. Administrators can grant access to users through specific levels of permission. The administrator can set up new users as a *Reader*, *Editor*, or *Administrator*.

✔ The Administrator has full access to your site. He can set up new users, decide which areas of Office Live users can access, and then access, add, modify, and delete any information that he wants.

✔ Editors have full access to the areas assigned to them by the Administrator; they can add, modify, and delete information.

✔ Readers (unfortunately) don't always read the instructions — so they have no more than read-only access to information to the areas assigned to them by the Administrator.

Synchronize your Office Live data to your software

I'm the first to admit that I am not a workaholic. I think my Type A personality combined with my intrinsic need to be lazy resulted in my love for Office Live. To me, the only thing worse than working is repeating the same work again a second time. Office Live very nicely synchronizes with several other popular software products allowing you to avoid the "that was so much fun let's do it again" syndrome.

If you are currently using Outlook or Outlook's Business Contact Manger, you can import your contacts directly from Outlook to Office Live. If you continue to use Outlook to schedule your appointments, you can synchronize your Outlook calendar with Office Live so you can view activities scheduled in Outlook from Office Live. If you want to see your Office Live activities in Outlook, that can also be arranged as well. You can even view your Office Live address book in Outlook, or your Outlook address book in Office Live.

For you accounting types out there, double-entry means some fancy thing you do with your accounting software. To the rest of us, double-entry sounds like double-work, and that does not sound like a good thing! By using Microsoft Accounting 2007 you can share your contact information among Office Live, the main computer in your office, and your accountant.

My PDA is Pretty Darn Amazing

Sometimes no one is around to share with so you just might want to share information with yourself. One way to do this is to purchase a Personal Digital Assistant (PDA) or a *smart phone* that is so smart that it combines the power of a cell phone with a PDA. Some of you might have already nicknamed your smart phones "My Life" because that is exactly what it contains. Office Live can synchronize with virtually any handheld device that uses the Windows Mobile operating system so that you can enter — or view — information from either your phone or from Office Live. See your address book! See your calendar! See your task list! See how easy it is to get a life.

What Are all These Darn Ads Doing Here?

It's pretty hard to escape advertising in this day and age. You see it on the sides of buses, before the coming attractions at the movies, and even hanging from an airplane as you sit watching a sporting event. Someone is paying big time for all those advertisements, so you'd think they're at least marginally effective.

You don't pay a fee to use an Office Live Basics account. So how can Microsoft pay for your domain register, host your Web site, and allow you to create 25 e-mail addresses for free? Easy. Microsoft places advertisements on your site that you see each and every time you log on to it.

The good news is that even though you see ads from your site when you log on to it, any visitors to your Web site are not subjected to advertising. They do, however, know that Microsoft is hosting your Web site; Microsoft adds a small Office Live logo to the bottom-right corner of your site.

You can bid those pesky ads adieu by subscribing to a fee-based account (Essentials or Premium). Apparently, however, Microsoft doesn't consider ads touting other Microsoft products to *be* advertisements because you're still treated to a bit of up-selling even after you upgrade to a fee-based account.

Terms You Need to Know

There's a toss-up as to who uses more acronyms and special naming conventions: an IT department or our Federal government. Now you might want to become a bit more proficient in MOL (Microsoft Office Live)-ese.

Here are a few terms you need to know when using Office Live:

✔ **Site:** This is the main area where you store your data. Depending on the version of Office Live that you use, you can create multiple sites to divide your business into separate areas. For example, you can create sites for a specific project, vendor, customer, or employee. Sites allow you to control which people have access to its content. You'll also create a Web site, which is open to the public.

✔ **Templates:** Templates are predesigned forms for those of you who are hesitant to design your sites from scratch.

✔ **Dashboard:** In much the same way the dashboard on your car gives you a bird's-eye view of how your car is running, Office Live's shows you the various facets of your business in one central location.

✔ **Web part:** You can customize dashboards to provide you with the information that you specifically want to see. A *Web part* is one of those sections of information.

✔ **List:** A *list* is a collection of data arranged in columns and rows. Typically you enter your data into a form; after you've input it, you can view it in list format — and even determine which pieces of data you'd like to see. For example, once you start adding contacts to Office Live, you might want to see their phone numbers and mailing addresses — and then arrange them alphabetically by their company names.

✔ **Applications:** The fee-based versions of Office Live provide you with a bunch of business applications that help you with everything from contact management, sales, and marketing to such daily concerns as employees, timesheets, and company asset management.

Help Me, Rhonda! (Getting Support)

No matter how easy a piece of software is to use, you're bound to have a question from time to time. Of course, this book answers the majority of those — but should you run into problems, you have several places to turn for additional support.

All users of Office Live can access help via e-mail, through an interactive chat session with one of the Microsoft support staff or through a public support forum. Only users with a paid subscription can access phone support; you'll have access to a 24/7 toll-free phone number that you can use and abuse until you find the answers to your questions.

Good help is hard to find and nowhere does that adage hold truer than in Office Live. You'll find the link to the public forum on your home page. You can find the various support options by clicking the help button at the top-right corner of Office Live and typing **Tech Support** in the search box. You're prompted to indicate the type of plan you have, and then you finally get to the support options.

Office Live offers several great areas for you to explore:

✔ The Help button is located in the upper-right corner of the Member Center page. You can search for the answers to your most earth-shattering questions. Figure 1-2 shows what the Office Live Help looks like.

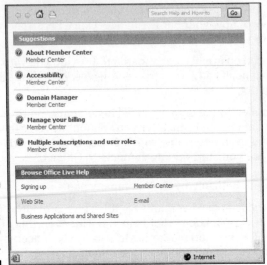

Figure 1-2:
Office Live's
Help
window.

✔ You'll find a few of the commonly used Learning Center lessons prominently displayed on the right side of the Member Center page. These are
designed to get you up and running on Office Live in a jiffy.

✔ The Learning Center link, located on the Navigation bar of the Member
Center page, takes you to the whole series of Learning Center articles
(see Figure 1-3). These articles help you to become an Office Live power
user.

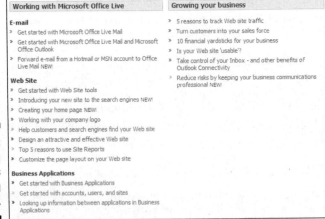

Figure 1-3:
Exploring
Office Live's
Learning
Center.

Chapter 2

Picking a Flavor of Office Live

In This Chapter

▶ Picking out an Office Live flavor

▶ Incurring extra charges

▶ Canceling your subscription

Many years ago, my daughter fell off the jungle gym at school; the school nurse suggested that I call an orthopedic guy. I conquered the phone maze and finally spoke to a nurse who asked whether my daughter had injured her hand, wrist, finger, arm, elbow, or shoulder so that she could schedule an appointment with the appropriate doctor. (Yikes. It seems that even falling from playground equipment is a specialized sport!)

You get almost as many options with Office Live; it comes in three distinct flavors. In this chapter, you find out about them all — and then decide which flavor is right for you!

Taking the Taste Test

Before launching a new business — or inaugurating a new software system — it's always a good idea to sit down and determine your goals and needs. Office Live offers various levels of service to subscribe to — you have to decide which flavor of Office Live best fits your needs.

Office Live comes in three flavors: Basics, Essentials, and Premium. They come equipped with slightly different features — and slightly different price tags. Remember, Office Live is a subscription service — which means you sign up to use the service and can discontinue it at any time.

Making the choice between these services is fairly easy. Plus, you don't have to feel like this decision is set in stone. You can start with any of the subscription plans and move up — or down — to a different plan at any time.

So what are the features you want to look for when you're deciding which subscription level is right for you? You might ask yourself the following questions:

✔ **How much do I want to pay for the service?** Pricing for Office Live ranges from free to $40 per month. Want more services? Shell out a few more bucks. Want to test drive Office Live for free? Start with a Basic account.

If $40 a month seems an astronomical price tag to you, consider this: A typical Web site can cost you around $20 per month to host; in addition, you'll probably pay around $10 to register your site — and around $15 a year to *re*register the site.

✔ **How much storage space do I need?** All subscription plans come with a generous amount of storage space. Typically, the larger your business the more storage space you need. Here are a few of the factors that determine how much space you're going to need:

- The number of pages in your Web site

- The amount of graphics in your Web site

- The number of visitors who come to your Web site

- The number of users who access your Office Live data

- The number of shared "spaces" you'll be setting up for your company

Not sure how to calculate how much space you'll need? Don't worry. Microsoft cheerfully informs you if you exceed your space limits — or are coming close to exceeding them!

✔ **Do I have — or want to have — a professionally created Web site?** Although Office Live comes with a large variety of Web-site templates you might prefer to have a more customized site.

✔ **Do I want my Outlook data to integrate with my Office Live content?**

✔ **Do I want to create customized workspaces that my employees can access to view information about current projects or to access detailed information about my customers?**

✔ **How many users will be accessing Office Live?**

✔ **Do I need business applications to help track projects, sales, documents, time, and/or contacts?**

✔ **Do I want 24/7 telephone help?**

After you make the determination how you'll be using Office Live, your next step is to pick the subscription plan that works best to help you achieve your goals.

Vanilla: Office Live Basics

If you're trying to decide whether or not Office Live is a viable alternative for your business, start with Basics. The question here is not why you *would* use Office Live but rather, why you *wouldn't* use it? The Office Live Basics subscription is *free* — as in *nothing* — as in, "You don't have to pay a dime for it!" Just in case you didn't hear me the first time: Office Live Basics won't cost you a thing.

So what do you get with a free Basics account? Enough to start a business — or to embellish an existing one. Among the features you'll start to drool over are these:

- **A domain name:** A Web site needs a name, something along the lines of `www.mycoolwebsite.com`. Microsoft gives you the domain of your choosing at no cost — and pays the yearly registration as long as you continue to host it with Microsoft.

   If you don't already have a Web site, run — don't walk — to Office Live and register one immediately. Most of the good Web-site names have already been reserved by other businesses and individuals. The longer you wait, the harder it will be to get a good Web-site name!

- **Web hosting:** After you decide a name for your Web site, you need someone to host it for you so the rest of the world can see it. Microsoft does that for you as well — free of charge.

- **Web site design:** Having a Web site is a three-pronged attack: You need to find and register a name, have someone host it for you, and then work on the actual Web-site design. Office Live Basics comes with templated designs you can choose. Once you decide on a design, you can go back and add a graphic or two, as well as a few words about yourself.

   Don't worry if this entire process seems way too complicated. Microsoft holds your hand as you try to come up with Web site names; in fact, if you find that all cool names you had in mind are already in use by someone else, Microsoft even suggests a few names. Once you choose the name, it's automatically up and running. Your only task at that point is to start fiddling with the content. (And, if you scurry over to Chapter 5, you find the precise details of how to create a killer Web site.)

- **Site reports:** The whole purpose of having a Web site is to attract visitors to it. Office Live gives you a variety of site reports that allows you to track the number of visitors to your Web site on a daily, weekly, or monthly basis. You can also determine which search engines and keywords are driving traffic to your Web site.

- **Office Live adManager:** adManager is an online tool that helps you set up pay-per-click ads on Windows Live Search.

- **Storage space:** You get 500MB of space with your Office Live account to house your Web site. Trust me — 500MB is sufficient to build a fairly large Web site!

- **E-mail accounts:** You receive up to 25 e-mail accounts, each with a full 2GB of space. How much is 2GB of space? A lot! It's hard to imagine anyone outgrowing that much e-mail storage space.

- **Instant messaging:** If you need to chat with your coworkers while you're on the phone with a client, or are trying to reach someone who is sequestered in an all day meeting, you might want to take advantage of Office Live's instant messaging service.

- **Shared contacts:** Although the address book that comes with Office Live Basics isn't as robust as the one that comes with Essentials and Premium, you can share it with up to ten of your coworkers.

- **Calendar:** Keeping up with your own busy schedule is a daunting task for many of you. Keeping up with the schedules of all the busy people in your organization is an impossibility — unless you can go online and access their calendars — which is exactly what Office Live lets you do.

- **Windows Mobile-powered phone e-mail access:** Who doesn't have a cell phone in this day and age? And, if you purchase one with the Windows Mobile operating system in it, you can access your e-mail wherever your travels take you.

- **Office Accounting Express 2007:** If you have a business, you need some sort of accounting software. Feel free to go out and buy one — or use the free version that comes with Office Live Basics. (Even though it's free, it still allows you to list items for sale on eBay, view their status, and process orders.)

- **Online and e-mail support:** Just in case you lose your copy of this book, you might need to contact Office Live's support for a little extra TLC. Basics allows you to do just that via e-mail or online chat. You can also view Online Communities to read questions — and answers — that have been posted by other Office Live users.

Chocolate: Office Live Essentials

Whew! With all the neat features that you get with Office Live Basics it's really hard to imagine that Microsoft left anything out, or that you'd feel the urge to upgrade to a fee-based service. Well, Microsoft added the Essentials subscription if you would like to have a few higher-end tricks up your sleeve.

Office Live Essentials runs you a whopping $19.95 a month. Considering that the price to host a typical Web site is about the same, however, Essentials represents a tremendous bargain. Office Live Essentials includes *all* the features in Basics — and then some. It's almost like having a "buy one, get one free" coupon for your favorite ice cream store!

Here's a rundown of those additional features:

- ✔ **More Web site flexibility:** If you already have a Web site, you can import it into Office Live Essentials. Or, if you want to create an extra-snazzy-looking Web site, you can use Web-designing software (such as FrontPage) or hire someone to do it for you.

- ✔ **More Web site storage space:** If you thought that the 500MB allotted with the Basics account was generous, you'll think you've died and gone to heaven with the 1GB of storage space that Essentials gives you.

- ✔ **More e-mail accounts:** Essentials increases the number of e-mail accounts that you can create with your subscription from 25 to 50.

- ✔ **Business Contact Manager:** Essentials adds Business Contact Manager (BCM) into the mix of things. Instead of a simple address book, you now reap the benefits of a full-fledged contact manager. You can create accounts as well as contacts, and keep track of all your sales opportunities.

- ✔ **Organize customer data:** You can share the status of your accounts, contacts, and sales opportunities with other members of your company or organization.

- ✔ **Create workspaces:** You can create *workspaces* (an online work area) that you can use to store and share information about a specific project. Up to ten users can access these workspaces.

- ✔ **More and better Help:** In addition to online and e-mail support, you can take advantage of a 24-hour, toll-free support line.

Banana split: Office Live Premium

Just when you thought it couldn't get any better, you find out about Office Live Premium — and all the cool features that it includes. Office Live Premium truly is the icing on the cake. The *crème de la crème*. The Big Kahuna. The cherry on top of the sundae — because Premium has all the features found in Essentials, and then some.

Office Live Premium sets you back a whopping $39.95 a month. However, when you consider that it feeds, er, supports twenty users you'll think that it's a steal of a deal.

Here's the skinny on the Premium features; thankfully, they won't make you gain any weight!

- ✔ **More Web site storage space:** 2GB of Web-site storage.

- ✔ **Up to 50 e-mail accounts**: Each with a full 2GB of space.

- ✔ **Synchronize your information with Outlook:** If you're using Outlook — and who isn't? — you can synchronize your e-mail, calendar, and contacts to your Outlook data so that you're up to date no matter where your travels take you!

- ✔ **More workspaces:** The Premium account increases both the number of workspaces you can create — and the number of users who can access them — to 20.

- ✔ **Online business applications:** Essentials gives you a whole bunch of nifty online business applications that allows you to manage your projects, sales, employees, and company.

Adding a topping

Microsoft is hoping that you will fall so in love with Office Live that you'll never switch over to another product. Their thinking is that you'll start with a Basics or Essentials account and eventually end up with a Premium account. But what happens if your company continues to grow? Well, after you take that extended cruise you've always dreamed of, you'll be happy to know that Office Live can expand right along with you.

Of course, expansion does not come without a price. You can exercise a number of fee-based options to expand the size of your Essentials or Premium account:

- ✔ **Additional domain names:** You can register additional domain names for your business. Perhaps you've added another division to your company and want to have a Web site for it. Or maybe you just want to have a second Web site as another way of luring potential customers to your primary Web site. Whatever the reason, you can purchase additional domains at $8.95 per domain per year.

- ✔ **More e-mail accounts:** It's almost hard to believe that you could outgrow the 50 e-mail accounts that Office Live Premium allots. If you find yourself in that situation, however, you can purchase additional e-mail accounts — in bundles of five — for $2.95 per bundle per month.

✔ **Additional Web site storage:** The Essentials and Premium accounts come equipped with generous amounts of storage space (1GB and 2GB respectively) to house the pages of your Web site. However, should your Web site expand beyond those perimeters you can purchase more space in 100MB increments for $4.95/month.

✔ **Additional shared sites and business applications storage:** If you're storing a whole lot of shared documents on your Office Live site — or if you want to create more workspaces — you can increase that storage space as well in increments of 100MB for $4.95/month.

✔ **Additional shared site users:** As your business grows — thanks no doubt to Office Live — you might need to expand between the ten and twenty user limits of the Essentials and Premium accounts. You can add more users, in bundles of five at a time, for $11.95/month.

✔ **Additional bandwidth:** When someone views your Web site or down-loads a file, bandwidth is used. If your Web site attracts a whole lot of visitors and/or they are downloading large files you might be putting a strain on the bandwidth that Microsoft has allotted you. Never fear — you can increase that as well, if necessary. You can purchase additional bandwidth in 24GB increments for $1.95 per month.

Signing On the Dotted Line

It's always scary to submit your credit-card information online. All Office Live subscriptions require that you submit your credit-card information, even if you're only registering for the free, Basics version. Microsoft has gone to great lengths to make sure that this information remains safe and secure — but then again, there are no guarantees in life (except for death and taxes). If you want to play the Office Live game, you'll have to abide by the Office Live rules and fork over that credit-card information.

May I see your credit card, please?

You might be wondering exactly why Microsoft is requiring you to submit your credit-card information for a free, Basics account. Microsoft wants to make sure that you are a real, live, human being and not some spammer hoping to set up *hundreds* of Web sites. Should Microsoft detect some risky business originating from your Web site, the guys in black trench coats track you down and put a stop to the nefarious dealings.

When you sign up for a Microsoft Office Live account, Microsoft performs a $1 authorization check on your credit card to verify that the card information you are using is valid and up to date. A temporary $1 charge may appear on your online credit-card statement for a short period, but won't appear on your final billing statement.

Many spammers take advantage of free Yahoo! and Google e-mail accounts — as well as Microsoft's very own Hotmail e-mail service — and Microsoft doesn't want to allow that to happen. Microsoft also limits you to one account per credit card as an added way of deterring the scoundrels in this world from signing up for multiple accounts — and then using them for spamming purposes.

Microsoft collects your credit-card information for another reason as well. They are banking — literally — on the expectation that you'll want to upgrade from the Basics account and/or add a few of the extra services. Or they're hoping you'll be so happy with adManager (Office Live's version of "pay-per-click") that you'll want to waste no time in giving Microsoft the go-ahead to add a few more charges to your account.

What happens next year?

Typically, you need to pay a renewal fee for your domain name once a year. The good news is that Microsoft automatically picks up the tab for your renewal fee for you as long as you continue to subscribe to Office Live. And, if you already own a domain name and wish to transfer it to Office Live, Microsoft pays for any future renewals.

By now you're probably wondering what happens to your domain name if you decide *not* to continue with Office Live. Legally, that domain name belongs to you. If you cancel the Office Live service, you maintain full control of your domain name — but you'll have to transfer your Web site to another hosting service. You are also responsible for paying the new company to host your Web site, as well as for paying the annual registration fee.

Chapter 3

Getting Office Live Up and Running

*Y*ou've signed up for Office Live, you have your domain name, you've thought about what you want to accomplish with your Web site . . . now what? You've already done your homework by studying all that Office Live has to offer and deciding on the flavor that best suits your need. Now you need to get your Office Live site up and running. Fortunately, you'll find that setting up your account is a snap. This chapter walks you through the initial setup, gives you a guided tour of Office Live, and even leads you through adding a few new users to the mix.

Creating a New Account

Starting at the beginning is always a good idea, so that's exactly where you should start — by going to the Office Live Web site at www.officelive.com (shown in Figure 3-1). You can set up your Web site with the Getting Started Wizard.

If you have previously used Hotmail or MSN or created a Microsoft Passport, you can skip this step. Simply log in to Windows Live ID before starting the Office Live setup. It saves you a couple of steps down the road.

Figure 3-1:
The Office
Live Web
site.

Follow these steps to set up your new Office Live database with the Getting
Started Wizard:

1. **Select the plan you want by clicking the appropriate Sign Up Now
   button.**

   Not sure which plan is for you? Read Chapter 2 to get a full rundown of
   each plan. In any event, the sign-up page appears, as shown in Figure 3-2.

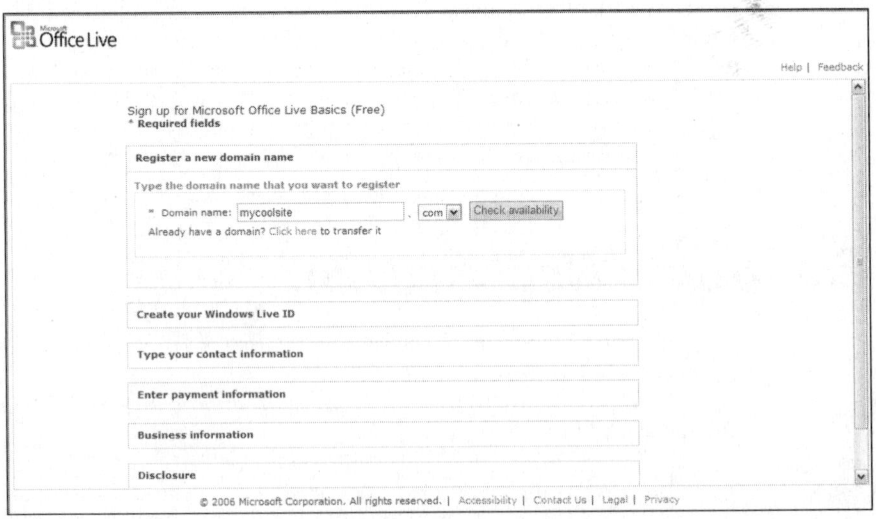

Figure 3-2:
Signing up
for Office
Live.

© 2006 Microsoft Corporation. All rights reserved. | Accessibility | Contact Us | Legal | Privacy

Tips for picking a good domain name

I'm not sure which is harder — naming your kid or naming your Web site. Hopefully, both will be with you for a long time to come! You'll probably have to try half a dozen possibilities before you find a great domain name that someone isn't already using. Here are a few tips:

✔ **KISS (Keep it Simple, Stupid):** Remember: People are going to have to type your domain name into a browser, or use when they send you an e-mail. You're going to have to spell it to people over the phone. This is a true case of less being more!

✔ **Put two words together:** Consider combining words. For example, you could add `world` or `universe` as a second word to make your business sound even bigger than it really is.

✔ **Use the .com or .net extensions:** There are a lot of newer extensions such as `.biz`, `.info` and `.us`. You'll probably want to avoid using them unless you want to send potential clients over to your competitor's site!

✔ **Use keywords:** Your domain name should include one or more of your keywords. Search engines can find you more easily this way.

2. **Fill in the domain name that you'd like to register and then click the Check Availability button.**

There are a few rules to follow when selecting a domain name:

- You can't use any spaces.

- Your name can use characters, numbers, and hyphens. After all, nobody wants to go to `*&$%!!@.com` (unless they stubbed their toe in the middle of the night).

- The domain name should be less than 49 characters. Again typing in `www.a-really-ridiculously-long-boring-drawn-out-website-name.com` is just not fun!

If the domain you suggested is available, go on to Step 4. If the domain you suggested is not available, Office Live presents you with the bad news; see Step 3.

3. **(Optional) If necessary, type another domain name.**

If at first you don't succeed, try, try again — and again and again — until you come up with something that works.

A good domain name is hard — if not impossible — to find. You'll probably find that most of the domain names that you try have already been taken by someone else. Choose wisely. Wait a day or two if necessary. That domain name is going to be with you for a long time to come!

You might not be thrilled with the domain name you came up with. If that's the case, you can hit the Back button and keep trying.

4. **Click the Confirm button if you are excited and happy about the domain name that you have chosen.**

5. **Log into your Windows ID by filling in the Windows Live ID box (see Figure 3-3).**

In order to use Office Live you must have a Windows Live ID. You'll use this ID every time you log in to your Office Live account. If you already have a Windows ID you can use it, or you can create a new ID associated with the Office Live account.

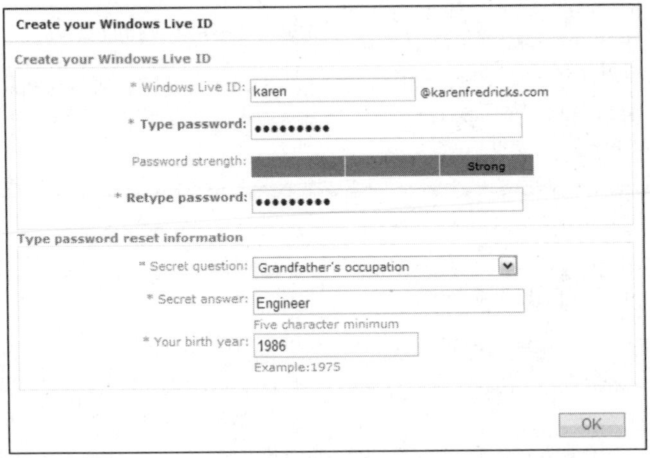

Create your Windows Live ID

Create your Windows Live ID

* Windows Live ID: `karen` @karenfredricks.com

* Type password: ••••••••

Password strength: Strong

* Retype password: ••••••••

Type password reset information

* Secret question: Grandfather's occupation

* Secret answer: Engineer
Five character minimum

* Your birth year: 1986
Example:1975

OK

Figure 3-3:
Creating a
Windows
Live ID and
password.

---

6. **Fill in — and repeat — your password.**

Your password must be between 6 and 16 characters long and be case sensitive. Office Live even has a rating system for grading your passwords:

- **Try again:** It's really not called *try again*, but if you come up with an unacceptable password (such as your name or `1234`), Office Live won't even bother to rate it — which is not a good sign!

  Office Live rejects any password that contains all or part of your e-mail address.

- **Weak:** Office Live is none too thrilled with passwords that consist of all-lowercase letters (`coolbeans`), all-uppercase letters (`DOLLARS`), all numbers (`007007`), or even all symbols (`$$&$$!`).

- **Medium:** Office Live perks up slightly if you create a password based on two keystroke types such as *dummy0101* or *money!!.*

- **Strong:** Office Live is thrilled with a password that includes three types of keystrokes such as *Dummy1234* or *Money!* that consists of upper- and lowercase letters and symbols. You can even get clever and use something like *h3!Lpm3,* which is a "strong" way of spelling *Help Me!*

7. **Fill in your top secret password reset information and click OK to continue.**

   Just in case you forget your super special password, Office Live can reset it for you if you're able to answer some top secret questions. Guess if you forget the answers to those questions you'll be plumb out of luck!

8. **Fill in your contact information and click OK.**

   Hopefully, entering such information as your name, address, and phone number doesn't leave you scratching your head too much. Fortunately, you're not asked to give your blood type.

9. **Fill in your credit card information and click OK.**

   Your computer buzzes and hisses for a few moments but you're soon prompted to type your password (see Figure 3-4) so you can access your brand-new Office Live site!

Figure 3-4:
Signing in to
Office Live.

Taking the Office Live Tour

Most country clubs have nice reception areas with comfy chairs that you can lounge in when you first enter. Office Live has a similar reception area. Basically, the Home page of a Basics account is pretty much the same as the Essentials and Premium accounts with a few small-but-noticeable differences:

- ✔ You'll see fewer ads floating across an Essentials or Premium home Page.
- ✔ You have fewer features to access in the Basics account.

Exploring a new piece of software is very much like buying a new car. You might feel a flutter of nervousness the first time it gets dark; you fumble for the light switch and watch as the windshield wipers turn on. But before long, the controls on your new car — and Office Live — start to feel like second nature to you.

Figure 3-5 shows you what the Office Live Home page looks like.

Help link

Search box

Account information

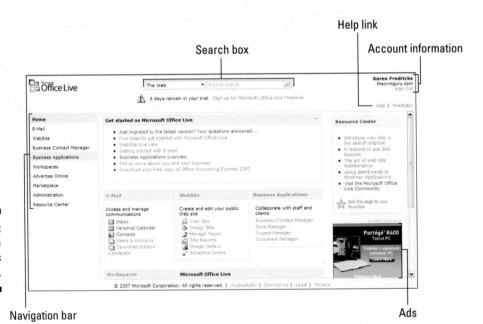

Figure 3-5:
The Office
Live Basics
Home page.

Navigation bar

Ads

Although most of the items on the Home page are fairly self-explanatory, it's always nice to have a guided tour — so here you go. Just keep walking and follow me!

✔ **Search box:** A search box is conveniently located at the top of the Home page. You can use it to search the Internet or to search for help on Office Live.

✔ **Account information:** The top right-hand corner includes your name, and the name of your Web site. For example, you might register one Office Live account to help you manage your business and another one to help you organize your daughter's Brownie troop. Seeing the appropriate Web site name assures that you won't send your best client four dozen boxes of Girl Scout cookies by mistake.

To switch between accounts, click the Sign Out button that is located beneath your account information. From there you can log in to one of your other accounts.

✔ **Help:** Like all good programs, Office Live comes equipped with a help utility designed to give you just that. You can search for the answers to your questions. You're offered a few suggestions based on the area of Office Live that you're in when you cry for help. You can also browse some of the most important topics.

✔ **Navigation bar:** Just like Hansel and Gretel threw bread crumbs into the forest to keep from getting lost, Office Live provides you with a site-Navigation bar on the left side of your screen.

If you leave the Home page and navigate to another area of Office Live, the Navigation bar changes slightly (compare Figure 3-6, which shows the E-Mail page, to Figure 3-5); click Home and you'll land with a plop back on the Home page.

Figure 3-6:
The
Navigation
bar shows
where
you are.

✔ **Get Started on Office Live:** This area gives you several help articles, smack dab in the middle of your Home page. These articles are "how-to" instructions, aimed at setting up and using key Office Live elements.

✔ **Resource Center:** The Resource Center at the right side of your Home page contains articles designed to increase your productivity.

- ✔ **Ads:** With the Basic subscription you get a free Web site, 25 e-mail addresses — and lots of ads. Because they tend to be in bright colors and dance around a lot on your screen, they're pretty hard to miss. With Essentials and Premium accounts, you only have to deal with one small ad in the lower-right corner.

- ✔ **E-mail:** Here's where you find the tools you need to access your e-mail Inbox, create a calendar, view your contacts, and invite other users to join the party.

- ✔ **Website:** Not surprisingly, this area sets you on your way to creating — and maintaining — your Web site.

Adding Office Live Users

Remember when you were a kid and got that great new bicycle for your birthday? You probably couldn't wait to show it off to your friends. The same thing holds true with Office Live. You signed up, logged in, and explored the ins and outs a bit. Now you're ready to roll up your sleeves and get to work — or maybe get a few of your employees to work.

The first thing you'll need to do is to set up additional users to access your Office Live account.

Being the subscription owner gives you some additional perks — besides seeing a service charge on your credit-card statement each month if you subscribe to a fee-based account. You're the one who gets to decide who else can access your site. In addition, you are the person who can grant those users permission to perform various tasks by assigning them roles.

Adding a user to a Basics account

To add a new user to an Office Live Basics account, follow these steps:

1. **Click Administration on the Navigation bar and then click Users & Permissions in the Navigation bar on the Administration page.**

   The Permissions page appears.

2. **Click the Add User icon.**

   The Add User page opens, as shown in Figure 3-7.

3. **Fill in the new user's e-mail address.**

   You have two options here:

   - Fill in the user's permanent, non-Office Live e-mail address if the user is using the Office Live site but doesn't need an Office Live e-mail address.

   - The user's Office Live e-mail address if the user already has an Office Live e-mail address. Not sure how to make that happen? Chapter 4 gives you the lowdown on creating a new Office Live e-mail address.

4. **Fill in the display name that you want to use for the new user.**

   Typically this is the person's first and last name, but you might prefer to use first name only, or the first initial and last name.

Figure 3-7:
The Add
User page.

5. **Click Next to continue.**

   The User Permissions page opens (see Figure 3-8). By now you might be thinking that you follow a whole lot of steps to create a new Office Live user. You're right — but the steps are really easy!

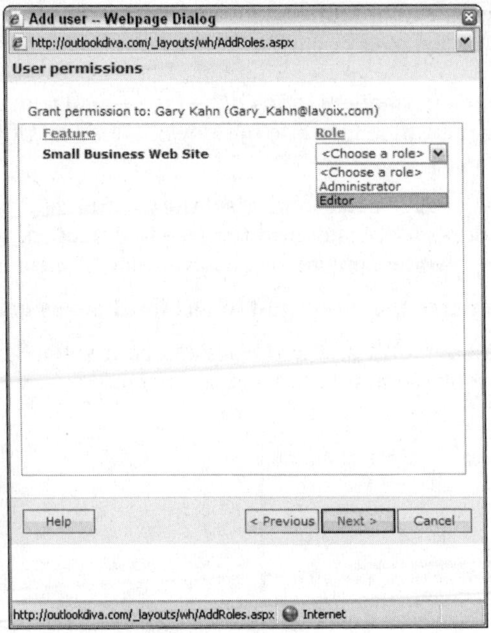

Figure 3-8:
The User
Permissions
page.

6. **Assign the user's role.**

   A *role* is a predefined set of permissions that allow users to perform various tasks in Office Live. A person's role also determines what they have permission to see when they sign on to Office Live: You must assign each user a role. You can't modify the permissions for a role or create new roles.

   Office Live has two roles:

   • **Administrator:** An administrator is a person who needs full control over all aspects of your Web site. They have permission to view, modify, add, and delete files, in addition to adding users and assigning their roles. For example, your company's Web administrator would most likely fill an Administrator role on Office Live for your Web site. When an administrator signs on to Office Live, they can see all the information that's necessary to manage your site.

   • **Editor:** An editor is a person who has permission to view, modify, add, and delete files on your site but can't add users or assign roles. When editors sign on to Office Live, they have access to the files on your site and Web Site tools.

7. **Click Next to continue.**

   The Invite User page opens (see Figure 3-9).

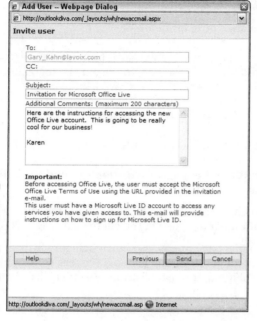

Figure 3-9:
Invite
another
person to
the Office
Live Web
site.

8. **Fill in the e-mail invitation and click the Send button.**

   This is really cool — at least it seems cool to me! Here's where you get to compose the e-mail to send to the new user. Office Live has already filled in the e-mail address based on the one you added in Step 3. Office Live even suggests a subject line, which you can change if you like. All you need to do — if anything — is to fill in a word or two of explanation.

9. **Wait for the Summary Web page to appear and then click the Finish button.**

   If all systems are go, you receive a congratulatory window summing up the new user's name, e-mail address, and role.

Adding a user to an Essentials or Premium account

The procedures for adding a user to either an Office Live Basic or to an Essentials or Premium account are fairly similar. However, you might want to make note of these differences:

✔ New users automatically receive an Office Live e-mail account.

✔ The entry screens are a little bit different.

These differences are pretty logical if you think about it. Theoretically, a Basics account is geared towards a one person business, recreational group, or organization that doesn't have a need to share a lot of data. Typically, the Basic user might already have an e-mail address — and might not even need an e-mail address linked specifically to the organization.

Here's the steps you'll follow to set up a new Essentials or Premium user:

1. **Click E-Mail from the Home page Navigation bar and then click the Users & Accounts icon on the E-Mail page.**

   Not sure where to find Users & Accounts? You have two places to look — it's on the Navigation bar and also in the center of the E-mail page.

   The Users & Accounts page opens, as shown in Figure 3-10. In addition to showing a list of all your existing users, the Users & Accounts page shows you the total number of e-mail address you've already used.

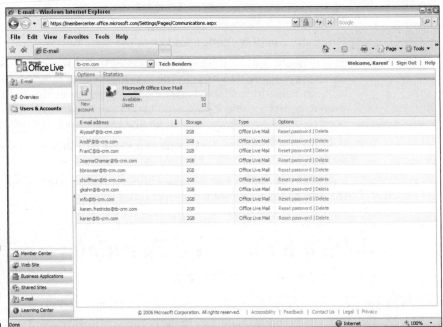

Figure 3-10:
The Users &
Accounts
page.

2. **Click the New Account icon on the Users & Accounts page.**

   The Create E-mail Account page opens (see Figure 3-11).

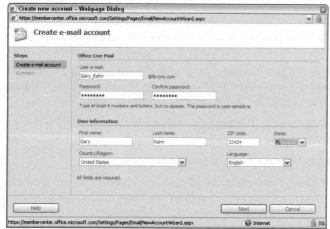

Figure 3-11:
The Create
E-mail
Account
page.

3. **Fill in the fields of the Create E-mail Account page:**

   • **User e-mail:** The end part of the address is already filled in with your Web site's name.

   • **Password** and **Confirmation Password:** Hopefully the user won't lose the assigned password — but just in case, the next section of this chapter shows you how to reset it if necessary.

   • **Basic user contact information**: Be prepared to supply the user's first and last name, zip code, state, country, and native language. (As of this writing, English was the only available language.)

4. **Click Next to continue.**

   After seeing a brief progress indicator, you land back at an empty Create E-mail Account page. Fill in the information for the next user account you want to create, or click Cancel to return to the Users & Accounts page.

Modifying User Accounts

One of the nice things about Office Live (from the administrator's point of view) is that it's so easy to change user information should users either forget their passwords or stop accessing Office Live altogether. Because there is no traditional software to install, the Office Live administrator can change user settings without even making contact with the users.

To change information in a Basic Office Live account, follow these steps:

1. **Click Administration on the Navigation bar and then Users & Permissions in the Navigation bar on the Administration page.**

   You access the user accounts a bit differently in the Essentials and Premium Accounts. Click E-mail from the Member Center Navigation bar, and then click Users & Accounts from the E-Mail Web page.

2. **Find the user in the list of e-mail addresses and click the appropriate option.**

   You don't have a lot of choice here:

   • **Reset Password:** Clicking this option opens the Reset Account Password page. Fill in the new password, type it again to confirm that you typed it correctly the first time, and then click OK.

   • **Delete:** You guessed it — this option deletes the user account as well as the user's e-mail address. When you click Delete, the Delete Account page opens. Click the Delete icon if you are really sure you want to rid yourself of this user.

Part II
Getting Down to Basics with Office Live Basics

The 5th Wave   By Rich Tennant

"I really think the Basics version will work for you. Besides, there's no Yurt Basic version of Office Live."

In this part . . .

Although it's named Basic, the Basic level of Office Live is anything but that! You start by adding an e-mail account and sending, receiving, and organizing your e-mail. Then you move on to building a great-looking Web site. After you have the site, you discover how to analyze it through the use of Site Reports. You get to see just how effective a marketing tool your Web site actually is. You can even add adManager if you'd like to become an instant hit with the search engines. If you have a small — or even a large — business, you can throw in the free Office Accounting Express to help you count a few beans. Finally, you find out how to schedule everything from a simple meeting to a large event.

Chapter 4

Working with Basic E-Mail

*O*ffice Live accounts provide you with lots of e-mail accounts so you may as well take advantage of them. After you set up those accounts, your Office Live users can access their e-mail anywhere their travels take them — as long as they have Internet connectivity. Office Live includes many of the features you'd expect from an e-mail program, including the capability to sort mail automatically and use a spam filter. There's even an address book to help keep track of all those burgeoning e-mail addresses.

Creating and Maintaining E-Mail Accounts

If you are the subscriber to the Office Live account, you can create, modify, and delete e-mail accounts. Office Live lets you set up lots of e-mail accounts (25 for Basic accounts and 50 for Premium and Essentials accounts). You can create e-mail accounts for your employees so that when they send e-mail to customers, the address reflects your organization's Web site. You can even set up a few generic accounts such as *info* or *service*.

Once your e-mail is configured, you can access and manage it from any Internet-connected computer, anywhere in the world. You can keep your messages for as long as you'd like. You also have the same functionality associated with other e-mail accounts you may have, including the ability to send file attachments.

The current Microsoft plan is to have Office Live Mail replace the existing MSN Hotmail e-mail service. When you use your Hotmail account, you have the option of using Office Live Mail. You can create an Office Live Mail account without having an Office Live account. Therefore, when you access the mail portion of Office Live, you actually leave your Office Live account.

Adding an e-mail account

Here's all you have to do to set up a new e-mail account using an existing Office Live subscription:

1. **Sign in to Office Live with the owner e-mail address and password that you used to subscribe to Office Live.**

   Only the original subscriber can create a new e-mail address — so if that's not you, scurry around the office until you find whoever plunked down the credit-card information to create the Office Live account.

2. **Click Administration on Office Live Home page Navigation bar.**

   The Office Live Administration page opens.

3. **Click E-Mail Accounts on the Navigation bar.**

   The E-Mail Accounts page opens, as shown in Figure 4-1.

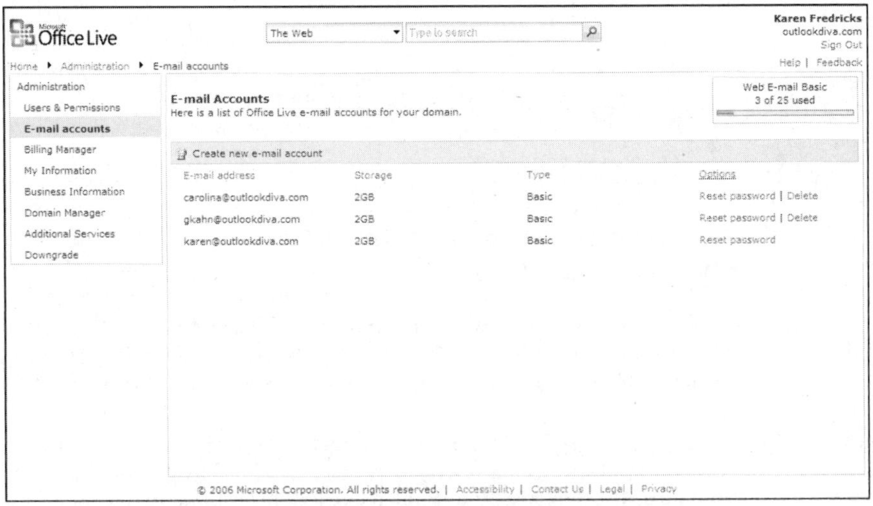

Figure 4-1:
The Office
Live E-Mail
Accounts
page.

E-mail address	Storage	Type	Options
carolina@outlookdiva.com	2GB	Basic	Reset password	Delete
gkahn@outlookdiva.com	2GB	Basic	Reset password	Delete
karen@outlookdiva.com	2GB	Basic	Reset password

© 2006 Microsoft Corporation. All rights reserved. | Accessibility | Contact Us | Legal | Privacy

4. **Click the Create New E-Mail Account icon.**

   The Create New E-Mail Account page opens; see Figure 4-2.

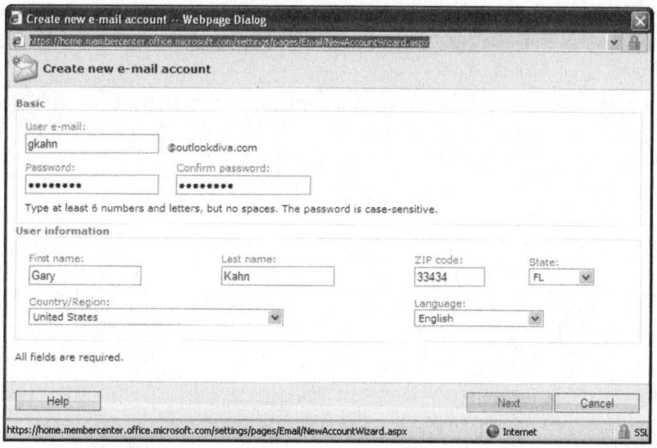

Figure 4-2:
Creating a
new e-mail
account.

5. Complete all the fields.

Stop groaning! You only have a few pieces of pertinent information to enter:

- *User E-Mail Name:* You only need to enter the first part of the e-mail address because Office Live already provides the @ and the domain name for you.

- *Password:* Think of — and remember — a good password. Make it at least six characters long, and remember: It's CASE-SENSITIVE. (Sorry to yell.)

- *Confirm Password:* Because this is a very secretive operation, your password appears as a series of dots just in case an evil spy is lurking behind you. Type your password a second time to avoid accidentally creating an unintentional password.

- *User Information:* Setting up 25 to 50 e-mail accounts can get confusing so adding a bit of information for the e-mail account user helps you tell them apart.

6. Click Next to continue.

This might take a moment or two so you might want to examine your fingernails or twiddle your thumbs while Office Live creates your new e-mail account. Eventually the Summary screen of the Create New E-Mail Account page opens (see Figure 4-3).

7. Read the fine print on the Summary screen.

The summary basically says the following:

- Jot down the new e-mail address and password.

- Scurry over to your Office Live Users & Accounts area to assign additional access to your new e-mail user.

- The new user has to log in with his or her new e-mail address and new password to access any new e-mail that might be coming in.

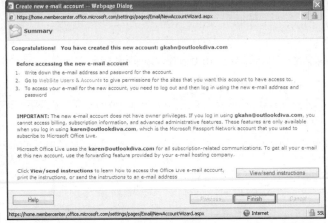

Figure 4-3:
Reading
the fine
print after
creating a
new e-mail
address.

8. **(Optional) Click the View/Send Instructions button if you created this account for another user.**

A new window springs open with instructions that show the user how to access the e-mail account. At this point, you have one of two options:

- Choose File⇨Print to print the instructions for the user.

- Type the user's current e-mail address in the box and click Send to send the person the instructions in an e-mail.

9. **(Optional) Close the new user instructions page if you had it open.**

10. **Click Finish to finish setting up the e-mail account.**

The original account that was created when you signed up for Office Live is the only account with owner privileges. Any additional e-mail accounts that you create for yourself or anyone else don't have access to billing and subscription information, or access to the advanced administrative features. You can, however, allow them access to other areas of your Office Live site; flip back to Chapter 3 for more details.

Deleting e-mail accounts

You can easily delete an e-mail account that you created for yourself or others. However, you can't delete the original e-mail address you used when you created the Office Live account — unless you decide to unsubscribe from Office Live.

Deleting an e-mail account is easy if you follow these steps:

1. **Sign in to Office Live with the owner e-mail address and password that you used to subscribe to Office Live.**

2. **Click Administration on the Office Live Home page Navigation bar.**

   This should seem like familiar territory — you followed the same set of instructions when you *created* the e-mail account.

3. **Click E-Mail Accounts on the Navigation bar.**

   The E-mail Accounts page opens.

4. **Find the e-mail address of the account you want to delete and click the Delete link.**

   A scary-looking Delete Account page opens, as shown in Figure 4-4. It warns you that you will lose all the e-mail associated with the account — and won't be able to set up another e-mail account with the same name for another 30 days.

Figure 4-4:
The scary-looking message you get when trying to delete an e-mail account.

5. **Click Delete and then click Close to close the Account Deleted page that appears.**

Resetting an e-mail password

As the administrator of the Office Live account you'll probably need to reset an e-mail password for a variety of reasons:

✔ You had a change in personnel and one of your generic e-mail accounts is now being accessed by someone else.

✔ You found out that a user has shared his or her password with an army of "closest friends."

✔ The user of the e-mail account forgot the password.

Passwords are particularly important in Office Live. In addition to accessing your e-mail, your e-mail account and password give you entrée into the portions of the Office Live site that you have permission to access. The best way to avoid changing e-mail passwords is to make it abundantly clear to your Office Live users just exactly how important that password is.

Okay, even if you're tempted to consider threatening your users with corporal punishment, here's how you can reset their passwords should you deem it necessary:

1. **Sign in to Office Live with the owner e-mail address and password that you used to subscribe to Office Live.**
2. **Click Administration on the Office Live Home page Navigation bar.**

   The Office Live Administration page opens.
3. **Click E-Mail Accounts on the Navigation bar.**

   The E-mail Accounts page opens.
4. **Find the e-mail address of the account for which you want to reset the password and click the Reset Password link.**

   The Reset Account Password page opens, as shown in Figure 4-5.

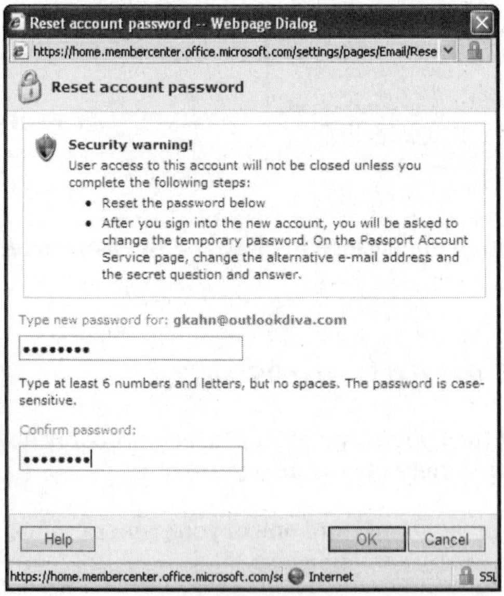
Reset account password -- Webpage Dialog
https://home.membercenter.office.microsoft.com/settings/pages/Email/Rese
Reset account password
Security warning!
User access to this account will not be closed unless you complete the following steps:
• Reset the password below
• After you sign into the new account, you will be asked to change the temporary password. On the Passport Account Service page, change the alternative e-mail address and the secret question and answer.
Type new password for: gkahn@outlookdiva.com
Type at least 6 numbers and letters, but no spaces. The password is case-sensitive.
Confirm password:
Help
OK
Cancel
https://home.membercenter.office.microsoft.com/se
Internet
SSL

Figure 4-5: Resetting an e-mail password.

5. **Type the new password in both the Type New Password For and Confirm Password text boxes.**

   You probably know the drill by now, but here it is again — as you type your password, all you see is a dot for each character you type. You need to confirm your password just in case you typed in an incorrect character.

6. **Click OK to reset the password.**

7. **Click Close to close the Reset Account Password Confirmation page.**

Using Your E-Mail Account

After the main Office Live subscriber has set up an e-mail account for you, you're probably chomping at the bit to use it. You're excited by the knowledge that you can access your e-mail no matter where your travels take you — as long as you have Internet connectivity. So what's your next step? I'm glad you asked — because this section is designed to help you with just that.

Logging into Office Live for the first time

After the main subscriber creates a new e-mail account for you, all kinds of exciting things start to happen. First of all, you'll receive a welcoming e-mail, which gives you the blow-by-blow account of what it takes to access Office Live.

One thing that is missing from the introductory e-mail, however, is your password; after all, this is top-secret stuff and you wouldn't want it to land in the hands of the wrong person. You'll need to ask the Office Live subscriber for that information; hopefully he or she has jotted it down somewhere and/or committed it to memory. If not, hand this book to that person and mention that the previous section explains how to reset a password.

The first time you log into Office Live you'll have to do a bit of extra work:

1. **Log in to Office Live.**

   Because this is your first time logging in, you'll have to change your password. Guess this extra ounce of prevention is just in case the Office Live subscriber jotted down your password and posted it somewhere for all the world to see.

   The Change Password Reset Information page (shown in Figure 4-6) appears.

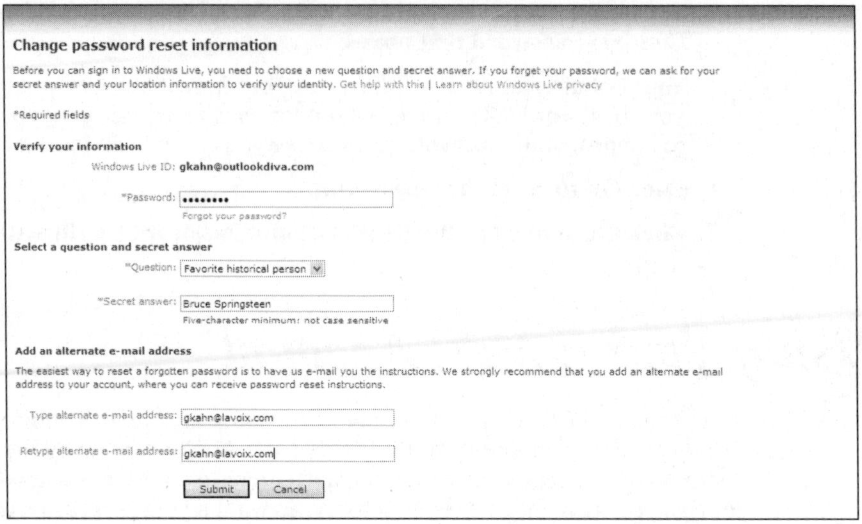

Change password reset information

Before you can sign in to Windows Live, you need to choose a new question and secret answer. If you forget your password, we can ask for your secret answer and your location information to verify your identity. Get help with this | Learn about Windows Live privacy

*Required fields

Verify your information

Windows Live ID: **gkahn@outlookdiva.com**

*Password: ●●●●●●●
Forgot your password?

Select a question and secret answer

*Question: Favorite historical person ▾

*Secret answer: Bruce Springsteen
Five-character minimum; not case sensitive

Add an alternate e-mail address

The easiest way to reset a forgotten password is to have us e-mail you the instructions. We strongly recommend that you add an alternate e-mail address to your account, where you can receive password reset instructions.

Type alternate e-mail address: gkahn@lavoix.com

Retype alternate e-mail address: gkahn@lavoix.com

[Submit]   [Cancel]

Figure 4-6:
Office Live's
prompt to
change your
password
the first time
you log in.

2. **Fill in a few critical pieces of information.**

   Office Live asks you to supply three pertinent pieces of information:

   - Your new password.

   - A secret question and its secret answer (you just have to love all this counterespionage activity).

   - An alternate e-mail address just in case you need to reset your password because you can't access this e-mail account.

3. **Click the Submit button.**

   Just when you think it's safe to start using Office Live, the Office Live Terms of Use page opens.

4. **Check the *I agree to the Microsoft Office Live Service agreement and Privacy statement* check box, and then click the I Accept button to return to the Home page.**

   Smile, happy in the thought that you'll never have to do all of *that* again!

Logging in to Office Live e-mail for the first time

The very first time you do something can be kind of scary. After all, you don't know what to expect and you haven't learned the ropes yet. Not to worry.

Office Live provides you with a Getting Started Wizard that helps you every step of the way.

When accessing your e-mail account for the very first time, follow these steps:

1. **Click E-Mail on the Office Live Home page Navigation bar.**

   You're greeted by the Welcome to Office Live Mail Welcome page (see Figure 4-7).

   The Welcome page gives you a sneak peek at what your e-mail will look like as well as providing you with four key Office Live E-mail features. If you click any of those features, the corresponding area lights up on the graphic.

2. **Click Next to continue and indicate your Inbox preferences.**

   The Customize Your Inbox page opens (see Figure 4-8). Office Live leaves nothing to chance, and here's your chance to select a few preferences.

   • Select your color theme.

   • Choose your preferred location for your reading pane.

   • Indicate whether you'd like to keep a copy of your sent messages.

3. **Click the Take Me to My E-Mail button.**

   Wait momentarily while Office Live Mail opens.

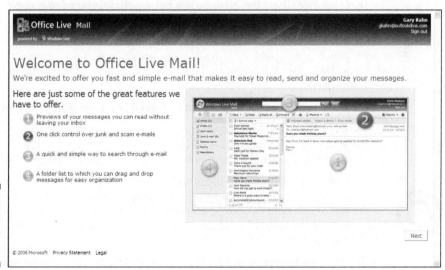

Figure 4-7:
Welcome to
Office Live
Mail.

Figure 4-8:
Customizing
your Office
Live Mail
page.

Reading your Office Live mail

After you successfully log in to Office Live for the first time, you'll want to check to see if you have received any new e-mail. To do this, start once again at the Office Live home page and follow these steps:

1. **Click E-Mail on the Navigation bar or click Inbox from the E-Mail section of the Office Live Home page.**

   All roads lead to Rome — or in this case the Office Live Mail Today page, which now opens. The Today window gives you a synopsis of how much e-mail space you've used, and shows you any contacts you've recently updated.

2. **Click Inbox on the folder list of the Office Live Mail Today window.**

   The Office Live Mail page opens, as shown in Figure 4-9. The Office Live Mail page consists of three columns: the folder list, the message list, and the Preview pane. Your messages appear in the message list column.

   If you'd like to change the width of one of the mail columns, place your cursor on the vertical line separating the columns until your cursor transforms into a double-pointing horizontal arrow. Hold down your left mouse button and drag the column border to the left or right to resize the column.

3. **(Optional) Sort your messages by clicking the Sort By drop-down arrow and choose Date, From, Subject, or Size.**

4. **Click one of the messages to select it.**

   The contents of the message now appear in the Preview pane.

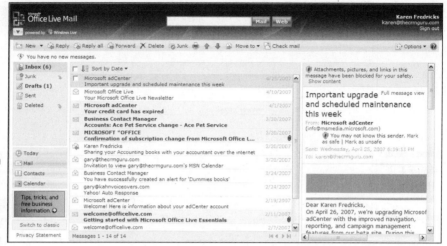

Figure 4-9:
The Office
Live Mail
page.

5. **(Optional) Select an e-mail option from the Office Live Mail toolbar:**

   • *New*: Create a new message, folder, contact, or group of contacts.

   • *Reply*: Allows you to send a response to the e-mail sender.

   • *Reply all*: Allows you to send a response to everyone who received the e-mail in addition to the sender.

   • *Forward*: Forwards the e-mail on to a new recipient.

   • *Delete:* Deletes the currently selected message.

   • *Junk*: Labels the e-mail as junk mail and sends it to the Junk folder.

   • *Print:* Prints the currently selected message.

   • *Up or Down Pointing Arrows:* Allows you to view the Next or Previous Message.

   • *Move to:* Allows you to move the message to another folder.

   • *Check Mail:* Refreshes the Office Live Mail window to check for any new mail messages that you might have received.

You can select several messages by clicking their check boxes — or (if you'd like to delete a bunch of messages at the same time) click the check box to the left of the Sort by Date button to select *all* messages.

6. **Click Reply or Forward if you'd like to reply or forward a message.**

   The Reply or Forward window opens, as shown in Figure 4-10. If you're replying to a message you only have to type the body of your message and click Send. If you're forwarding a message, type the recipient's e-mail address in the To address field, type you message, and then click Send.

Figure 4-10:
Replying to
a message.

Sending Office Live mail

When you've mastered the art of *reading* your mail, you'll probably want to start *sending* some. If you've used other programs to send e-mail you'll find that Office Live has all the bells and whistles you'd normally associate with sending e-mail.

Follow these steps to create a brand, spanking-new e-mail message:

1. **Click Inbox in the E-Mail section of the Office Live Home page.**

   The Office Live Mail page opens.

2. **Click New on the toolbar at the top of the Office Live Mail page.**

   A New Message page opens; see Figure 4-11.

3. **In the To line, type the e-mail address of the person you want to send the message to.**

   If you have already added contacts to Office Live, you can click the book icon to the left of the To line to reveal a list of your contacts. Feel free to click one of the contact names — and watch the e-mail address magically fill in for you in the To line.

4. **(Optional) Click the Show Cc and Bcc button to reveal the Cc and Bcc lines.**

   If you're sending an e-mail to multiple other recipients this is where you'll want to put their addresses.

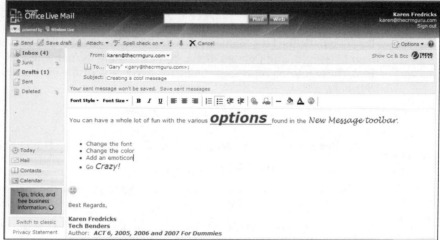

Figure 4-11:
Sending an
Office Live
e-mail
message.

5. **In the Subject line, type a brief description of the message.**

6. **Type your message in the main message box, and then click Send.**

   If you have an artistic streak, you can format the message in a number of ways. The New Message icon bar helps you change the font, its size, its color, and other attributes including bolding, italicizing, and underlining. You can number or bullet a list of items, and even add an "emoticon" if you'd like.

Faster than a speeding bullet your e-mail message hurtles through cyber-space and lands in the recipient's Inbox.

Organizing Your E-Mail

After you start using your Office Live Main account, it's likely your Inbox will soon fill to the brim with e-mail. If you are an eager beaver, you can respond to each message as it arrives. However, many of you might need a little bit of extra help to keep all that mail organized.

Office Live Mail includes most of the same features that are in more sophisti-cated e-mail clients. You can divide your Inbox and Sent messages folders into smaller, more manageable parts. After you create the folders, you can have your messages sent to one of them automatically. Or, should the mes-sage be spam, Office Live Mail can send the offending e-mail packing.

Creating new folders

By default, Office Live Mail comes with five folders: Inbox, Junk E-Mail, Drafts, Sent Messages, and Deleted Items. You can create as many new folders as you like. These folders represent the major parts of your life such as *Personal* and *Business*.

Here's how you set up additional folders:

1. **Click Inbox in the E-Mail section of the Office Live Home page.**

   The Office Live Mail page opens.

2. **Click the New drop-down arrow on the toolbar at the top of the Office Live Mail page and select Folder.**

   A new folder appears at the bottom of your folder list with the appropriate name New Folder.

3. **Fill in the name of the new folder.**

   The new folder appears alphabetically under the Deleted Items folder.

After you create a folder, you can rename or delete it at any time. Simply right-click the folder you want to delete or rename and then click Rename Folder or Delete Folder.

 All the folders you create are top-level folders — you cannot create subfolders within another folder. Because the folders appear alphabetically you might take that into consideration when naming your folders. For example, if you want to set up ten separate folders (one for each client) you might name them *Client 1* and *Client 2* so all your client folders appear together.

Moving mail automatically

For most of you, any time someone volunteers to do some of your work for you is a good thing. Office Live Mail might just become your new best friend because it sorts your mail according to your specifications. For example, you might want all the correspondence that comes in from tom@mycompany.com to move automatically to the Client — My Company folder or mail with that includes the word *contract* to move to the VIP folder.

After you set up some new e-mail folders, here's how you can have Office Live Mail sort your incoming e-mail for you automatically:

1. **Click Inbox in the E-Mail section of the Office Live Home page.**

   The Office Live Mail page opens.

2. **Click Options in the toolbar.**

   The Options menu expands to show you lots of e-mail options.

3. **Click More Options.**

   The Options page opens.

4. **Click the Automatically Sort Email into Folders link in the Customize Your E-Mail section of the Options page.**

   The Automatically Sort E-Mail into Folders page opens. (Before you start grousing about all the steps you have taken to arrive at this point, remember that this will save you lots of time in the long run!)

5. **Click New Filter.**

   The Edit Filter page opens; see Figure 4-12. You'll notice that any new folders that you have created are listed there.

6. **In Step 1: Which Messages Are You Looking For?, specify where the e-mail is coming from, the matching criterion you want Office Live Mail to use, and the person's name or e-mail address information.**

7. **In Step 2: Where Do You Want to Put These Messages?, select the folder that you'd like the incoming e-mail to move to.**

   You can even select the New Folder option and indicate the name of the new folder you'd like Office Live to create for you. Or, if you prefer, you can select the Delete These Messages option to have Office Live Mail delete messages coming in from your enemies and/or ex-spouse!

Figure 4-12:
Creating a filter to move incoming e-mail messages.

8. **Click Save to save your changes.**

   You land back in the Automatically Sort Email into Folders page. Then click Edit to edit an existing rule, Delete to delete a rule, or click the Mail icon to return to your Inbox.

Junking your junk mail

The proliferation of spam in this day and age is truly amazing. Office Live's junk e-mail filter helps keep that nasty stuff out of your Inbox. You can specify the level of security you want, and how you want Office Live to handle those pesky messages.

Here's how you can change the Office Live Mail spam filter:

1. **Click Inbox in the E-Mail section of the Office Live Home page.**

   The Office Live Mail page opens.

2. **Click Options in the toolbar.**

   The Options menu expands to show you lots of e-mail options.

3. **Click More Options.**

   The Options page opens.

4. **Click Filters and Confirmation in the Junk E-Mail section of the Options page.**

   The Filters and Confirmation page opens, as shown in Figure 4-13.

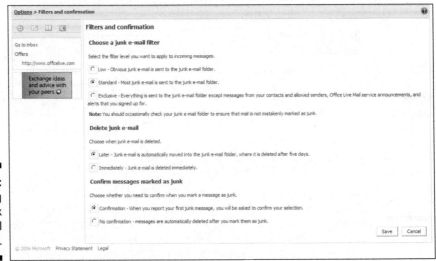

Figure 4:13: Changing the Junk E-mail filters.

5. **Select the level of security, when you'd like to see the spam deleted, and what kind of confirmation you'd like to receive when the deed is done.**

   If you specify the Low level of filtering, Office Live filters only the most flagrant messages. If you set the level to Exclusive, you receive only e-mail from people you have approved in advance. By default, the level is set to Standard.

   Because no junk e-mail system is perfect, you'll probably want to leave the Delete Junk E-Mail option set to Later rather than to Immediately. Should the junk e-mail system erroneously mark something as junk you won't have a chance to retrieve it if you have the option set to Immediately.

6. **Click Save to save your changes.**

   You land back in the Options page.

7. **(Optional) Click Allowed and Blocked Senders.**

   The Allowed and Blocked Senders page opens. Here's where you can create lists for both the *allowed senders* (those people you want to make sure are allowed past your spam filter) and your *blocked senders* (those people from whom you never want to receive e-mail). You can even indicate any mailing lists that you have signed up for to ensure that you get their monthly newsletters.

Remember to check your Junk E-Mail folder every time you check your mail to make sure that important mail has not landed there by accident. If you find a message in this folder that is not spam, click the message and then click Allow Sender from the toolbar.

Working with Basic E-Mail Contacts

Office Live comes equipped with a basic address book. You can use the address book alone, or use it in conjunction with your e-mail.

The Essentials and Premium Office Live accounts come with Business Contact Manager, which you might think of as the basic e-mail address book on steroids. You can read all the details about Business Contact Manager in Chapter 8.

Making contacts

You can add people by going directly to the address book and filling in their information. Alternatively, you can add new contacts when you are sending or receiving e-mail. You can even import contacts from a file if you have one. After you enter your contacts in the address book, you can type their names in the To box when composing an e-mail message, or select their names in the contact list, in order to send an e-mail.

Entering contacts manually

Follow these steps to add a contact manually:

1. **Click Contacts in the E-Mail section of the Office Live Home page.**

   The Office Live Mail address book opens.

   If you are already in Office Live Mail, you can click the address book icon.

2. **Click New on the address book toolbar.**

   The address book opens.

3. **(Optional) Click Show All Fields.**

   Selecting this option displays all the fields you see in Figure 4-14 rather than just the four basic name and e-mail fields.

4. **Enter the details of your new contact, and then click Save.**

   You end up back in Office Live Mail. The next time you send e-mail, you can access the address book without having to strip-search your desk for the sticky note that holds the contact's e-mail address.

Importing contacts

Unless you've been living under a rock somewhere, or are under the age of ten, chances are pretty good that you've been using e-mail prior to using Office Live — and that you already have an address book. If you are currently using Outlook, Outlook Express, Windows Contacts, Live Mail, Yahoo!, or Google, you can export your information into a text file and then import the information directly into Office Live.

Figure 4-14:
Adding a
contact to
the Office
Live address
book.

Office Live Mail	Karen Fredricks
powered by Windows Live	karen@thecrmguru.com
	Contacts Web	Sign out

Save ✗ Cancel   Options ▾

You
All contacts (14)   **Edit contact details**
Coworkers (1)   First name
Family (2)   Last name
Friends (2)   Nickname

                     Personal Information

                      Personal e-mail
                      Windows Live ID   ☐ Use this address with Windows Live Messenger
                      Home phone
                      Mobile phone
                      Home address
Today   City
Mail   State/Province
Contacts   ZIP/Postal code
Calendar   Country

Exchange ideas   **Business Information**
and advice with
your peers ○   Company
Switch to classic   Work e-mail
Privacy Statement   Work phone
                      Pager

Here's all you need to do:

1. **Click Contacts in the E-Mail section of the Office Live Home page.**

   The Office Live Mail address book opens.

2. **Click Options and select Import Contacts.**

   The Import Contacts page, shown in Figure 4-15, appears on the scene.

3. **Select an import option from the list in Option 2: Import from a File section.**

4. **Click Browse and navigate to the spot where you saved the export file.**

5. **Click the Import Contacts button to import your contacts.**

   After a few seconds of whirring and hissing, your contacts now appear in your Office Live address book.

Adding a contact from an incoming e-mail message

Perhaps the easiest method of adding a new contact into the Office Live address book is to add it when you receive an e-mail message. The Add Contact link appears next to the header of every message that you receive from someone who is not currently in your address book (in the Preview pane and in the header area of the message itself). Click the link to add the name and e-mail address of the sender automatically to your address book.

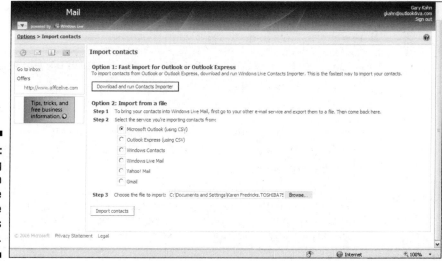

Figure 4-15:
Importing
information
into the
Office Live
address
book.

Removing or changing contacts

It's just as easy to edit or remove contact information from the Office Live address book as it is to enter the information in the first place.

Here's all you need to do:

1. **Select a contact by clicking it.**

   If your plan is to delete multiple contacts you can speed up the process by holding down the Ctrl key, and then clicking each contact that you want to remove to select contacts that are not next to each other. Click the first contact in a sequence of contacts, hold down the Shift key, and then click the last contact to select consecutive contacts.

3. **Click Delete to delete the contact or Edit to change the contact information.**

4. **Click Yes to confirm the deletion or Save to save your changes.**

Printing your contact information

After you spend hours and hours slaving over the computer inputting your contacts — or maybe you just clicked a button and imported a whole slew of them in one fell click — you might have the urge to print your address book for posterity. As you might have guessed by now, just about anything is possible in Office Live — including the ability to print an address book.

Here's all you have to do to print your contacts:

1. **Click Contacts in the E-Mail section of the Office Live Home page.**

   The Office Live Mail address book opens.

2. **Click Print on the toolbar.**

   If you're not sure what the icon looks like, you'll find it cleverly disguised as a printer. A printable copy of your address book opens in a new page.

3. **Click Print.**

   As you would suspect, your printer responds accordingly and starts spitting out paper containing your contact information. The size of each entry depends on the information you entered for the contact. For example, if you only added the first and last name and the e-mail address of the contact, that's all that appears. If you added further information (such as an address and additional e-mail addresses for a contact), all that information prints as well.

Creating a group of contacts

Any feature that saves me time gets special recognition in my book. Creating a group of contacts is one such feature. You can organize your contacts into groups so you can send mail to everyone in that group at the same time. You can create multiple groups, and contacts can belong to more than one group. For example, if you're on the planning committee of the Chamber of Commerce, you can create a Planning group. If you're also on the Board of Directors, you can create a Board group. A contact can belong to either group — or to both.

All contacts that you create in the address book automatically belong in the All contacts group. And, as you add more groups and add contacts to them, you can still access all your contacts in the All Contacts group.

Although using a group saves you lots of time, it takes very little time to set one up. Here's how you do it:

1. **Click Contacts in the E-Mail section of the Office Live Home page.**

   The Office Live Mail address book opens.

2. **Click the New drop-down arrow and choose Group.**

   A new group appears in the address book Navigation bar.

3. **Type a name for your new group, and then press Enter.**

   Your new contact group appears under the All Contacts folder. The groups appear in alphabetical order.

4. **Select one or more contacts from your contact list and drag them to the group you want them to be in.**

   The contacts remain in both the All Contacts folder and in the new group folder.

5. **(Optional) Click the contact that you want to remove from a group and then click Remove from Group on the toolbar.**

   The contact remains in the All Contacts folder but disappears from the group.

To send e-mail to a whole group, type the group name in the To box when composing an e-mail message, or select the group from the To drop-down list.

Chapter 5

Everyone Needs a Web Site

. . . .

In This Chapter

▶ Boosting your business with a Web site
▶ Checking off things to include on your site
▶ Working with the templates
▶ Using the Document Gallery

. . . .

Chapter 3 shows you how to choose a name and register a Web site. This chapter shows you how to get your Web site up and running. You'll want to think a bit about the purpose of your Web site, and then design it accordingly. You can start by using the numerous Web site templates that come with Office Live — or import an existing Web site if you have one. Add a few graphics and you're ready to go — unless, of course, you decide to tweak it a bit.

In order to work on your Web site, you must have the proper permissions. The person who subscribed to Office Live is by default an administrator and can work on the site. In addition, any other users with Editor or Administrator permissions can also work on the site. If you don't have those access levels, you might skip this chapter — or pass this book on to the person who does. (Better yet, make him or her buy an "administrator's" copy!)

So Why Do You Need a Web Site?

If your business has flourished in spite of not having a Web site, you're probably wondering why you need one — or why you should take the time to develop one. Those of you who already have a Web site might not have seen any noticeable increase in your business. That's exactly where Office Live comes into play.

Office Live offers you a free and easy way to create a Web site. If that alone doesn't convince you to create one, there are plenty of other reasons why small businesses today should have a Web presence. Keep these benefits in mind as you start to design your Web site:

- ✔ **Keep your name in front of prospects:** More and more people are using the Internet to research products and services; phone book and newspaper advertising are becoming a thing of the past. If you don't keep up with technology you'll soon be left behind.

- ✔ **Expand your territory:** A Web site represents a great way for you to expand the territory that you can cover. Unlike a newspaper or yellow page ad that only reaches a limited geographical area, the Internet is global. If you're selling products you no longer have to sell just from one location, you might even be able to eliminate the need for a storefront. Consider if your business can offer services remotely as well as locally.

- ✔ **Provide 24/7 customer service:** A Web site can be as much about customer service as it is about selling products and services. Prospects and customers should be able to access your Web site and find the information they want — whenever they want it. You can add pictures of your products, pricelists, and any pertinent information you want.

- ✔ **Keep up with the competition:** Chances are good that most — if not all — of your competitors have a Web site. A good Web site can help level the playing field for smaller companies as they try to compete against larger companies. You might even check out the Web sites of your competitors to get an idea of what types of information their sites include.

- ✔ **Credibility:** First impressions are important and for some of your prospects your Web site will be their first introduction to your company. Having a professional-looking Web site gives your company a professional image — even if you are working out of a back bedroom!

Getting Your Site Up and Running in a Jiffy

Before Office Live, creating a Web site entailed a lot of time, effort, and money. You'd have to research and hire a Web designer, register a URL, figure out how to have the site hosted, and pay someone to keep your site updated. If all that seems a bit much, here's good news: Office Live has removed all those barriers that might have kept you from having a Web site. Chapter 3 shows how easily you can register a Web site with Office Live. In addition, Office Live includes over a hundred predesigned Web site templates; these templates are geared towards small business owners and managers who are either technically challenged, artistically challenged — or both! And there's more — after you choose a template, easy-to-understand tools help you modify your site.

Rome wasn't built in a day — or so I'm told — and you're not going to finish your Web site in a day, either. Consider your Web site to be a work in progress.

Doing a bit of Web-site decorating

Before you work on individual pages, it's a good idea to design the elements common to each page in your site. This helps give your site a more professional appearance. In addition, visitors will find it easier to navigate your Web site if all its pages have the same basic look and feel.

Here's how to get started on your Web-site design:

1. **Click WebSite in the Navigation bar of your Office Live Home page.**

   The Page Manager page opens, as shown in Figure 5-1.

2. **Click Edit next to the page you'd like to edit.**

   The Office Live Web Designer opens. Although you can add as many pages as you'd like to your Web site, Office Live very nicely starts you out with four Web pages:

   - *Home Page:* This is the first page visitors will see when they land on your Web site.

   - *About Us:* This page is a good place to describe the services and products you offer.

Figure 5-1:
Creating an
Essentials
or Premium
Web site.

- *Contact Us:* This is a good place to list your contact information.

- *Site Map:* Having a site map page will ensure that the visitors to your site will be able to find their way around your site quickly and easily.

3. **Click the Site Designer icon.**

   The Site Designer opens, as shown in Figure 5-2. The Site Designer toolbar is where you find the tools you need to make site-wide design changes.

4. **Click one of the Site Designer icons on the toolbar, fill in the desired information, and then click OK.**

   Here's where the fun and games begin because you can choose the basic look and feel of your Web site. You can choose any and all of the elements that appear on the Site Designer toolbar. Experiment with the different look each gives your site.

   - *Header:* This is where you can add the name of your company, a slogan if you have one and indicate whether or not you want a Search box to appear on your Web site. Figure 5-3 shows the Customize Header page.

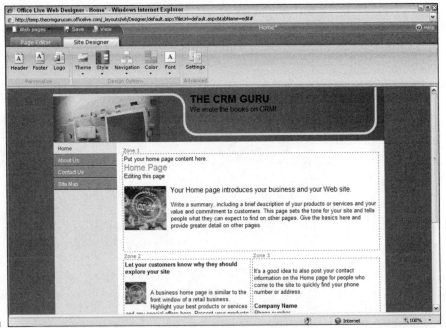

Figure 5-2:
The Site
Designer.

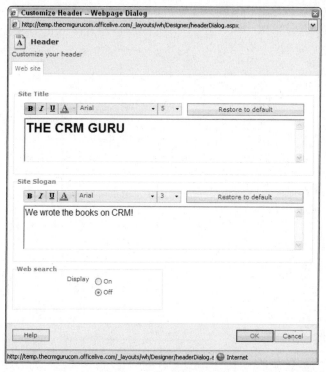

Figure 5-3:
Creating
a header
for your
Web site.

- *Footer:* Add any disclaimer information that you want to appear on the bottom of each page of your site. You can also add links to other sites if you'd like. Figure 5-4 shows the Customize Your Footer page.

- *Logo:* You can add a graphic to your Web site by clicking the Upload Pictures icon in the Change Your Logo page, navigating to the graphic you'd like to include on your site, and then clicking OK.

- *Theme:* If you are artistically challenged, you're going to love choosing a theme for your Web site! Click the Theme button and a list appears. Office Live comes with over twenty theme industries; each industry has six suggested Web-site designs that include graphics and layout designs. Start by choosing a basic Web site template. This is not an earth-shattering decision; you can easily change it at a later date if you decide you'd like to convey a different image.

  Changing one option may change some of the other options as well. For example, if you select a different theme you may find that the header style is no longer the one you had previously selected.

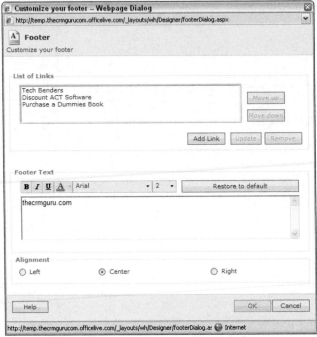

Figure 5-4:
Adding
a footer
to your
Web site.

- *Style:* Click the Style button and select a header style. Choosing a style allows you to select a slightly different header designer than the one that appeared with the theme you chose. Click the different styles to see how each one looks; the changes you make are dynamic so that you can see immediately what they look like.

- *Navigation:* This option allows you to place the navigation buttons (the links to the other pages of your Web site) at either the top or left side of your Web site.

- *Color:* True to its word, the Color button allows you to change the color scheme of your Web site simply by clicking one of the color themes.

- *Font:* Here's where you get to pick the default font for your Web site. Don't be surprised when you only see a handful of choices. Although you may have lots of fonts on your computer, it's better to stick to the Web-compatible fonts — which is exactly what Office Live does.

5. **Click the Save icon when you are finished making changes to your Web site design.**

An asterisk appears after the page name in the Site Designer title bar in the upper-right of the window. This indicates that the page you are working on has unsaved changes. Remember to save your changes and make the asterisk disappear!

6. **Close the Site Designer by clicking the X in the upper-right corner of the Site Designer when you finish making all the desired changes to your Web site.**

Conveying a message in your Web site

After you settle on the basic *look* of your Web site, you can start working on your Web site's *message*. Unfortunately, you're going to have to do a bit of homework here. The best way to add content to your Web site is to start small and expand as the need — and inspiration — arises. At the very least, you can start out with a "business card" Web site that contains very basic information about your company:

Here's a quartet of basic information items you'll want to include:

- ✔ Name
- ✔ Location
- ✔ Contact information
- ✔ Brief description of products or services

Your Web site appears on the Internet as soon as you sign up for an Office Live account. Make sure that you replace the instructional content that is displayed on your site pages before you announce your Web-site address to the world!

To modify the text on your Web pages, follow these steps:

1. **Click WebSite in the Navigation bar of your Office Live Home page.**

   The Page Manager page opens.

2. **Click Edit next to the page you'd like to edit.**

   The Page Editor tab opens. You'll probably want to start out by making changes to the home page.

3. **Click the Layout icon on the Page Editor toolbar and select a column layout for the page.**

   Unfortunately, you don't have a lot of choice here; Figure 5-5 shows an example of a three-"zone" layout.

4. **Edit the existing text by placing your cursor in the area you want to edit and start typing away.**

   You find all the comforts of your favorite word processor right on the Page Editor toolbar. Click a button to change font attributes such as bold, italic, underline, and font color. You'll find icons to help you create bullets or numbers as well as to center or right justify your text.

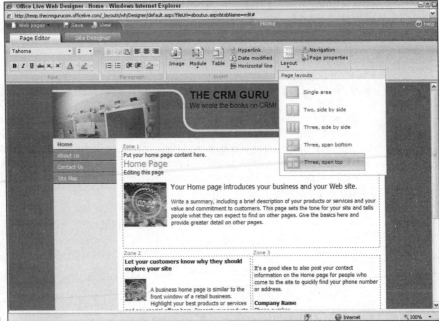

Figure 5-5:
Making
changes to
Web site
content in
the Page
Editor.

Office Live's Page Editor is a very easy way of creating your Web site. Many Web designers rely on HTML to design sites. You might be wondering about the font size which seems kind of tiny. That's because Office Live is displaying HTML font sizes; click the Font drop-down arrow and you'll see the more common equivalent to the traditional HTML sizing.

5. **Click the Save icon when you are finished making all your editing changes.**

6. **Close the Office Live Page Editor by clicking the red X in the top-right corner of the window.**

   You can go back and edit the rest of the pages of your Web site by clicking one of the navigation links on the left side of your Web site.

All work and no play makes you, well, cranky. To ease the strain of all of the hard work that is going into your Web site you might want to sit back for a minute and enjoy the fruits of your labors. Click the View icon to see your Web site exactly as your visitors will see it.

Doing a Bit of Web Site Redecoration

It's always good to start with a basic Web site and then expand it as the need arises. After you have your basic design down, and you've added your basic contact and product information, you're ready to start expanding your horizons. There are lots of neat ways to improve the look of your site; try as many of them as you'd like.

Working with the pages of your Web site

Office Live starts you with four Web-site pages: Home, About Us, Contact Us, and Site Map. These pages appear as navigation aids on every one of your Web site pages, making it easy to navigate from page to page. You may find the default pages are perfect as they stand, but odds are you'll want to add more pages. Or you might wake up in the middle of the night with the burning desire to change the names of the pages. You might even decide that the default page names are perfect, but the order of the pages needs a bit of tweaking. No problemo — these are all easy feats to accomplish.

Adding new pages to your Web site

Scrollitis is a condition that affects many Web sites. Scrollitis occurs when a Web page has so much content that you have to scroll down to view the bottommost contents of a page. If your Web site suffers from this malady, rest assured that there's a simple cure — add more Web pages.

Adding a new page to your Web site is just about effortless if you follow these steps:

1. **Click WebSite on the Navigation bar of the Office Live home page.**

   The Page Manager opens.

2. **Click New Page.**

   The Select a Template page opens (see Figure 5-6).

Figure 5-6:
Adding a
new page
to your
Web site.

3. **Select a Web-page template.**

   For your Web-site-creation pleasure, Office Live has included templates for areas that are common to most Web sites. Select the one that pertains to the page you'd like to add, or just choose the General template.

4. **Click Next to continue.**

   The Choose Page Properties page opens (see Figure 5-7).

5. **Give the new page a title, and decide whether it's going to appear in the Navigation bar.**

   If you give the new page the same name as an existing page, you can opt to overwrite the existing page.

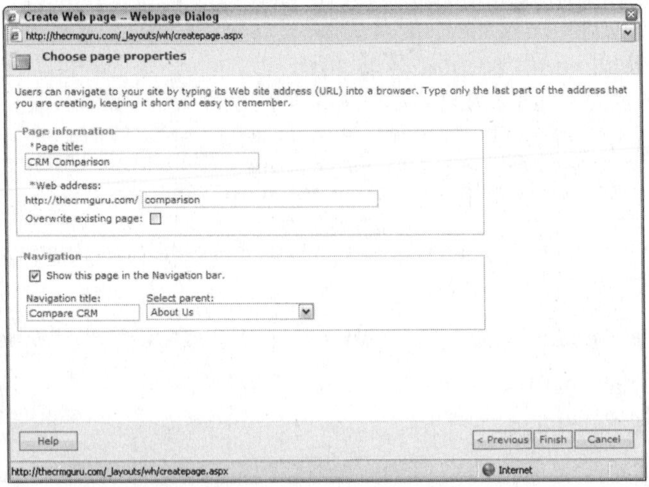

Figure 5-7:
Choosing
the page
properties
of the new
Web page.

6. **Click Finish to close the wizard.**

   You land with a plop back at the Page Manager. And — wonder of wonders — you see the new page listed with all your other existing Web pages.

Changing the order of your Web-site pages

Although I can't provide you with a quick and easy way to move your living room furniture, I can show you how easy it is to move around the pages of your Web site. You might want to think of the Navigation bar as your Web site's table of contents because it lists your Web pages in the order of their appearance.

To change the order of your Web pages, follow these steps:

1. **Click WebSite on the Navigation bar of the Office Live Home page.**

   The Page Manager opens.

2. **Click Navigation from the Page Manager toolbar.**

   The Navigation page opens; see Figure 5-8.

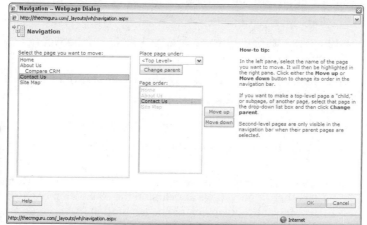

Figure 5-8:
Changing
the order of
your Web
pages.

3. **Make the appropriate changes to the page order.**

   • *Move a page:* Select the page you want to move from the appropriately titled Select the Page You Want to Move section.

   • *Select a parent page:* Select <Top Level> from the Place Page Under drop-down box (if you want the page to appear in the Navigation bar) or select the name of another page (if you want this page to be visible only when the parent page is being viewed).

   • *Change the parent page:* Select a different page from the Place Page Under drop-down list and click the Change Parent button if you decide that you would like to change the parent page that a page is associated with.

   • *Change the order of the pages:* Select a page and then click Move Up or Move Down to change the order of the Navigation bar.

4. **Click OK when you're finished.**

   Your changes are saved and you return to the Page Manager.

Renaming a page

Being able to change your Web site as your business changes is important.
And being able to make these changes without having to call in the somewhat
surly (and definitely overpriced) IT guy is, of course, an added bonus.

In addition to adding new pages and rearranging them, you might want to
rename your pages from time to time. Accomplishing that is extremely easy:

1. **Click WebSite on the Navigation bar of the Office Live Home page.**

   The Page Manager opens.

2. **In the Page Manager area, click Properties to the right of the page you
   want to rename.**

   The Choose Page Properties page opens, as shown in Figure 5-9.

3. **Fill in the pertinent information.**

   You have three key pieces of information to add here:

   - *Page Title:* This is the name of the page that is shown in your
     browser's address bar.

   - *Show This Page in the Navigation Bar:* This check box determines
     whether or not a page appears on the Navigation bar. Use this option
     if you want to keep certain pages hidden from public access.

   - *Navigation Title:* This is the official name that appears on the
     Navigation bar.

   Optionally, you can also click the Edit Navigation Position button to
   change the order of your pages.

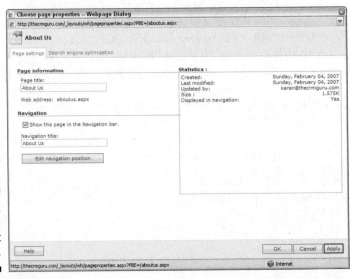

Figure 5-9:
Changing
the name of
a Web page,
in this case
the About
Us page.

4. **Click OK when you finish renaming the Web page.**

You end up back at the Page Manager that now reflects the new name you've given to your Web page.

Getting hyper about hyperlinks

A *hyperlink* is a link to another page on either your own or a different Web site. You can generally recognize hyperlinks because the font color is slightly different from the color of the rest of the text on a page. And behold! If you happen to hover your cursor over a hyperlink and it changes to a hand, you can click the hyperlink — and then hurtle through cyberspace to land on another Web site in an Internet galaxy far, far away.

Hyperlinks are an easy way to provide more information to the visitors to your Web site. You might even create an entire page of hyperlinks linking to recommended products or informational sites. Or you might create hyperlinks to link to other sites; Chapter 6 explains why this is a great way to improve the traffic to your Web site.

Here's all you need to get started linking your way through cyberspace:

1. **Click WebSite on the Navigation bar of the Office Live Home page.**

The Page Manager opens.

2. **Click Edit next to the name of the page to which you'd like to add a hyperlink.**

The Page Editor tab of the Web Designer opens.

3. **Create the text that you want to transform into a hyperlink, and then select it.**

If you want to be really boring you might type text such as "visit my Web site at www.yadayada.com for more information." Of course, if you want to be a bit spiffier, you might consider something along the lines of "Click Here to Learn More."

You can also create a hyperlink from a graphic. Instead of highlighting text, simply select the graphic you'd like to transform into a hyperlink.

4. **Click the Hyperlink button on the Page Editor toolbar.**

The Insert Link page opens, as shown in Figure 5-10.

5. **Select the type of link that you want to insert and fill in the corresponding information.**

- *Web:* Link to any Web site other than your own; fill in the URL address in the Link field.

- *My Page:* Link to a page on your Web site; click the Select Page icon that appears and choose the page you want to link to based on the sample provided.

- *Email:* Link to an e-mail address; fill in the e-mail address in the Link field based on the sample provided.

- *Document:* Link to a file that you've uploaded to the Document Gallery (see the later section called "Documenting Documents with the Document Gallery"). Click the Select Document icon to select the appropriate document.

- *Other:* Link to other, less typical sites types such as HTTPS or FTP.

Figure 5-10:
Adding a
hyperlink.

6. **Click OK to create the hyperlink and return to the Page Editor.**

7. **Click Save to save your changes and close the Page Editor.**

Creating a table

Tables are a great way to organize the content of your Web site. A table consists of equally sized columns and rows. For example, you might want to list six products and include a picture, the product name, item code, and a price for each product. You could create a table consisting of six rows (one for each product) and four columns (representing the graphic, name, item code, and price) making it a no-brainer for Web site visitors to get the lowdown on each of your products.

You can insert a table into any area of your Web site by following these steps:

1. **Click WebSite on the Navigation bar of the Office Live Home page.**

   The Page Manager opens.

2. **In the Page Manager area, click Edit next to the name of the page to which you'd like to add a hyperlink.**

   The Page Editor tab of the Web Designer opens.

3. **Put your cursor on the spot where you'd like to insert a table, and then click Table on the Page Editor toolbar.**

   The Create Table page opens, as shown in Figure 5-11.

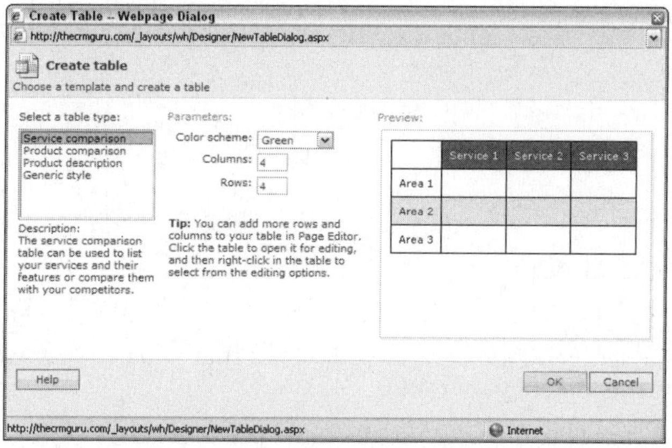

Figure 5-11: Inserting a table on your Web site.

4. **Fill in the table information.**

   As usual, you have a few choices here. The object of the game is to select the choices that you think look best on your Web site. The preview window changes to reflect your changes as you make them.

   - *Select a table type:* Select a product or service style table if you want to insert a preformatted table; select Generic style if you want an unformatted table.

   - *Select the color scheme:* You have over a half dozen color choices.

   - *Select the numbers of columns and rows:* Remember, rows run horizontally and columns run vertically.

5. **Click OK to close the Create Table page.**

6. **Click in an empty cell and type your content.**

   You can use any of the text-formatting tools to customize your text. If you type more text than a cell can hold, the cell widens automatically to accommodate your text. If you hit the Enter key, the cell elongates.

7. **Right-click the table and choose Properties to change how a table looks.**

   The Table Properties page opens, as shown in Figure 5-12.

Figure 5-12: Changing the table properties.

Here's a handy bunch of table properties that you can play with to change the look of your table:

- *Width:* Sets the width of the table cell in pixels.

- *Height:* Sets the height of the table cell in pixels.

- *Cell Padding:* Determines the amount of space between your text and the edge of a cell.

- *Cell Spacing:* Changes the distance between the cell borders.

- *Border Color:* Allows you to select the border color for the table.

- *Border Width:* Changes the thickness of the border.

- *Background Color:* Lets you select the table background color.

- *Use Background Image:* Select this check box to use an image file as the background for your table.

- *Image File:* Allows you to browse for an image that is placed in the selected cell.

8. **Click Apply to save your table changes and return to the Page Editor.**

9. **Click Save to save the changes to your Web site, and then click the red X to close the Page Editor.**

Improving your image with images

No one wants to look at a boring Web site. You'll probably want to add a few graphics to yours to give it a bit more interest. If you have pictures of your products, a logo, or even a photo of your building on your computer, you can upload those pictures to your Web site.

Adding graphics to your Web site is actually a two-step process:

1. You must upload the graphic from your computer to your Office Live site. You can then access them again in the Image Library.

2. You place the graphic on the appropriate area of your Web site.

Having graphics on your Web site adds to the time it takes for a page to download. Professional Web designers use "thumbnail" software to make image file sizes as small as possible before adding them to a page. This reduces the time it takes for a visitor to load those images — and your Web site.

Web images are considered intellectual property; it is against the law to use copyrighted images. You may be able to use or buy images that you find on the Internet. Be aware that unless otherwise stated, you should assume that a graphic is copyrighted.

Although there are many types of graphics, the most common ones used on Web sites include these file extensions:

- **.bmp:** This is one of the most common image file types, giving a good image quality with a relatively small file size.

- **.jpg or .jpeg:** This format reduces the image's file size without an appreciable loss of image quality.

- **.gif:** These graphics provide the best quality for most images but are typically not used for photographs.

Follow these steps to upload an image and then add it to your Web site:

1. **Click WebSite in the Navigation bar of your Office Live Home page.**

   The Page Manager opens.

2. **In the Page Manager area, click Edit next to the page you'd like to edit.**

   The Page Editor tab of the Web opens.

3. **Click the spot in the page where you'd like the new graphic to appear, and then click Image on the Page Editor toolbar.**

   The Pick an Image page opens; see Figure 5-13. If you have not uploaded any images to your site, the page is empty.

Figure 5-13:
Adding
a graphic
to your
Web site.

4. **Click the Upload Pictures button.**

   The Image Uploader opens, as shown in Figure 5-14.

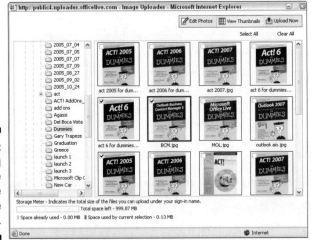

Figure 5-14:
Uploading
an image
using the
Image
Uploader.

5. **Browse to the folder using the navigation tree on the left that contains the image that you want to upload, and then select the check box in the upper-left of the box of the graphic(s) you want to upload to your Web site.**

If you look very closely, you'll notice a check mark appearing in the upper-left corner of any graphic file(s) you select.

6. **(Optional) Click the Edit Photos button on the Image Uploader toolbar. Rotate, adjust the contrast or brightness, and crop your photos as needed.**

   The Edit Photos page opens, as shown in Figure 5-15. You'll find icons on the toolbar to rotate, adjust the contrast and/or brightness, and crop the graphic.

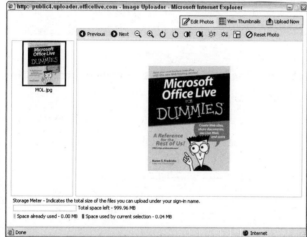

Figure 5-15: Editing a graphic for use on your Web site.

7. **When you've selected one or more images, click the Upload Now button in the upper-right of the Image Uploader.**

   The graphics you selected now appear on the Pick an Image page.

8. **Click an image to select it on the Pick an Image page, and then click OK.**

   Your image now appears on your Web site. If you decide you don't want the graphic, simply click it one time to select it and then press Delete — presto-change-o, it's gone.

9. **Click Save on the Page Editor toolbar and then close the Office Live Page Editor by clicking the red X in the top right.**

If you find that the size of your graphic is too large or too small for your Web site, you might need to edit the graphic before uploading it. There are a number of free utilities available to create thumbnail copies of your graphics — reducing their size without risking distortion.

Documenting documents with the Document Gallery

You have lots and lots of information that you want to impart to your Web site visitors. However, you might be concerned that adding too much text to your site will make it appear cluttered and hard to read. A simple solution is to upload informational documents that your visitors can download at their discretion. For example, you might want to include your company brochure and price list in PDF format. Or you might want to offer an executable file to update software if you are a software developer.

Here's all you need to do to upload a file and then make it available to the public at large:

1. **Click WebSite in the Navigation bar of your Office Live Home page.**

   The Page Manager opens.

2. **Click Document Gallery on the Page Manager Navigation bar.**

   The Document Gallery page opens, as shown in Figure 5-16.

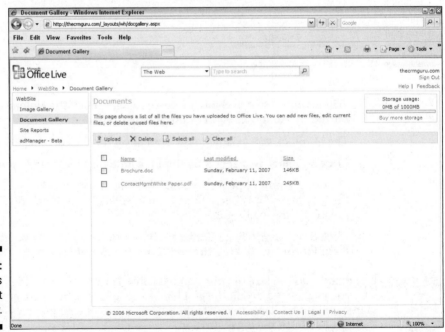

Figure 5-16:
Office Live's
Document
Gallery.

3. **Click Upload on the toolbar of the Document Gallery.**

   The Document Uploader page opens; see Figure 5-17.

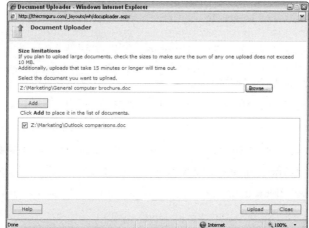

Figure 5-17:
The
Document
Uploader.

4. **Click Browse to locate the file you want to add, and then click Add.**

   The document appears in the documents list on the bottom portion of the Document Uploader. You can continue to add more documents if you'd like.

5. **Select the documents to be added, and then click Upload.**

   You can tell that a when a document is selected because a check mark appears in front of the filename.

   Uploading your files might take a moment or two depending on the number and size of files you are trying to upload. The Document Uploader closes and you land with a thump back in the Document Gallery (fortunately, the thump won't hurt!).

After you upload documents to the Document Gallery, you can create a hyperlink to them anywhere on your site. Not sure how to create a hyperlink? Turn to the "Getting hyper about hyperlinks" section, earlier in this chapter.

Using the Web Site Modules

If you love a challenge, think nothing of doing something the "hard way," and are willing to spend hours reading directions, this section isn't for you.

However, if you believe the shortest distance between two points is a straight line, you might want to take a look at the Page Editor *modules*. In a nutshell, an Office Live module is a cool, easy way for you to add some of the bells and whistles generally found in the most professional Web sites.

You can use modules to create anything from a driving direction link (say, from a visitor's location to your office) to a contact form designed to help you build a database from visitors' contact information.

To add a module to your Web site, follow these easy steps:

1. **Click WebSite in the Navigation bar of your Office Live home page.**

   The Page Manager opens.

2. **Click the Page Editor icon on the Page Manager section's toolbar.**

   The Page Editor springs to attention.

3. **Click Module on the Page Editor toolbar and click the module you want.**

   There are several modules you can choose:

   - *Contact Us:* Creates a contact form in which a visitor can send you an e-mail without you having to put your e-mail address on your site for the world — and the spammers — to see.

   - *HTML:* Allows you to insert a block of HTML code — should you have one!

   - *Map & Directions:* Creates a map and directions from the visitor's location to yours.

   - *Slideshow:* Creates a slideshow of graphics for your visitors. This is a real easy way to add excitement to your Web site.

   - *Stock List:* Lists the current stock prices for the stocks you've selected.

   - *Weather:* Displays the current weather forecast based on your zip code.

   - *Collect Data:* Allows you to create a form to collect data that will be entered into a list you have created in Office Live.

   - *Display Data:* Displays the data in a list that created in Office Live.

4. **Fill in the information required for your selected module and click OK.**

   The required information is fairly self-explanatory. For example, Figure 5-18 shows the Map & Directions page. Fill in your address (following the form of the sample provided) and you're good to go.

5. **Click Save on the Page Editor toolbar to save your changes and then close the Page Editor by clicking the X in the upper-right corner.**

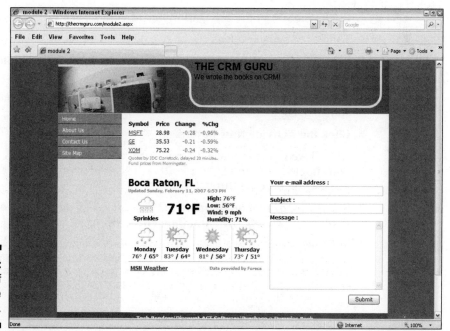

Figure 5-18:
Creating an
address
module.

Figure 5-19 shows a finished Web page that contains the Stock list, Weather, and Contact Us modules.

Figure 5-19:
Samples of
Office Live
modules.

Importing an Existing Web Site

An Essentials or Premium Office Live account allows you to create a Web site in one of three ways:

- ✔ You can use Office Live's Web Designer.
- ✔ If you're proficient in Web design, you can use software specifically designed for Web-site creation, such as Microsoft Expression Web or Macromedia Dreamweaver.
- ✔ You can hire a Web design professional.

If you want to use your own Web-site design software, you have to change that option in Office Live:

- ✔ You lose the capability to use the Office Live Web Designer.

    Any pages created using the Web Designer are permanently deleted (although any images or documents you've uploaded to the Image Gallery or the Document Gallery are still saved).

- ✔ If you decide to return to the Office Live Web Designer, any pages you created using your third-party design software are deleted — as are any files associated with the site, including images and documents. Then you have to re-create your entire Web site, using Office Live's Web Designer.

Here's how you can change your Web Designer preferences:

1. **Click WebSite in the Navigation bar of your Office Live Home page.**

    The Page Manager opens.

2. **Select Activate Third-Party Design Tools from the Site Actions drop-down menu.**

    You're rewarded with the very scary and ominous warning message shown in Figure 5-20.

3. **Click the Activate Now button.**

    Office Live wants to make it abundantly clear that this is not a matter you should enter into lightly. You see a second warning window — just in case you breezed through the first one.

4. **Select *I want to deactivate the Office Live Web designer tools and delete my existing files* and then click OK.**

    You might want to take a deep breath before clicking that OK button. An indicator bar scrolls across your screen, indicating that you have just lost your existing site and disabled the Office Live Web Designer. You end up back at the Page Manager.

5. **Click Go to Your Web Site folder.**

   A folder containing your new Web pages opens (see Figure 5-21). After you've switched to using a third-party Web designer, you no longer have access to the Page Manager. Instead, your Web pages are stored in a folder on the Office Live servers.

   When you first open your Web Site folder, you find three folders and one file:

   - *Shared folder:* This folder contains all the files necessary to make your pages play nicely with Office Live; to keep it that way, make sure you do not delete this folder.

   - *Documents* or *Images folder:* If you have already uploaded documents and images to Office Live, you find those in these folders.

   - The `default.aspx` *file* is your temporary home page. You can delete this file once your new `default.htm` Web page is in the folder. Files that you previously uploaded to your Document and Image Galleries also appear in the Documents and Images folders.

   You'll notice the `default.aspx` file in your Web Site folder. You must name your home page file `default.htm`.

6. **Drag the HTML files from your computer to the Office Live Web-site folder.**

   Be sure to include all the files — such as images and documents — necessary for viewing your Web site.

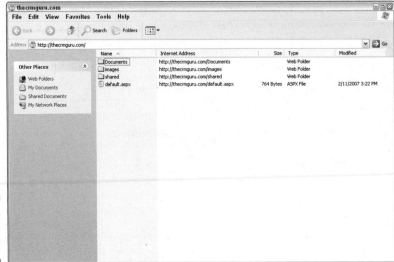

Figure 5-21:
The Web
Site folder.

Do not delete the Shared folder from the Office Live Web site folder. The folder contains hidden files that are used by the system to direct visitors to your public Web site. If you delete this folder, your service will be interrupted and you will need to contact Office Live Customer Support to fix the problem.

Maintaining Your Web Site

After you design and tweak your Web site, you might feel you're ready to relax, enjoy, and take a well-deserved break. But before you head out to the beach with your bottle of suntan lotion, you need to take in a bit about *Web-site maintenance* — the process of keeping the content on your site current. Think of your Web site as a work in progress. Your Web site has an edit date; search engines do not look highly upon Web sites with old edit dates. Along the same lines, visitors don't want to read about last year's news.

Updating Web site content

Updated content is a great way to lure potential clients back to your site. Search engines regularly pay visits to Web sites; however, if they visit your site several times and don't find any new information, they may decide not to come back — which adversely affects your search-engine rankings.

If you are not the most creative of writers, you might find yourself with a bad case of writer's block when it comes time to edit your Web site's contents. Here's a bit of fodder that might help you with your next edit:

- ✔ List new accreditations or licenses.
- ✔ Talk about new products or services or, at the very least, update your price list.
- ✔ Mention any changes to your business including new employees that you might have recently hired.
- ✔ Add a recent case study.
- ✔ Add a few client testimonials
- ✔ Write an informative article — and make sure that it contains lots of your keywords.
- ✔ Post your press releases.

Keeping up with the times

In addition to changing the content of your Web site, you should also check the site itself periodically to make sure that no glaring mistakes have surfaced. Among the first things you should check are these:

- ✔ Make sure that all the links on your Web site still work.
- ✔ Ensure that any time references on your site are still timely. For example, if you mention how many years you've been in business, you'll want to change that reference.

Chapter 6

Optimizing Your Web Site

In This Chapter

▶ Submitting to the search engines

▶ Linking to others

▶ Creating search words

▶ Viewing the site reports

▶ Using adManager

*B*uilding a Web site is only half the battle. The other half of the fun comes when you hang out the welcome mat to attract prospects to your Web site. In this chapter, you find out how to create reciprocal links to other sites, submit your site to the search engines, and create some traffic-stopping keywords. You discover how to assess your efforts by looking at the Office Live site reports. Finally, should you really want to jumpstart your e-marketing, you can use Ad Manager to make sure that your Web site shows up at the top of the search heap.

Working with the Search Engines

Imagine building a great new restaurant, hiring a wonderful chef, decorating to the *n*th degree — and then having no one show up when you open your doors for your Grand Opening. Your Web site is just like any other undertaking. You've put a lot of time and thought into creating a great-looking Web site, you're ready for business — but no one's visiting. The few "hits" you get are probably from you or one of your friends. Try searching for your main product in a popular search engine. Does your name appear on the first page? On the *tenth* page? At this point you're wondering what all the fuss was about — you built it and they most definitely *didn't* come.

The search engines probably don't know that your site exists yet. Don't feel bad — you are not alone. Many new site owners face the same obstacle. After you build your Web site, you need to submit it to search engines so other people can search for and find your site. If you understand how search engines work, you'll soon have lots of visitors to your site.

Checking to see whether your site is indexed

Simply stated, search engines consist of huge, alphabetical listings of various Web site names and key words. A search engine needs to index your site in order for it to appear in a search. Sometimes a search engine can index your site without your knowledge; however, if your site isn't indexed it doesn't show up in a search on that search engine. Therefore it's good practice to see which of the major search engines have indexed your site before you bother with anything else.

Determining whether your site is indexed is fairly easy — although the process varies somewhat between the search engines.

- **On MSN (www.msn.com) or Google (www.google.com):** Open the appropriate Web site in your browser and type **site:*yourdomainname*.com** in the search box. (For example, if you wanted to see whether my company, Tech Benders, was indexed on MSN, you would type **site:techbenders.com** and click Search.) If your site isn't indexed, you get a message like the one you see in Figure 6-1.

- **On Yahoo! (www.yahoo.com):** Type **domain:*yourdomainname*.com** in the search box. To see (for example) whether my company is indexed by Yahoo!, you would type **domain:techbenders.com** in the search box and click Search. If your site is indexed, you see the various pages of your Web site listed (see Figure 6-2).

If no results come back for your site or you get a message saying no results were found, then your site isn't listed on that engine. At this point you can do two things to correct this. First, submit your site name to the search engines directly. Second, do what you can to get links built from other recognized sites to your site. You find out how to do just that later in this chapter.

Figure 6-1:
Uh-Oh! The site isn't indexed.

Keying in your keywords

You should add keyword metatags and a page description for each page
on your site. *Keyword metatags* are words and combinations of words that
search engines use to index your Web site and help people get better search
results. Placing clear keyword metatags and a description on each page can
help you increase your position with the search engines.

Concocting your list of keyword metatags and writing a page description is
the hard part; adding them to your Web site is easy if you follow these steps:

1. **Click WebSite from your Office Live Home page.**

   The Page Manager opens.

2. **Click the Properties link for the page that you'd like to edit.**

   The Choose Page Properties page opens for the page you selected. You
   can have different keyword metatags and page descriptions for each of
   the pages of your site. In fact, having a different focus for each page
   might make your site even more appealing to the search engines.

3. **Click the Search Engine Optimization tab.**

   Figure 6-3 shows the Search Engine Optimization tab. You might want to
   read the helpful hints that appear along the right side of the window.

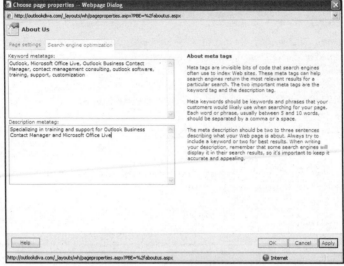

Figure 6-3:
Adding
keyword
metatags
and a page
description
to your
Web site.

4. **Fill in your keyword metatags, using commas as separators.**

As you fill in your keyword metatags you might want to keep these thoughts in mind:

- *Your keyword metatags should reflect the words that you think people might use to search for your products or services.* Think outside the box. If you offer great prices you might want to add the word "discount" or "cheap" in front of your product name. Put yourself in the shoes of your prospect; he will be more familiar with a generic product name than with a specific product code.

- *Limit the number of keyword metatags to 25 or fewer.* Search engines do not want to sort through hundreds of words.

5. **Fill in your page description metatags.**

Your page description is a brief synopsis of the purpose of your Web site. Here's where to mention exactly what you do and how you do it. Search engines often ask for your page description when you submit your site so be prepared.

6. **Click OK to save your changes and return to the Page Manager.**

7. **Click the Properties link for next page that you'd like to edit, and then repeat Steps 3-6.**

Add metatags (for both keywords and description) for each page of your site.

Submitting your keywords

After you determine that your site isn't listed on a search engine, and you've chosen the keywords that you think potential customers will use to find you, it's time to submit your site to the various search engines. The good news is that this part is easy; all you have to do is go to their submission pages and follow the instructions. Here's the drill for the Big Three search engines:

- ✔ Google Search:

    1. **Go to** www.google.com/addurl/?continue=/addurl.

    2. **Fill in your Web site address and any optional comments you might have (see Figure 6-4).**

        Don't forget to fill in the entire address of your Web site including the *www* portion!

    3. **Type the secret code word that Google automatically displays.**

    4. **Click the Add URL button to submit your site.**

- ✔ Yahoo Search:

    1. **Go to** https://siteexplorer.search.yahoo.com/submit.

        You'll have to submit your Yahoo! username and password or, if you don't have one, sign up for a free account.

    2. **Fill in your Web site address.**

    3. **Click the Submit URL button to submit your site.**

- ✔ MSN Search:

    1. **Go to** http://search.msn.com.sg/docs/submit.aspx?FORM=WSDD.

    2. **Type the secret code word that MSN automatically displays.**

    3. **Fill in your Web site's address and any optional comments you might have.**

    4. **Click the Submit URL button to submit your site.**

After you submit your site name, you might wait a few weeks and then check to see whether your site is indexed. If, after four to six weeks, you're still not listed, you may want to resubmit to the search engines and try building some more links.

Getting added to an index can take anywhere from one day to a month or more; the time can vary depending on the search engine. You might grow impatient waiting for your site to appear. However, avoid the temptation to keep resubmitting your site. Many of the search engines have very stringent rules determining how often is "too often" to submit a site. Make sure you read the fine print on the search engine's submission page to avoid "oversubmitting" your site.

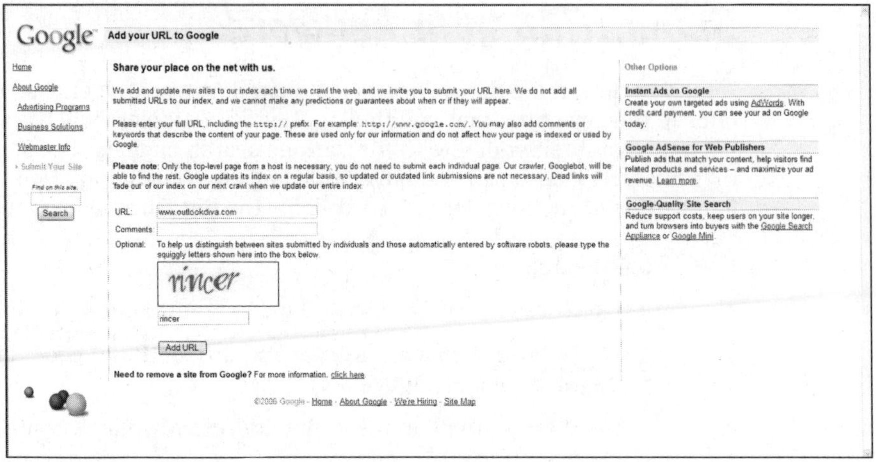

Figure 6-4:
Submitting
your site to
Google.

 You may only think of the "Big Three" (Google, Yahoo!, and MSN) when think-ing of Web-site submission. However, you can also list your site on literally thousands of other search engines and directories. Some directories focus on specific topics that might be applicable to your business; although they may charge a small fee for listing, they can improve your Web site's visibility. Many local organizations also provide directories; Chambers of commerce, for example, often have a page of links to local businesses.

Getting Reciprocal Links

Submitting to the search engines can *get* your site indexed quickly, but with-out a few incoming links your site may not *stay* indexed. Reciprocal links help *keep* your site indexed for the long term.

When it comes to Web sites, *networking* isn't just a software term. Social net-working is an important part of optimizing your Web site. Here's how recipro-cal linking works. You add links to other companies on your Web site — and in turn ask those sites to add links to your site. Building the right kind of links to your site improves your search-engine results.

Search engines love links — especially links from other sites. A link to your site from another site indicates to the search engine that your site is valuable to someone else; search engines see this as a sign of quality. The more quality links you have to your site, the higher your placement is with the search engines.

Unfortunately, cultivating links to your site can be difficult. Talk to everyone you know who has a site. Ask friends, family, suppliers, and business associ-ates. Ask your customers. It's best if the site is somehow related to yours, but any link (within reason) helps.

If you're really serious about creating reciprocal links, you might consider adding a link page to your Web site. That way potential link partners see exactly where you'll place *their* links.

Here are a few tips that might make your site a bit more desirable to other sites. The best part about building great content is that some sites might link to your site without your even having to ask:

- ✔ **Add informative content:** Your site should offer something of value to entice other sites to link to yours. As fascinating as you might find your own products and services to be, that may not enough to keep visitors' attention; get busy creating some informative content that they might use. Add how-to articles, product reviews, and general tips related to your industry. Try to teach without selling. If you just can't get into writing, consider linking to informative articles that you've found elsewhere on the Internet.

- ✔ **Offer a freebie or two:** Nothing entices visitors to your site faster than free stuff. Add a free tool or download.

- ✔ **Find good tie-ins to your industry:** It's good business to figure out all the different types of sites that could potentially trade links with you. Focus on sites that are related to your target market. For example, if you sell real estate you might trade links with a mortgage company, title company, and real estate attorney. Include decorating tips and link to an interior decorator.

- ✔ **Link to quality sites:** Make sure the sites with which you are going to reciprocate are indexed. Better yet, see if they show up relatively high on the search engines. The higher a page appears, the better. Try to affiliate your site with sites that have pages ranked as high as (or higher than) your own.

- ✔ **Link to sites that already link to other sites:** The span of your Web site expands proportionately if you link to sites that are already taking advantage of reciprocal linking to other sites.

After you set up reciprocal links on your Web site to other sites, check those other sites and make sure that links to *your* site appear on them. Hopefully, those people who said they would add links to your site have actually added them, but sometimes people forget!

Reviewing Your Site Reports

After you submit your site name to the search engine and build some reciprocal links to your site, you want to see if your e-marketing plan is actually attracting new visitors to your site. Office Live includes several Site Reports that analyze the traffic to your Web site. Site Reports track statistics about several key areas of your Web site. Site Report information clearly shows the results — or lack thereof — of your efforts.

Much of the traffic to your Web site will likely come from search engines and directories. Site Reports provides data on search engines, listing all the engines that send visitors to your site and top *keywords* (the words or phrases visitors typed into search engines to find your site). It's useful to know information about the various search engines because that way you can customize your pages to include keywords that they find attractive. Also, many engines have services that allow you to pay for preferred listings for specific phrases and you'll want to see whether your marketing dollars are paying off.

Knowing the Site Reports

Site Reports capture information about other referring sources. You see not only what other Web sites are throwing business your way, but also the specific pages — and even the domain types (`.com`, `.org`, `.edu`) — that people are using to find you. With that information in hand, you can focus your efforts. For example, if you are a real estate agent and find that you get more referrals from title companies than you do from mortgage companies, you might solicit other title companies to include links to your site.

The site reports focus on two major areas:

- ✔ **Visitors:** This measurement tells you the number of unique visitors for any time period so you can see how many people visit your site by hour each day, by day each month, and by month each year. Site Reports count unique visitors and not how many times a visitor accesses your site. For example, if the same person visits the site at 9:00 a.m., 11:00 a.m., and 4:00 p.m., it's counted as three visits in the day as viewed by hour — but only one visit for that day in the month view. If the same person visits the site on February 2, 14, and 21, it would count as one visit for that month in the year view.

- ✔ **Page views:** This measurement shows you the number of times a page has been viewed, regardless of the number of visitors.

Although Site Reports come with all three versions of Office Live, only the original subscriber can view them. Users with Administrative, Editor, or Reader permission cannot view Site Report information.

To access your site reports, follow these steps:

1. **Click WebSite on the Navigation bar of the Office Live Home page.**

   The Page Manager opens.

2. **Click Site Reports from the Navigation bar.**

   The Web Site Statistics Summary page opens, as shown in Figure 6-5.

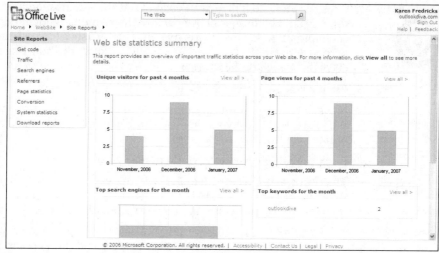

Karen Fredricks
outlookdiva.com
Sign Out
Help | Feedback

Figure 6-5:
The Web
Site
statistics
summary
Web page.

If you scroll down the page, you find all kinds of interesting — and useful — tidbits about your site. This information is particularly useful if you've been working your little fingers (or other parts of your anatomy) off trying to get your Web site's name out to the Internet world.

The statistical summaries include these:

- *Unique visitors for past 4 months:* This graph shows how many different individuals wandered into your Web site over the course of the last four months.

- *Page views for past 4 months:* This graph show how many pages were viewed during the last four months. For example, you might have had ninety unique people access your site, representing over a thousand hits on your various pages.

- *Top search engines for the month:* Talk about useful — here's where you can see a list of the search engines that your visitors used to find you.

- *Top keywords for the month:* Here's where you get a list of the specific keywords that visitors are using to find your site.

- *Top referring domains this month:* If you're sharing reciprocal links with other Web-site owners (see the earlier section, "Getting Reciprocal Links") you might want to see whether your efforts are bearing any fruit. Here's where you see a list of all the domains that are sending traffic in your direction.

- *Top referring pages this month:* In addition to having Web site visitors find you from other Web sites, you might want to know exactly which pages on those Web sites they used. Here's where you'll learn exactly that.

Click the View All link next to each of the statistical summaries to get more detailed information for each of the sections — including statistical information for the entire year. In addition, should you become bombarded with traffic, here's where you'll find both the Top Ten and Top 200 lists of each of these areas.

3. **Click a category from the Site Reports Navigation bar.**

   As useful as the various statistical summaries are, they represent only the proverbial tip of your analysis. (You can find additional site-report options via the Navigation bar.)

4. **Click the Site Report that you'd like to view.**

   The best way to become familiar with the various site reports is to view the content in each one. However, to help get you on your way, here are the site report categories and the corresponding reports:

   - *Traffic:* The Visitors report shows how many visitors came to your site and how many pages they viewed, and the Views report displays how many views the individual pages get (on an hourly, daily, monthly, or yearly basis).

   - *Search engines:* The Engines report shows which search engines have sent traffic to your site. The Keywords report lists the keywords that visitors used to find your site.

   - *Referrers:* The Referring Pages report shows the exact Web pages that are sending traffic to your site. The Referring Domains report shows you the Web sites that are referring traffic to you. The Referring Domain types report shows the domain types (.edu, .com, .org) that are sending visitors to your site. Figure 6-6 shows the Referring Pages report.

   - *Page Statistics:* The Page Statistics section includes the Most Requested Pages report (showing the pages within your site that most visitors access); the Entry Pages report (showing the first page visitors see) and the Exit Pages report (showing the page that visitors are on when they exit your Web site). Figure 6-7 shows the Most Requested Pages report.

   - *Conversion:* If you sell products on your Web site, or allow visitors to sign up for additional services such as a newsletter, the conversion reports can prove helpful to you. The Conversion Referrers report lists the referral sources that sent you a visitor that purchased or signed up for something on your site. The Conversion Points report shows you the pages visitors are on when they make a purchase.

   - *System Statistics:* These reports provide you with information about the types of operating systems (Operating systems report), browsers (Browsers report) and screen resolutions (Screen resolutions report) that your visitors use. If you are using your own software to design your site, this information can help you design it in such a way so as to make it usable for visitors who use various browsers and screen resolutions.

Although Get Code appears as one of the Site Reports, this item isn't really a site report. Any Web page you created with the Office Live Web Designer includes code that allows you to create Site Reports. However, if you used your own software to design your site, you have to embed a piece of tracking code into the HTML so that you can create Site Reports.

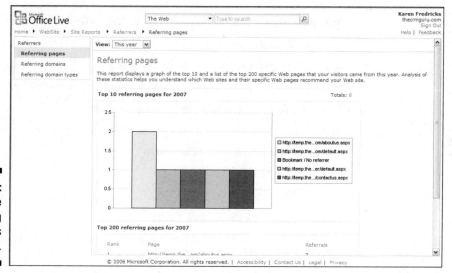

Figure 6-6:
The Referring Pages report.

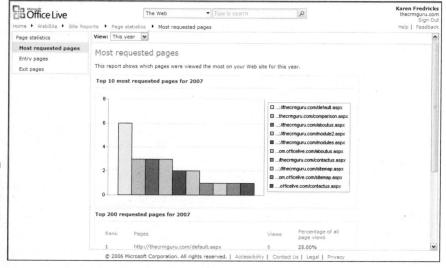

Figure 6-7:
The Most Requested Pages report.

Creating a copy of a Site Report

Office Live restricts the ability to run a Site Report to your account's main subscriber, so you may want to download a copy of a Site Report. You can save site reports in CSV (comma-separated value) format for later review.

To download a site report, follow these steps:

1. **Click WebSite on the Navigation bar of the Office Live Home page.**

   The Page Manager page opens.

2. **Click Site Reports from the Navigation bar.**

   The Web Site Statistics Summary page opens (refer to Figure 6-5).

3. **Click Download Reports in the Navigation bar.**

   The Download Reports page opens, as shown in Figure 6-8.

4. **Make your date and item selections.**

   Select as many reports as you'd like.

5. **Click the Run Report button.**

   The File Download dialog box opens.

6. **Click Save to save the report as a file, browse to the folder where you'd like to store the report, and then click Save.**

   If you want to open the file instead of saving it, click Open.

   When the download is complete, you can choose to open and view the report. Figure 6-9 shows a site report imported into Excel.

Figure 6-8:
The Download Reports page.

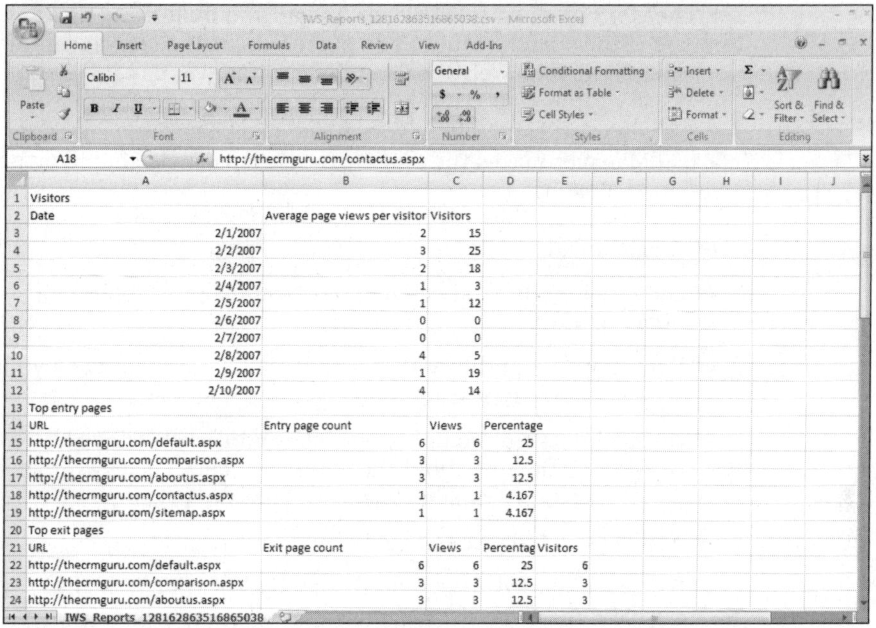

	A	B	C	D	E
1	Visitors				
2	Date	Average page views per visitor	Visitors		
3	2/1/2007	2	15		
4	2/2/2007	3	25		
5	2/3/2007	2	18		
6	2/4/2007	1	3		
7	2/5/2007	1	12		
8	2/6/2007	0	0		
9	2/7/2007	0	0		
10	2/8/2007	4	5		
11	2/9/2007	1	19		
12	2/10/2007	4	14		
13	Top entry pages				
14	URL	Entry page count	Views	Percentage	
15	http://thecrmguru.com/default.aspx	6	6	25	
16	http://thecrmguru.com/comparison.aspx	3	3	12.5	
17	http://thecrmguru.com/aboutus.aspx	3	3	12.5	
18	http://thecrmguru.com/contactus.aspx	1	1	4.167	
19	http://thecrmguru.com/sitemap.aspx	1	1	4.167	
20	Top exit pages				
21	URL	Exit page count	Views	Percentag	Visitors
22	http://thecrmguru.com/default.aspx	6	6	25	6
23	http://thecrmguru.com/comparison.aspx	3	3	12.5	3
24	http://thecrmguru.com/aboutus.aspx	3	3	12.5	3

Figure 6-9: A sample site report.

Adding in the adManager

Office Live's adManager is a service that allows you to create and purchase ads that appear on Windows Live Search by using Microsoft adCenter. This form of advertising is also known as *pay per click* because you only pay if a prospect clicks your ad.

You select and purchase keywords by bidding on them in an auction format. The keyword-bid price determines the location of your ad in the sponsored ad list. Higher bids are placed more prominently in the sponsored ad list. Currently, Windows Live Search displays a maximum of eight ads, three at the top of the page and five on the right side of the page. An ad with the highest keyword-bid price appears in the top-left position of the page.

Microsoft adCenter charges a $5 sign-up fee to activate your account. Additional billing occurs when users of Windows Live Search click one of your ads. The lowest bid permitted is $0.05 and the highest bid permitted is $1,000.

Office Live's adManager steps you through creating your ad, setting up your budget, and choosing your search keywords. AdManager lets you decide how much to pay for your ads and when to activate and deactivate them. As you create your ads, you'll bid on keywords. When a Windows Live Search user searches for one of your keywords, the ad you built using that keyword appears in the search results. The person doing the search can then click your ad to find your Web site (and that's when you pay the amount you bid).

In case you're still scratching your head over this whole concept of pay per click, adManager makes the entire process amazingly simple by helping you to do the following:

- Create an ad.
- Target your ads by specifying the location and language of your target market.
- Determine a monthly advertising budget; after you reach your budget, your ad stops appearing.
- Decide how much to bid on each keyword click. Office Live adManager provides estimates about the number of clicks a keyword might receive and the keyword ranking based on your bid price.
- Adjust your bid price to get better results.
- Suggest keywords based on the content of your Web site.
- Receive detailed reports on the keywords attracting the most clicks. This information helps you identify the most cost-effective keywords.

We're off to see the adManager Wizard

Now that you are frothing at the mouth in anticipation of all the great new business you can attract to your Web site, it's time to get going. Here's how you can do exactly that:

1. **Click WebSite on the Navigation bar of the Office Live Home page.**

   The Page Manager page opens.

2. **Click adManager from the Navigation bar.**

   If this is your first foray into adManager, the Welcome screen of the adManager Wizard opens (see Figure 6-10).

3. **Click Start to continue.**

   The second screen of the adManager Account Creation Wizard appears, asking you to fill in your vital statistics — including your name, address, and e-mail address. This should be a fairly easy window to deal with; the information is already filled in (based on the info you provided when signing up for your Office Live account). Feel free to tweak it if necessary.

Figure 6-10:
The
Welcome
screen
of the
adManager
Wizard.

4. **Check that your name, address, and e-mail address are correct and click OK to continue.**

   The Create Login Information screen of the adManager Account Creation Wizard appears (see Figure 6-11).

   If you click OK at any time and get an error message instead of moving to the next wizard screen, it means you forgot to fill in some information. Apologize profusely (or not), fill in the missing information, and click OK again. When you move on to the next screen, you've filled in all the information correctly.

5. **Create your adCenter account by supplying your login information.**

   Supply a username, password, select a secret question from the drop-down list — and then supply a super-secret answer to the super-secret question.

6. **Click OK to continue.**

   The Enter Payment Information screen of the adManager Account Creation Wizard opens.

7. **Fill in your credit-card information and click OK to continue.**

   For many of you, this is the most terrifying part of the entire wizard. Be brave.

   You're charged $5 to sign up for adCenter. You aren't charged for anything else until you have created an ad and someone has actually clicked it. In addition, you set a budget so you aren't hit with a large, unexpected bill in the future.

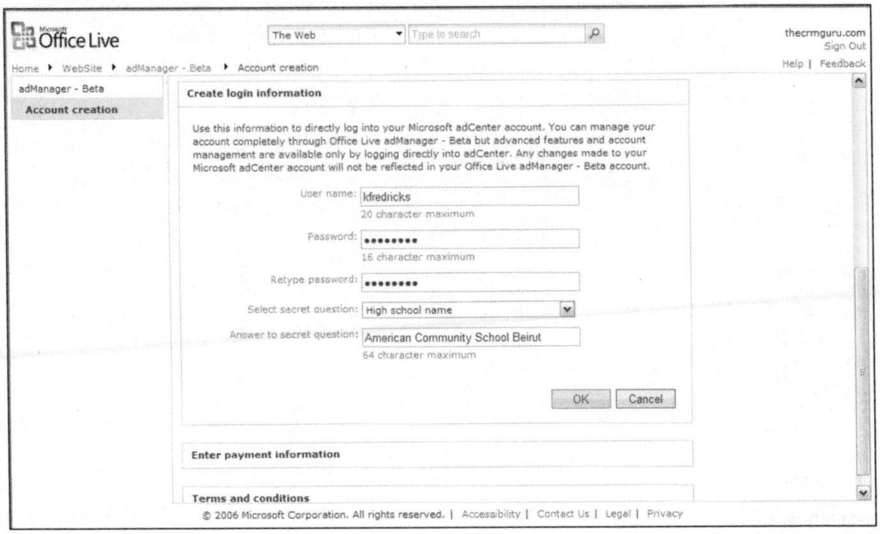

Figure 6-11:
Creating an
adCenter
account.

8. **Click the check box accepting the adCenter terms (on the Terms and Conditions screen of the adManager Account Creation wizard) and then click Finish.**

If you don't play by Microsoft's rules and click the check box, you can't play the adCenter game. After a moment or two of nail-biting anticipation, adManager's Ad Settings window appears — and you're ready to start creating an ad.

Managing the adManager settings

After you set up an account with the adCenter, you specify where the ad runs and set up a monthly budget. Creating a budget ensures that your advertising campaign doesn't end up costing you more than you anticipated. Depending on the keywords you use for your ads, you might not reach your monthly budget. Alternatively, in a very competitive environment, it's possible that customer clicks cost the maximum amount you specify.

Here's how you set the ground rules for your adManager account:

1. **Click WebSite on the Navigation bar of the Office Live Home page.**

   The Page Manager opens.

2. **Click adManager from the Navigation bar.**

   If you've previously plunked down your credit card information, adManager's Ad Settings page opens (see Figure 6-12).

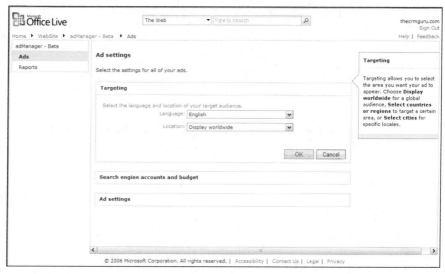

Figure 6-12:
Setting your
adManager
preferences.

3. **Fill in the language and area for your ad and click OK.**

   You can select a city, state, or country in which to display your ad from the Location drop-down list.

4. **In the Search Engine Accounts and Budget area of the Ad Settings page, enter the total amount you want to spend each month on all of your ads.**

   You can set your monthly budget amount anywhere from $1 up to $10,000. Your budget is divided by the number of days in the month. For instance, if you specify a $300 per month budget, your daily budget limit is automatically set at $10. If you don't reach your daily limit, the remainder is then divided evenly over the remainder of the month. (Sounds kind of complicated — you might pity the guy who is sitting with his abacus trying to figure the whole thing out.)

5. **Click OK to continue.**

   A summary screen appears showing your budget and letting you know that you can increase or decrease your monthly budget at any time.

6. **Click Next to continue.**

   You are now ready to start creating ads.

If, in the future, you'd like to change your monthly budget, follow these steps:

1. **Click WebSite on the Navigation bar of the Office Live Home page.**

   The Page Manager page opens.

2. **Click adManager from the Navigation bar.**

   Once you have signed up for an adCenter account, and specified your settings, the adManager Ad Summary page opens, as shown in Figure 6-13.

3. **Click Settings to open the Ad Settings page.**

4. **Click Edit in the Search Engine Accounts and Budget section of the Ad Settings page.**

5. **Fill in the new amount for your monthly budget and click OK to save your changes.**

Figure 6-13: The Ad Summary page.

Creating an ad in adManager

Whew! Now that you've created an adCenter account, you're ready to design your first ad. Don't worry if you count yourself among the ranks of the "artistically challenged." Designing doesn't require an in-house graphic artist, nor do you have to have a degree in marketing.

You can design as many ads as you like. However, all your ads are included in your monthly budget. For example, if you have a $30 monthly budget and you create two ads, each one has a monthly budget of $15.

Follow these steps to create your first ad:

1. **Click WebSite on the Navigation bar of the Office Live Home page.**

   The Page Manager page opens.

2. **Click adManager from the Navigation bar.**

   AdManager's Ad Summary page opens.

3. **Click New on the Ad Summary toolbar.**

   The Create Your Ad page opens.

4. **Fill in your ad content.**

   You need to fill in the headline, two lines of text, your display URL, and your destination URL. See the upcoming sidebar, "Tips for writing a good pay-per-click ad" to create an ad Microsoft will love. As you fill in each tidbit, a preview of your ad appears at the bottom of the page (see Figure 6-14). And, should you be confused, Office Live offers guidelines as well as a tooltip for each text box.

5. **Click OK.**

   The Pricing portion of the Create Your Ad page appears, as shown in Figure 6-15. Here's where you enter the maximum price per click that you are willing to pay. You may not end up paying your bid amount, but it is important that you are comfortable with your bid. For example, if you set a maximum bid at $2, and another advertiser sets a maximum bid for the same keyword at $1, you're charged $1.01 for each click — and your ad is placed higher in the list of sponsored links. If another advertiser sets its maximum bid for the same keyword at $3 per click, then you pay no more than $2 per click — and your ad drops in the sponsored list ranking. The cost-per-click rate can vary from minute to minute, day to day, or week to week, depending on when other advertisers bid on the same keyword.

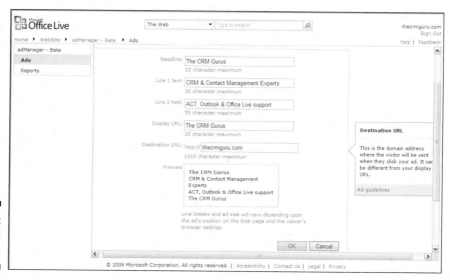

Figure 6-14:
Creating
an ad.

Figure 6-15:
Entering a
keyword bid
amount.

You bid amount must be between $.05 and $1,000. Think about your monthly budget before you enter your bid amount. It doesn't make a whole lot of sense to enter a bid amount of $100 if your monthly budget is $25.

6. **Enter your bid amount and click OK.**

    After a momentary pause (during which adManager combs through your Web site), the Keywords portion of the Create Your Ad page appears. If you're like me, you love it when someone does your homework for you — which is the case here. adManager suggests several keywords based on the content of your Web site, as shown in Figure 6-16.

7. **Scroll down the list of suggested keywords, select one you like, and then click Add. If you don't like the keywords adManager suggested, click the Custom Keyword option, type a keyword into the box, and click Add.**

    You can select as many keywords as you'd like; Office Live adds them to the list at the bottom of the page.

    As you add in keywords, Office Live races out to the Internet and tries to figure out the estimated position, daily cost, and number of clicks that your keyword can attract (see Figure 6-16). This information helps you to get the most bang for your buck.

8. **(Optional) To remove a keyword, click the rather large X that appears to the right of the keyword.**

    Your keyword is instantly deleted. Don't worry, though; you can resurrect it in a heartbeat by repeating Step 7.

9. **Click OK to continue.**

   A confirmation page appears listing the ad, bid price, and keywords that you selected.

10. **Click OK to confirm your selections.**

    You now land with a plop on the Ad Summary page. Your ad is listed there with *Pending* in the Status column, which means it's under consideration by Microsoft.

Tips for writing a good pay-per-click ad

Because using adCenter is so inexpensive, Microsoft has imposed very stringent rules. Your ad can be rejected for many reasons. Try to be accurate, truthful, and specific. For example, your ad content should provide a clear and accurate description of your Web site — and include some of your keywords. The landing page should reflect the content of your ad.

Adhering to the following guidelines helps ensure that your ad content is accepted:

✔ **Limit the number of characters in your ad:** Size matters. You must limit your title to 25 characters, each line of your ad text and display URL to 35 characters, and your destination URL to 1,015 characters.

✔ **Display family-friendly content:** Microsoft doesn't allow ads advertising adult or sexual content, profanity, online gambling, or weapons.

✔ **Don't duplicate ads:** Microsoft does not allow you to duplicate your other ads.

✔ **Don't violate trademarks:** Do not bid on trademarks, or include them within the text of your ads, unless your use of the trademark is lawful.

✔ **Include special or free offers:** Make sure your landing page prominently features any special or free offers that are described in the ad.

✔ **Check your grammar and punctuation:** Microsoft doesn't allow exclamation points in ad titles, repeated or unnecessary use of punctuation, symbols, or characters, or capitalization of entire words (unless they are normally written that way).

✔ **Avoid repetition of words:** Microsoft would most probably reject an ad that includes phrases like "Free, Free, Free."

✔ **Don't use offensive or inappropriate language:** Ugly words convey an impression that Microsoft wants nothing to do with.

✔ **Stay away from illegal products or services:** Do not advertise illegitimate or illegal products or services. Microsoft (in its wisdom) doesn't go looking for trouble.

✔ **Be honest:** Do not intentionally mislead customers or create the wrong impression.

✔ **Make sure your site is running as it should:** Check that your Web site is fully operational.

In addition, you might want to use these tips to create a compelling ad:

✔ Include your most important keyword in the first line of your ad. Make sure to include as many other keywords as possible in your ad text.

✔ Include the best feature(s) of your product or service.

✔ State any discounts you are offering.

✔ Avoid using terms that you can't prove, such as "best" or "cheapest."

Figure 6-16:
Selecting
your
keywords.

Looking at the Ad Summary

As its name implies, the Ad Summary page provides you with a summary of all your ads, as well as the activity for each ad. The Ad Summary page (refer to Figure 6-13) also lets you create new ads, edit your ads, and/or stop your ads from appearing in search-engine listings.

If you have created ads, the Ad Summary page also displays these features:

✓ **Title:** Lists the title of each of your ads.

✓ **Views:** Shows the number of times your ad has appeared in search engine listings in the past 30 days.

✓ **Clicks:** Displays the number of clicks your ad has received in the past 30 days.

✓ **Total cost:** Tells the total amount spent on clicks for each ad in the past 30 days.

✓ **Status:** Lists the current status of your ad passed on their current level of activity. Depending on the time of month, your ad might show one of the following status levels:

  • **Pending:** Ads are marked as pending until they are reviewed by Microsoft, which can take up to 24 hours.

- **Rejected:** If you ad does not meet Microsoft's guidelines (see the sidebar, "Tips for writing a good pay-per-click ad"), your ad is marked as rejected.

- **Active:** Congratulations! Your ad is online and available for searches.

- **Paused:** Your ad is unavailable for searches. This occurs when you've reached your monthly ad budget or you've removed your ad manually.

✔ **Actions:** Depending on an ad's status, it displays one of the following actions:

- **Refresh:** If an ad is pending, the Action displays as Refresh. Click it to update the contents of the Ad Summary page.

- **Pause:** If your ad is active, the Action displays as Pause. Click it to stop an ad manually.

- **Activate:** If you have paused an ad manually, you can click Activate to start the ad once again.

Chapter 7

Playing the Dating Game

· ·

In This Chapter

▶ Scheduling activities

▶ Viewing Office Live calendars

▶ Using the Task List

▶ Making notes

▶ Sharing your calendar

· ·

*T*he Basic Office Live subscription comes equipped with a personal calendar. In this chapter, I show you how to schedule activities with your contacts, how to view those activities and modify them if necessary. You also get a handle on the intricacies of navigating through the various Office Live calendars — and on how to create Tasks, Reminders, and Notes Lists to keep you on top of your activities. Finally, you discover the joy of sharing your calendar with others.

Using the Personal Calendar

You can get to the Office Live calendar in two ways:

- ✔ Click the Personal Calendar link in the E-Mail section of the Home page.
- ✔ Click the Calendar icon while in Office Live e-mail.

The calendar opens in Day view, showing you today's calendar (see Figure 7-1). The Personal Calendar includes five sections in the Navigation bar:

- ✔ **Calendar:** When you first open the Calendar, you always get the current day. Feel free to click another date — or use the right-pointing arrow to advance to the next month.

- ✔ **Sharing:** Lists the calendars of other people who have shared their calendars with you.

- ✔ **Tasks:** Lists all your tasks as well as their due dates.

> ✔ **Reminders:** Lists all appointments and tasks for which you've set reminders, as well as the dates they were scheduled for.
>
> ✔ **Notes:** Includes all personal notes you've created.

The Sharing, Tasks, Reminders, and Notes sections all have a set of double-pointing arrows. If they are pointing upward, the section is expanded and shows more information. When a section is expanded, each item appears as a link; click it and you see the item in its entirety. (You'll also see links that start you creating a new item or take you to the list view.) If the arrows are pointing downward, the section is collapsed and you don't see any of the items that are included in the list.

If you need more capabilities from your personal calendar, upgrade to the Premium account. Chapter 17 talks about the business applications found in a Premium account, including a supercharged scheduling system.

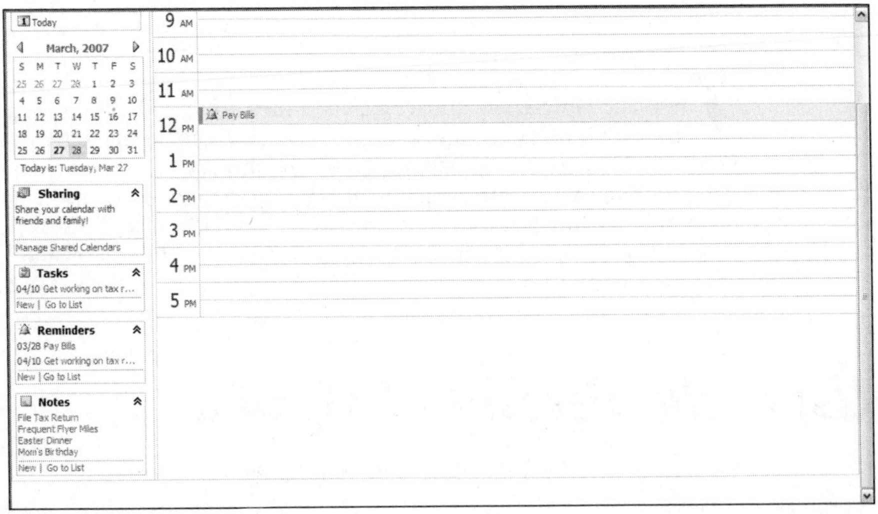

Figure 7-1:
The
Personal
Calendar
day view.

Scheduling a Meeting

If you want to rely on the Office Live personal calendar to keep track of your activities, you need to know how to add them into the calendar. The first thing you'll probably want to do when using the personal calendar is set up a new activity.

Here's what you do to add an activity to your busy schedule:

1. **Go to the date of the activity by clicking the appropriate date on the mini calendar.**

   The mini-calendar is pretty easy to locate — it's the small calendar of the current month located on the left side of the personal calendar. You can click a date if it's in the current month, or click the right arrow to advance to another month.

2. **Schedule an activity using one of these methods:**

   - Click New on the personal calendar toolbar.

   - Double-click the appropriate time slot on the Office Live calendar.

   Both roads lead to the Schedule Activity page, as shown in Figure 7-2.

3. **Fill in the appointment information.**

   The Schedule Activity page offers a myriad of scheduling options from which to pick. You can fill in as much information as you'd like, or leave any of the fields blank:

   - *Subject:* Give a brief title for your meeting.

   - *Location:* It never hurts to let everyone, including yourself, know where the big event is going to take place.

   - *Start:* The date you selected in Step 1 is displayed. To change the date, click the arrow to the right of the field to display the calendar and select the date of the big event. Alternatively, to save a bunch of clicking, you can use the drop-down arrows to change the month, date, or year. Enter a start time for the event. Check the All Day Event check box if the meeting will last all day.

   - *End:* The end date fills in automatically based on the Start date you provided. Feel free to change it if you need to.

   The End Date and End Time are automatically set based on the starting date and time you specify. If you change the Start date or time, Office Live automatically adjusts the end date and time.

   - *Notes:* Write down anything you need to bring to the table — especially if you are scheduling something way off in the future!

   - *Category:* You can sort your activities by calendar so feel free to pick a category, such as Birthday, Holiday, or Meeting.

   - *Show Time As:* Indicate whether you want to show the scheduled time as Free, Tentative, Busy, or Out of the Office.

   - *Private:* Later in this chapter you find out how to share your personal calendar with other people. If you decide to share — but don't want to share the details about this particular activity — make sure you check this option.

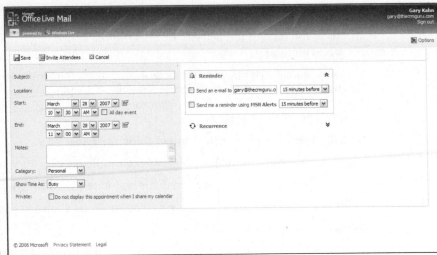

© 2006 Microsoft   Privacy Statement   Legal

Figure 7-2:
Schedule an
activity in
Office Live
here.

4. **(Optional) Click the Invite Attendees icon, enter the e-mail addresses of the recipients and then click Send.**

   If you want, you can ask others to join the party. Figure 7-3 shows the Invitation page that appears. You'll notice that most of the information is already filled out for you.

   If you don't know your recipient's e-mail addresses, click the Insert Addresses icon; your e-mail address book opens. Double-click a name to add it to the recipients list.

   The e-mail recipient receives an e-mail like the one in Figure 7-4. The recipient can choose to Accept, Tentatively Accept, or Decline the invitation; and the response is logged in your Office Live personal calendar. If the recipient(s) use Outlook, accepted invitations appear automatically in their Outlook calendars.

5. **(Optional) Click the Reminder link and decide what kind of reminder you want.**

   The Reminder area expands with two additional options:

   • *Send an E-Mail To:* Indicate who is to receive the reminder and how far in advance of the meeting they are to receive it.

   • *Send Me a Reminder Using MSN Alerts:* If you are using MSN Alerts you can have a reminder sent to your MSN Web page or your phone.

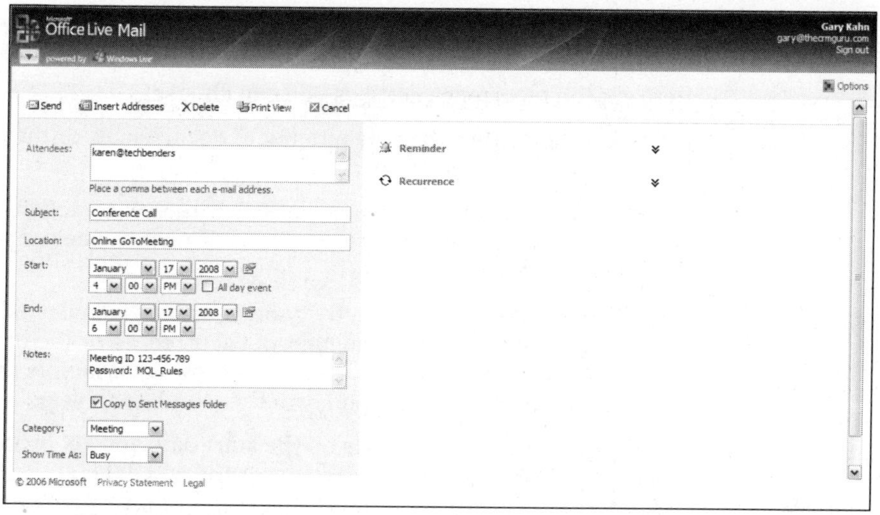

Figure 7-3:
Inviting
others to
join the
party.

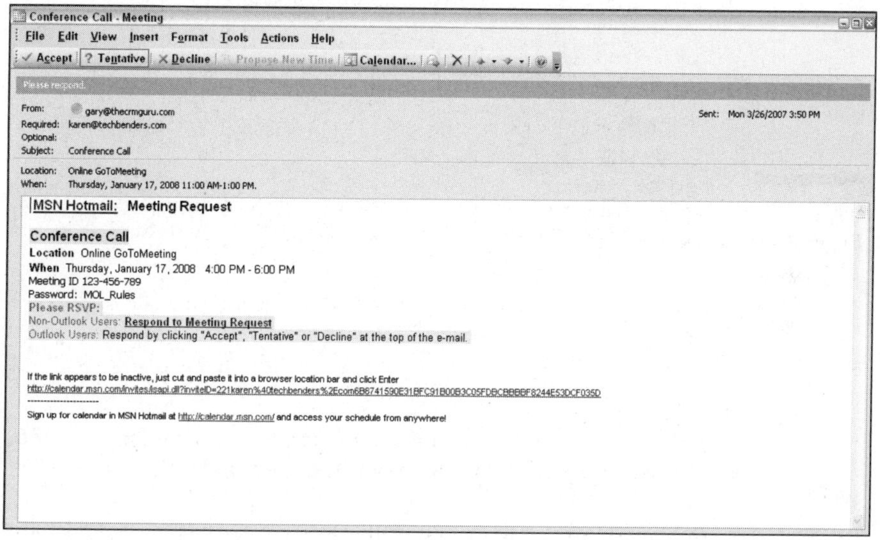

Figure 7-4:
Receiving
an e-mail
invitation for
a scheduled
event.

6. (Optional) Click the Recurrence link.

If the activity you're scheduling repeats on a regular basis, you can designate it as a *recurring* activity rather than setting up several separate activities for every time it comes around. For example, if you're taking a class that meets once a week for the next 12 weeks, you can designate the class as a meeting with a weekly recurrence.

7. **Select one of the Recurrence options from the drop-down list, and then other appropriate choices, depending on your recurrence rate.**

   Here are the recurrence settings you can choose:

   - *Daily:* Indicate either the number of occurrences or the date on which the activity stops.

   - *Weekly:* Indicate how many weeks between each activity, the day of the weeks, and either the number of occurrences or the date on which the activity stops.

   - *Monthly:* Indicate if the activity occurs on a given day of the week or date, and either the number of occurrences or the date on which the activity stops. Figure 7-5 shows an example of an activity that repeats the first Monday of the month for a year.

   - *Yearly:* The activity starts on the start date you set in Step 3; indicate the number of occurrences or the end date.

8. **Click Save.**

   You now have a real live *scheduled* activity!

Figure 7-5:
Scheduling
a recurring
monthly
meeting.

You can see your activities on your calendar. You can see any reminders you've set in the Reminders area of the Personal Calendar.

If you asked to receive e-mail reminders, be sure to look for them in your Office Live e-mail.

Editing your activities

Like all the best-laid plans of mice and men, your activities will change — and you need a way to make note of these changes in Office Live. Changing an activity is all in the click. If you can see an activity, you can edit it. That means you can edit your activities from the Day, Week, or Month calendars.

All of these calendars show your activities as a link. Click the link to open the Edit Appointment page, make your changes and then click the Save button. If you've invited attendees, they receive e-mail with the updated information. What could be easier?

Knowing the various calendar views

The various Office Live calendars are great for viewing scheduled tasks. You can easily access the various views by clicking the appropriate icon in the personal calendar tool bar. A scheduled activity shows up on all of the various calendar views; for example, if you used the weekly calendar to schedule an appointment, you can still view it in your monthly calendar.

Here are a couple of ways in which to view your calendars:

- **Day:** Shows you the time-specific activities of the selected day. The day is divided into half-hour intervals.
- **Weekly:** Shows the entire week, including Saturday and Sunday. (See Figure 7-6.)
- **Monthly:** Shows you the time-specific activities of the selected month.
- **Yearly:** Shows you a yearly calendar. Although you can't see your scheduled activities in this view, you can click any date to zoom into the daily view of that date.

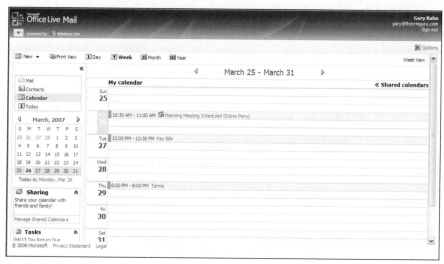

Figure 7-6:
Organize with a weekly calendar.

Using the Task List

Like the Honey-Do list hanging from every husband's workbench, the Office Live Task List gives you a listing of all those things you need "to get around to." In general, your calendar is the best tool for scheduling activities associated with specific dates and times; your Task List on the other hand, includes those timeless activities that you just plain *need to accomplish*. (When you get to them. Real soon now.)

You can access the Task List readily enough by clicking Tasks on the Office Live Navigation bar. Figure 7-7 shows a sample Task List.

Figure 7-7:
The Office Live Task List.

Follow these steps to create a new task:

1. **Click the New drop-down arrow and select Task.**

   The New Task page appears, as shown in Figure 7-8.

2. **Fill in the Task fields with the information about your task.**

   • *Subject:* It always helps to know what you're trying to accomplish.

   • *Start* and *Due Date:* Because tasks often take a while to complete, you have both a Start and Due date.

   • *Status:* This proves particularly helpful if you are sharing your Personal Calendar with others. You can choose a status of Not Started, In Progress, or Completed.

- *Notes:* Feel free to write a book to yourself with the nitty-gritty details of the task.

- *Category:* Because you can sort the Task List by category you might want to add one to your task.

- *Reminder:* Click the double down-pointing arrows to expand the Reminders area so you can have an e-mail reminder of the task's milestones.

3. **Click Save to save your task.**

   You arrive back at the Task List where the new tasks sit in wait — hopefully not surrounded by too many *other* tasks!

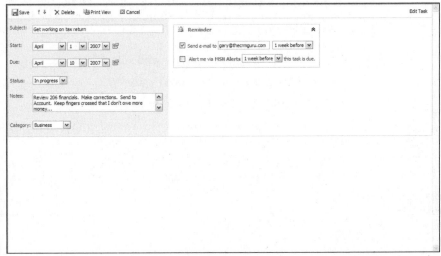

Figure 7-8:
The New
Task page.

Being Reminded by the Reminders

Scheduling an appointment or task is only half the battle — the second half takes place when you actually remember to *do* what you set out to do! So the Reminders section includes a list of all the reminders you set for your activities and tasks.

If you need to set up a reminder, click the New link in the Reminders section. You go to the New Reminder page, which looks exactly like the New Appointment page. Not surprisingly, anything scheduled via the Reminders section automatically appears on your calendar.

Click the Go to List link in the Reminders section to get a more detailed list of all the activities and tasks for which you included a reminder.

Taking Notes

If you live in Florida — or any place with an abundance of paddle fans — you've probably learned that a sticky note is not your best method of recording information. Even if you haven't fallen prey to a paddle fan, you might avoid sticky notes because they tend to stick to everything *except* what they're intended to stick to.

You can jot down a Note in the Office Live Personal Calendar in much the same way you create one on a sticky note or paper scrap — and it won't blow away. Here's how you do it:

1. **Click the New drop-down arrow and select Note.**

   The New Note page appears; see Figure 7-9.

2. **Fill in the note details and click Save.**

   Selecting a category from the drop-down list comes in handy if you decide to sort your notes by category later on.

   You return to the Notes page, as shown in Figure 7-10. Your new note sits along all the other notes that you've added along the way.

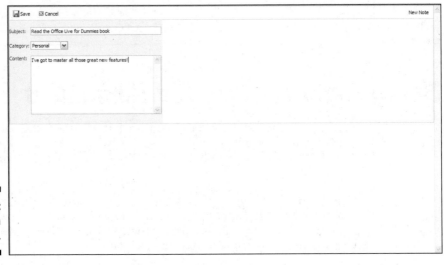

Figure 7-9:
Creating a
new note.

Figure 7-10:
The Notes
window.

Sending an E-Greeting Card

American Greetings has teamed with Office Live to make it easier to send e-cards. Click the New drop-down arrow and select Greeting Card. When you do, the MSN Greetings page opens, showing all sorts of card categories.

Although some of the greeting cards are free, Microsoft would love for you to become a paying member of the service. A yearly membership — which can be shared by two people — costs a whopping $13.95 per year. As an added incentive, you can create an unlimited number of electronic cards directly from your Office Live e-mail address book — or access your address book from the MSN American Greetings site.

Getting It in Writing

As great as Office Live is, it can be totally useless if you don't have access to a computer or handheld device. Or maybe you work with a technically challenged coworker (your boss?) who prefers to have a copy of his or her Task List printed daily. No need to fret; Office Live can easily print any of the lists in your personal calendar for you:

1. **Click the list view you'd like to print.**

   For example, if you want to print your Task List, click Tasks from the Personal Calendar Navigation bar. The appropriate list opens, complete with all the items you've so painstakingly entered.

2. **Click Print View.**

   You list transforms into a nice, clean-looking list.

3. **Click the Print button on your browser's toolbar.**

   Your printer window opens.

4. **Click OK to print your list.**

   If you'd like, feel free to pat yourself on the back and say, "*Darn*, I'm *good*" as you affix your beautifully designed list to the company bulletin board.

Sharing Your Calendar

When you were little, your mother taught you to share. Now that you're all grown up, sharing has become a necessity.

One of the great benefits of Office Live is that you can share your Personal Calendar with others. And you can decide not only *who* accesses your calendar, but *what* they can access.

You can share your calendar with others in several ways:

- ✔ **One-to-one free/busy:** A specific person can view the times on your calendar when you are free or busy, but can't view any of your appointment details (such as location or appointment title).

- ✔ **One-to-one full:** A specific person can view your complete schedule, including appointment details.

- ✔ **Public free/busy:** Anyone connected to the Internet can view the times on your calendar when you are free or busy, but can't view any of your appointment details.

- ✔ **Public full:** Anyone connected to the Internet can view your complete schedule, including appointment details.

Sharing your calendar with a single user

Your first decision when sharing your personal calendar is to decide whether select individuals can access your calendar, or whether you want to open it up to the Internet world at large. Typically you'll want to share your calendar with a single individual or two. As you set up the sharing, you can decide whether you want them to see the details of your activities, or just the fact that you are free or busy during any given time period.

If you want to share your calendar with a hand-picked list of individuals, you'll have to do so one at a time. Here's how you'll share your calendar with the first person:

1. **Click the Sharing link in the Personal Calendar.**

   The Sharing page, shown in Figure 7-11, opens.

2. **Click Share Your Calendar.**

   The first page of the Calendar – Options Wizard opens.

3. **Fill in the e-mail address of the person with whom you want to share your calendar.**

   You can select an address from Contacts if you've already entered him in your Address Book. You can only share your calendar with people who are MSN members or have a Microsoft Passport.

   You can usually recognize the Microsoft Passport crowd by their suitcases and hotmail.com or msn.com e-mail addresses. In addition, anyone sharing your Office Live account is also part of the In-Crowd who may share your calendar.

4. **Click Next to continue.**

   The Choose How Much Information to Display page opens.

5. **Select the level of appointment detail that you want to share.**

   You don't really have much choice here; you can either opt to let the invitees see all the juicy details of your appointments, or let your visitors know only that you are either free or busy.

6. **Click Next to continue.**

   The third page opens, as shown in Figure 7-12. Here's where you can type a personal e-mail to the person you are going to share your calendar with.

7. **Click Finish.**

   A recap page opens, confirming that your e-mail has been sent, which contains a link to your shared calendar.

8. **Click OK.**

   You return to the Calendar Sharing page where you can further configure your calendar or just call it a day. Your invitees can view your calendar by using their Microsoft Passport e-mail addresses and passwords.

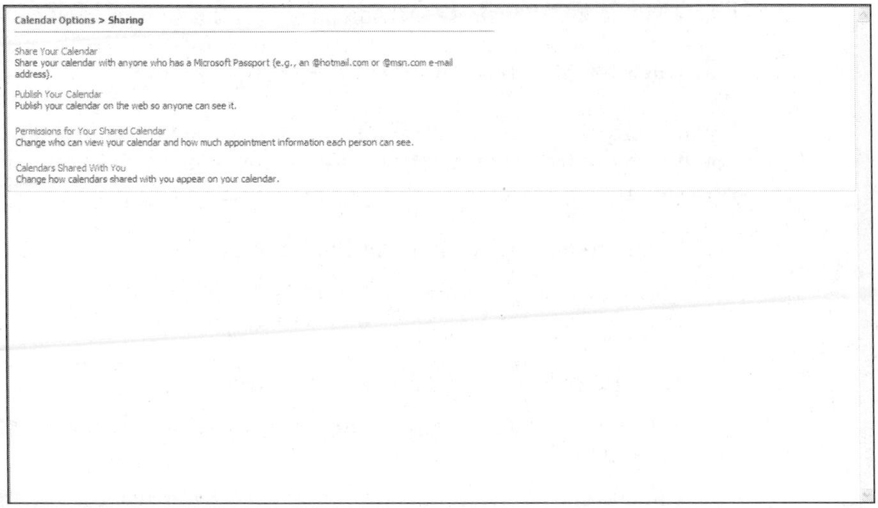

Calendar Options > **Sharing**

Share Your Calendar
Share your calendar with anyone who has a Microsoft Passport (e.g., an @hotmail.com or @msn.com e-mail address).

Publish Your Calendar
Publish your calendar on the web so anyone can see it.

Permissions for Your Shared Calendar
Change who can view your calendar and how much appointment information each person can see.

Calendars Shared With You
Change how calendars shared with you appear on your calendar.

Figure 7-11:
Sharing
your
personal
calendar.

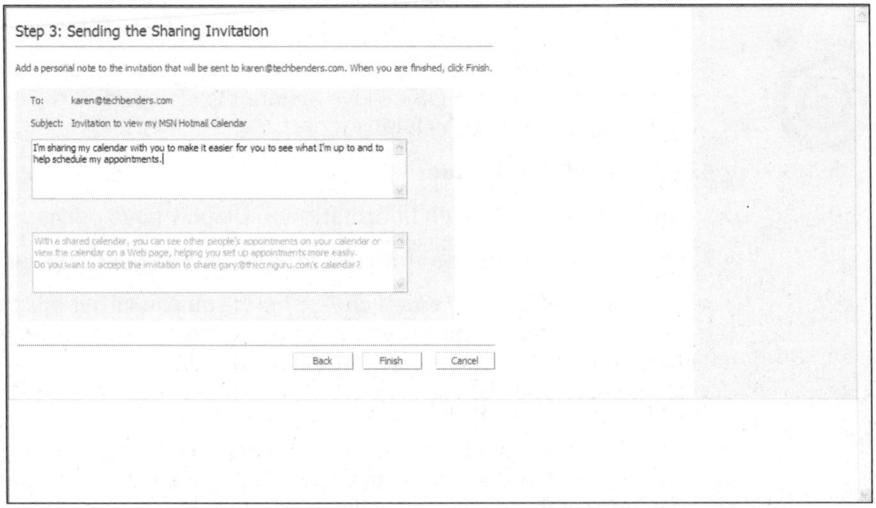

Step 3: Sending the Sharing Invitation

Add a personal note to the invitation that will be sent to karen@techbenders.com. When you are finished, click Finish.

To: karen@techbenders.com

Subject: Invitation to view my MSN Hotmail Calendar

I'm sharing my calendar with you to make it easier for you to see what I'm up to and to help schedule my appointments.

With a shared calendar, you can see other people's appointments on your calendar or view the calendar on a Web page, helping you set up appointments more easily.
Do you want to accept the invitation to share gary@thscmguru.com's calendar?

Back   Finish   Cancel

Figure 7-12:
Sending the
Sharing
Invitation.

After you've set up Personal Calendar sharing with a person, one of two thoughts will probably strike you:

✔ Eww. I've changed my mind — I *don't* want to share my calendar with *him*.

✔ Wow! This is so cool I think I'll share my calendar with a few other members of the In Crowd.

Either way, you'll follow these steps:

1. **Click the Sharing link on your Personal Calendar.**

   The Calendar – Sharing page opens.

2. **Click Permissions for Your Shared Calendar.**

   The Change Who Can View Your Calendar page opens, as shown in Figure 7-13.

3. **Click one of the option buttons.**

   Depending on your choice, another window opens:

   • *Add Person:* Share your database with another person. Follow Steps 3-8 in the previous list.

   • *Edit:* Change the sharing privileges of someone currently sharing your database.

   • *Stop Sharing:* Remove the sharing privileges for the selected contact.

4. **Click Save Changes to close the open window, and then click Finish to close the Change Who Can View Your Calendar window.**

Creating a calendar for the whole world to see

You might be wondering why you'd want to let the entire universe access your Personal calendar. The answer is to not get hung up on the *Personal* portion of the calendar. Clubs and businesses can enjoy the benefits of a Basic Office Live subscription. For example, a soccer team might publish its calendar on the Web so anyone — moms, dads, grandparents, players — can access the team's schedule. A dance studio might want to publish its class schedules. The possibilities are endless.

By making the calendar public, you don't have to worry about collecting everyone's e-mail addresses; instead, you provide them with a direct link to the calendar.

Here's all you need to do to get started:

1. **Click the Sharing link on your Personal Calendar.**

   The Calendar – Sharing page opens.

2. **Click Publish Your Calendar.**

   The Publish Your Calendar page opens.

3. Select the level of detail that you want to share with others.

The only options you have are to allow everyone to see the details of all your appointments, or only allow them to see when you're free or busy.

4. Save changes.

After you publish your calendar, anyone with an Internet connection can view it. Simply give them the link to your calendar — or consider putting a link to it on the Web site you create in Office Live!

You might decide that there are certain appointments you *don't* want everyone to see. To make an existing appointment private, double-click the appointment, and then select Do Not Display This Appointment When I Share My Calendar.

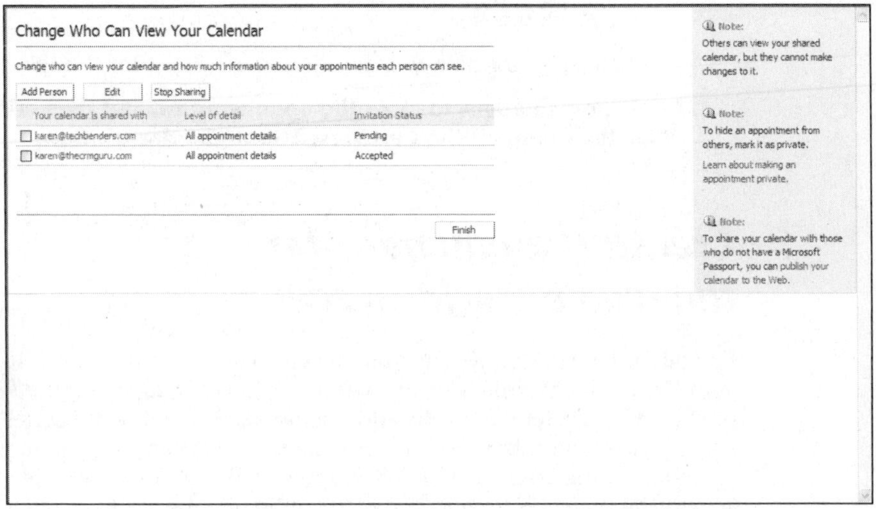

Change Who Can View Your Calendar

Change who can view your calendar and how much information about your appointments each person can see.

| Add Person | Edit | Stop Sharing |

Your calendar is shared with	Level of detail	Invitation Status
☐ karen@techbenders.com	All appointment details	Pending
☐ karen@thecrmguru.com	All appointment details	Accepted

Finish

Note:
Others can view your shared calendar, but they cannot make changes to it.

Note:
To hide an appointment from others, mark it as private.
Learn about making an appointment private.

Note:
To share your calendar with those who do not have a Microsoft Passport, you can publish your calendar to the Web.

Figure 7-13:
Changing who can view your calendar.

Part III
Adding a Few Essentials

The 5th Wave   By Rich Tennant

UBER-USER DWAYNE GRANTZ CHALKS
UP BEFORE PUTTING OFFICE LIVE
THROUGH ITS PACES.

In this part . . .

When you move from the Basic to the Essentials plan, a whole new world opens. You find out how to create a site that other members of your team can access. You can store your contacts and other pertinent information about your business in the online version of Business Contact Manager; if you already have a Web site, you can download it into Essentials. Finally, you can take your business on the road by synching all your Office Live info to Outlook or to your PDA.

Chapter 8

Working with Business Contact Manager

*I*f you have an Essentials or Premium Office Live account, you can use Business Contact Manager to organize your contacts and accounts in one central location. You can also create opportunities, track a sales pipeline, and store various product information with Business Contact Manager. In addition, Business Contact Manager includes a Business Documents library to store documents that are important for your customer relations.

Chapter 4 discusses the Address Book that comes with all Office Live accounts. In this chapter, you get a look at all the additional functionality of Business Contact Manager.

Welcome to the World of Contact Management

You might like to think of Contact Management as the last frontier in the world of software. When you start a business you probably have a certain hierarchy of software in mind. You probably start with the ability to e-mail and compose documents, throw in a spreadsheet or accounting software to track the dollars coming in and out of your business, and maybe even develop a Web site.

A successful business follows a steady path. You start with some prospects that hopefully turn into paying customers. As your business grows, so does your customer list. And as your business continues to grow, so do your headaches. You find that sticky notes and legal pads are just not an efficient way to conduct your business.

Enter the world of contact management — with the operative word being *contact*: a person you've encountered in the course of your business. A contact *record* is all the information you have collected about that person. Note, however, another meaning of the word *contact* — to communicate. To do business, you need to stay in touch with your contacts — and Business Contact Manager gives you all the tools to do just that.

Click the Business Contact Manager link from the home page Navigation bar to open the Business Contact Manager dashboard, shown in Figure 8-1. The dashboard provides you with a listing of all the newest information for the various BCM parts. In addition, the dashboard allows you to add new Accounts and Contacts quickly.

Figure 8-1:
The
Business
Contact
Manager
dashboard.

Business Contact Manager consists of five main areas, all of which you can access by clicking the corresponding tabs that run across the top of Business Contact Manager page:

- ✔ **Accounts:** The companies that you work with
- ✔ **Contacts:** The individuals that you work with
- ✔ **Opportunities:** Potential sales you're hoping to close
- ✔ **Products:** The items or services that you sell
- ✔ **Business Documents:** Documents that you upload to the BCM portion of Office Live to share with other users

Accounting for Your Accounts

Business Contact Manager includes the capability to add both *accounts* and *contacts*. An account record contains all the pertinent details about a company or an organization. A contact record collects information about an individual person. You can associate contacts with an account if you have a number of contacts in one company.

You might think of an account as an "uber-contact" because it represents the master contact. Some of your clients may be smaller businesses and you'll find that one contact record is sufficient. However, if you're dealing with larger organizations — those with a bunch of cubicles and a cafeteria — you might be dealing with several people in an organization. And chances are that the contacts working for a company might be "here today and gone tomorrow." The account record holds the critical information for the company, including a list of all the contacts associated with it.

Adding an Account record with all the bells and whistles

Creating an account is easy. Here's all you need to do:

1. **Click Business Contact Manager from the Office Live Home page Navigation bar.**

   The Business Contact Manager dashboard opens.

2. **Click the Accounts tab.**

   The Business Contact Manager Accounts list opens, as shown in Figure 8-2.

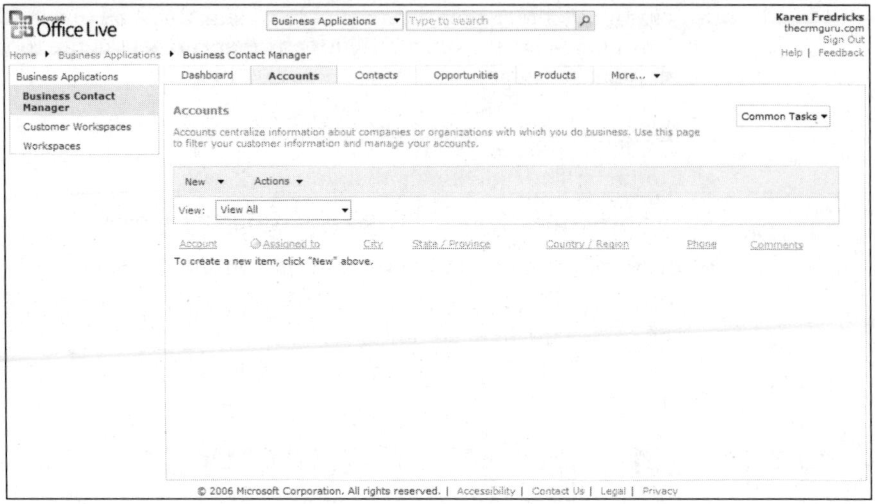

Figure 8-2:
The
Business
Contact
Manager
Account
tab.

3. Click New on the toolbar.

The Accounts – New Item page opens with the Communicate tab showing, as shown in Figure 8-3.

4. Fill in all the pertinent information.

The only field that you must fill in is the Account field — the rest of the
fields are optional.

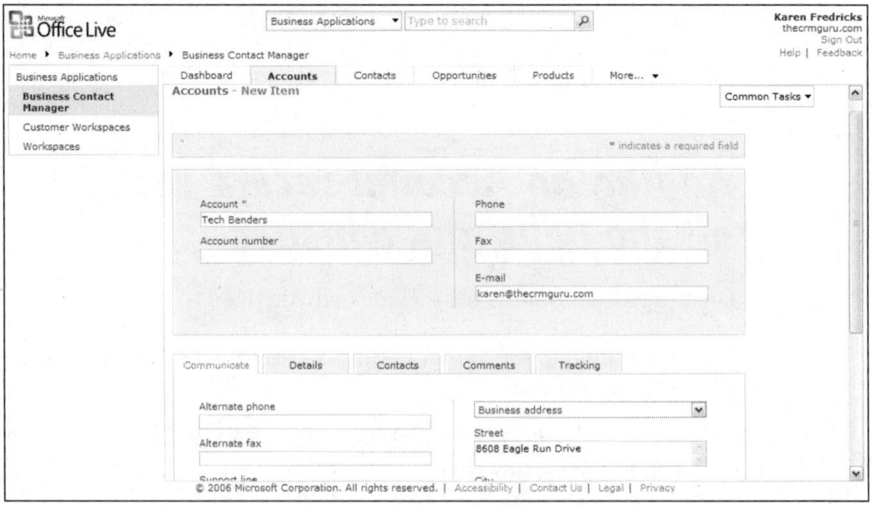

Figure 8-3:
The New
Accounts
page.

5. **(Optional) On the Communicate tab, click the Business Address drop-down arrow and choose Shipping Address if you'd like to fill in an additional address that you'll use for shipping.**

   Business Contact Manager allows you to enter both a business and shipping address.

6. **(Optional) Click the Details tab and fill in the account information.**

   Here's where you can add the pertinent account information, including projected revenue and payment status (see Figure 8-4). You can also assign an Office Live user to the Account; the users appear when you click the book icon to the right of the Assigned To field.

7. **(Optional) Click the Contacts tab and add any contacts that belong to the account.**

   If you've ever wondered which comes first — the chicken or the egg — you'll probably be just as inquisitive about knowing which comes first — the Account or the Contact? If you've added contacts to Business Contact Manager, you can associate them with the Account record by clicking the Add Existing link (see Figure 8-5) to see a list of all the contacts in Business Contact Manager. If you'd rather add a new contact, click the Add New link; the New Contact page opens and you can add a new contact that is then associated automatically with the Account record.

   Wondering why you don't see a contact listed here when you know you've added it already? If the contact you want to add is not in the list, you've probably already associated it with a *different* account.

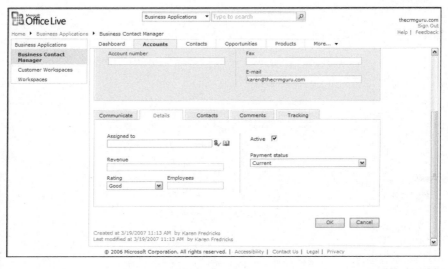

Figure 8-4:
The
Accounts
Details tab.

Figure 8-5:
The
Accounts
Contacts
tab.

8. **(Optional) Click the Comments tab and add a comment about the account.**

You can add a small comment — or write a book about — the Account just by filling in the Comment field (see Figure 8-6).

The Comment tab allows you to add *one* comment — and *only one* comment — to the Account record. The Tracking tab, however, allows you to add *multiple* notes to the Account record.

Figure 8-6:
The
Accounts
Comments
tab.

9. **(Optional) Click the Tracking tab.**

   The Tracking tab is where you turn to add opportunities, phone logs, and notes to an Account record. You can add an unlimited number of items to the Tracking tab. Need to add a lot of notes? No problem — add away!

10. **(Optional) To add a new tracking item, click the appropriate link, as shown in Figure 8-7.**

    For example, if you want to add a note, click the Add Note link.

    The corresponding form appears. Figure 8-8 shows the Opportunities form; to find out more about adding an Opportunity to either an Account or Contact record see the section, "Creating an Opportunity When One Comes Knocking" later in this chapter.

11. **Click OK to save your changes.**

Congratulations! You are now the proud owner of an Account record.

Adding an Account record on the fly

If you're chomping at the bit to start creating an Account record — or if you just don't have all the pertinent information at your fingertips — you might want to create an abbreviated Account record. After all, you can always go back later and edit the record to include any pieces of information you left out the first time around.

Figure 8-7:
The
Accounts
Tracking
tab.

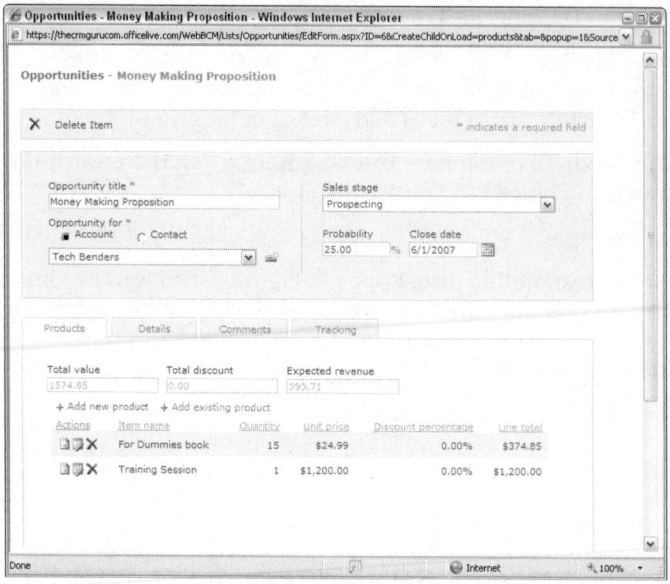

Figure 8-8:
The
Accounts
Opportunity
tab.

Here's what you need to do to add an Account record in a jiffy:

1. **Click Business Contact Manager from the Office Live Home page Navigation bar.**

   The Business Contact Manager dashboard opens.

2. **Fill in the pertinent information in the Quick Add: Account section.**

   Talk about abbreviated — there are only three fields (Account name, Primary E-mail, and Phone) to fill in.

3. **Click Save to save your new Account record.**

No pain, no gain. The more information you fill in now, the more information you can use later. Although this method is quick and easy, be sure to fill in the rest of the information later.

Contacting Your Contacts

While an *account* generally refers to a company, a *contact* is the actual person with whom you do business. Although you enter contact information in pretty much the exact same way as you do account information, some of the fields differ a bit. For example, you'll probably need to store more than one e-mail address — and possibly an IM address as well.

You'll use the account record to keep details about a company or an organization, and the contact record to capture information about the people with whom you have a business relationship.

If you shut your eyes while adding a contact record, you'd probably think you were adding an account record. (Actually, you'd probably better keep those eyes open when adding any kind of record into Office Live, but you get the drift.) You'll see very little difference between your account and contact records.

Follow these steps to add a contact to Business Contact Manager:

1. **Click Business Contact Manager from the Office Live Home page Navigation bar.**

   The Business Contact Manager dashboard opens.

2. **Click the Contacts tab.**

   The Contacts List appears, as shown in Figure 8-9.

3. **Click New on the Contact tab toolbar.**

   The Contacts – New Item page opens with the Communicate tab showing.

4. **Type the requested information on the Communicate tab.**

   The Communicate tab contains the fields you use when you want to communicate with someone: It gives you places for names, addresses, phone numbers, and e-mail addresses.

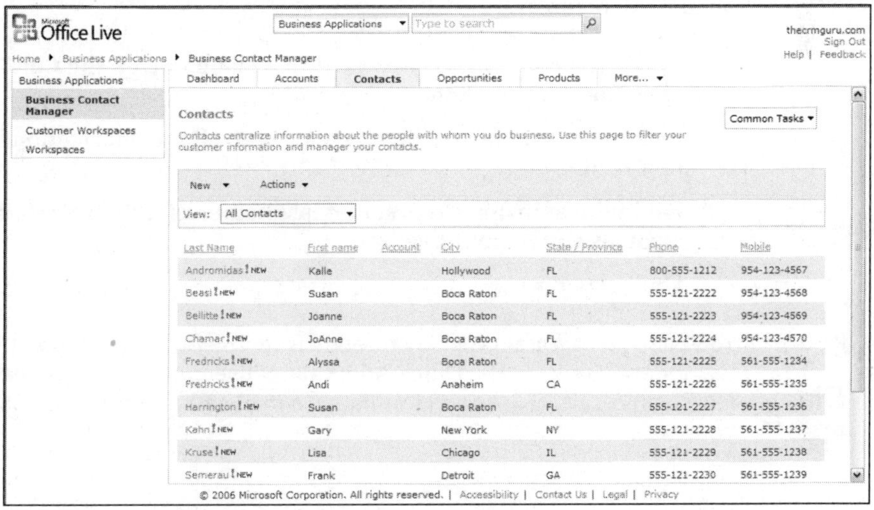

Figure 8-9:
The
Business
Contact
Manager
Contacts
List.

5. **(Optional) Click the Details tab and add more details.**

   Funnily enough, the Details tab lets you fill in a few more *details* about the contact — including the Office/Branch, Department, Manager, Profession, and shoe size. (Okay, they really don't ask for your shoe size — just wanted to make sure you were paying attention.)

6. **(Optional) Click the Personal tab and add more details.**

   If you have some personal lowdown on the contact, here's the place to put it. You can record everything from a Nickname and Hobbies to Birth and Anniversary dates on this tab.

7. **(Optional) Click the Comments tab to add a comment about the contact.**

   As the name implies, here's where you can create a big, fat comment — or a teeny-tiny little one — about the contact.

8. **(Optional) Click the Tracking tab to log in items about the contact.**

   The Tracking tab is used to keep a log of opportunities, phone logs, and notes for the contact. This tab works exactly like the Tracking tab of an Account record; there is no limit to how many items you can add.

9. **Click OK to save your changes and exit the New Item page.**

If you have several people who are all working for the same company, chances are pretty good that they all share the same business address. If time is not an object, feel free to add all those contacts in one by one — but if you're in a rush to fit in a few rounds of golf before the sun sets, you can duplicate a record:

1. **Click the drop-down arrow next to a last name on the Contacts tab and choose Copy Item.**

   A new record appears, already filled with all the information from the first record.

2. **Fill in the appropriate first and last name, as well as any other changes you might have.**

   You're good to go!

You can add a contact quickly directly from the Business Contact Manager dashboard. Look for the Quick Add: Contact section where you can add a few small details (Last and First name, e-mail and phone), and you'll be on your way.

Creating an Opportunity When One Comes Knocking

An *opportunity* is a prospective sale. Business Contact Manager lets you keep a running list of all those potential sales — including the potential cash that will potentially hit your wallet. You can use Business Contact Manager to capture the details of each opportunity and then view them all together in the Opportunities list. An opportunity usually consists of the various products or services, a sales stage, and the sales rep who was responsible for the deal. You can track notes and phone logs about the opportunity. Best of all, Business Contact Manager does all the calculating for you!

Opportunity records work just like Account and Contact records. You can view all your opportunities at once in the Opportunities list, or you can view a single opportunity in full detail. You can sort and view the Opportunity list in a number of ways, or customize it to your liking.

To create a golden opportunity — or at least one that will (hopefully) make you lots of money — follow these steps:

1. **Click Business Contact Manager from the Office Live Home page Navigation bar.**

   The Business Contact Manager dashboard opens.

2. **Click the Opportunities tab.**

   You'll end up with a loud *ka-ching* smack dab in the middle of the Opportunities list. Don't worry if there's nothing listed there yet — there will be soon!

3. **Click the New button.**

   The Opportunities – New Item page opens, as shown in Figure 8-10.

4. **Fill in the required information.**

   There are only two requirements here:

   - *Opportunity Title:* The title is up to you; you might name the opportunity something catchy like "Huge Money-Maker" or you might give it a more subtle name that corresponds to an invoice number.

   - *Opportunity For:* You must associate either an existing Account or Contact with the Opportunity but you can't associate both. Select the type of record you'd like to associate with the Opportunity; then choose an existing Office Live record. Click the icon next to the drop-down list to add a new record if you need to.

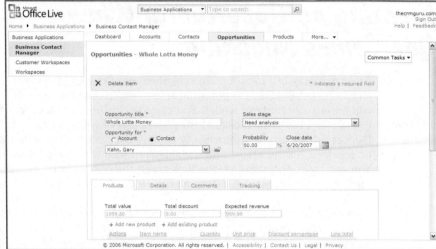

Figure 8-10:
The
Business
Contact
Manager
Opportu-
nities list.

5. Fill in the optional information.

This doesn't require a whole lot of effort but it can prove really helpful in the future. Business Contact Manager comes equipped with a Sales Stage drop-down list of common sales stages (everything from Prospecting down through Quoting and Negotiating, with a final stop at either Closed won or Closed loss). You can then manually input a closing probability and an estimated Close date.

6. On the Products tab, click the Add Existing Product link.

If you haven't saved your opportunity, Office Live prompts you to do so.

The Add Existing Product page appears, which provides a list of your products (see Figure 8-11).

7. Place a check mark next to the item(s) you want to add and then click OK.

For some unknown reason, any products you add from the Opportunity record are associated only with that opportunity. The product(s) don't appear in the Products list. If you want to add a product that you'll use with multiple opportunities, you have to add them prior to creating the opportunity.

Don't worry if you haven't added any new products — you can do so in the "Producing More Products" section later in this chapter.

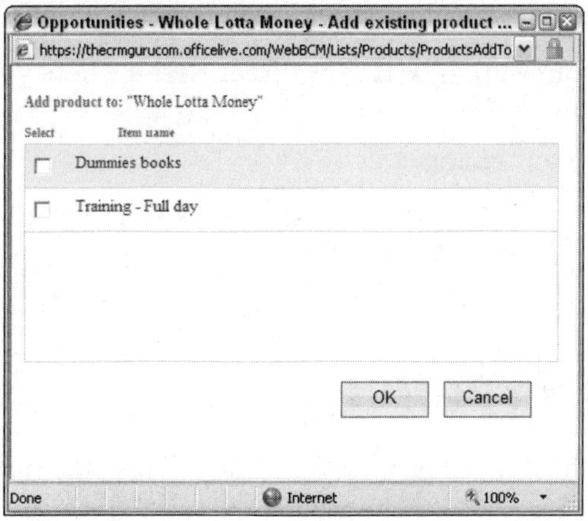

Figure 8-11:
The Add
Existing
Product
page.

8. **(Optional) Click the Details tab and add details about the opportunity.**

   Here's where you can enter additional information, including the sales rep's name and the payment terms (see Figure 8-12).

9. **(Optional) Click the Comments tab and add a comment about the opportunity.**

   Got something on your mind? Here's where to add any thoughts, comments, or complaints about the opportunity that you might have.

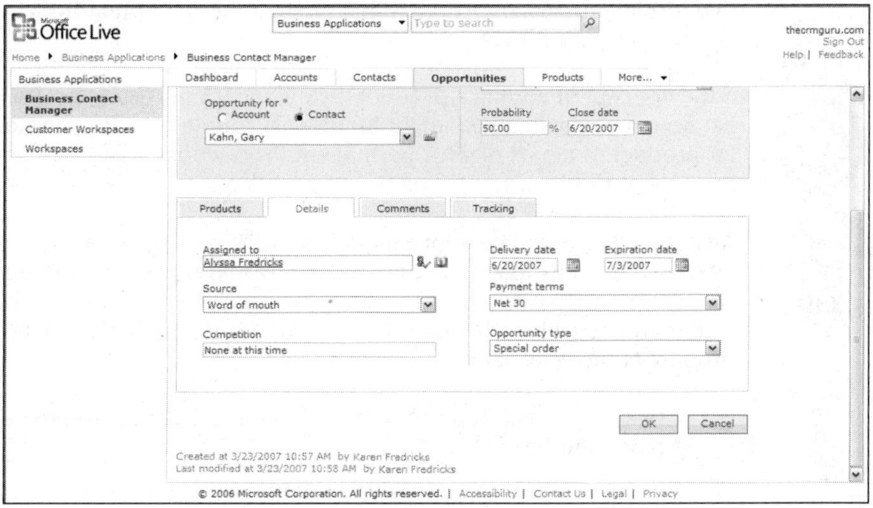

Figure 8-12:
The
Opportunity
Details tab.

10. **(Optional) Click the Tracking tab and make additional notes.**

   Need to make a follow-up — or two or three? Here's where you can add your phone logs and notes.

11. **Click OK to save your changes.**

   Home, sweet home — which (in this case) is the Opportunities list where your newly created opportunity now resides.

Producing More Products

A *product* is an item that you sell or a service that you provide. You can add products to the Business Contact Manager Products list to develop a centralized catalog, or you can add a product to an opportunity if you want to create a product that is only used with that opportunity.

Products work in much the same way as Contacts, Accounts, and Opportunities. You can view all your products in a list, or you can zoom in on any given product to see a bit more detail. You can access your products while adding or editing an Opportunity in the same way you access your Account and Contact lists from within an Opportunity.

However, there is one rather unique quirk you should recognize while working with products: Products that are created from within an Opportunity don't appear in the Products list. And when you edit the price or quantity of a product in an Opportunity, that change doesn't appear as a permanent change in the Products list.

If the concept of adding a product through an opportunity or the Products list seems confusing, you might follow this simple rule: If you want a particular product as a part of your permanent Product list, add it directly from the Product list.

Any changes you make to products from within an Opportunity list don't affect the main Product list, only the current Opportunity you are editing.

Understanding where to add a new product is the *difficult* part; creating a new product is the *easy* part:

1. **Click Business Contact Manager from the Office Live Home page Navigation bar.**

   The Business Contact Manager dashboard opens.

2. **Click the Products tab.**

   The Products list opens, displaying any products you might have already added.

3. **Click New.**

   The Products – New Item page opens, as shown in Figure 8-13.

4. **Fill in the required information.**

   This step should prove fairly easy; the only information you must add is a product name and the default quantity or amount. The product description isn't required.

   You can change the quantity or amount for each individual Opportunity when you create a new Opportunity or edit an existing one.

5. **Fill in any additional information.**

   When you add a product description, unit cost, unit price, and a discount percentage, and then indicate if the product is taxable, Business Contact Manager automatically calculates these things:

   • *Markup:* The difference between the unit price and cost.

   • *Line Total Before Discount:* The quantity times the unit price.

   • *Line Total:* The quantity times the unit price minus the discount percentage.

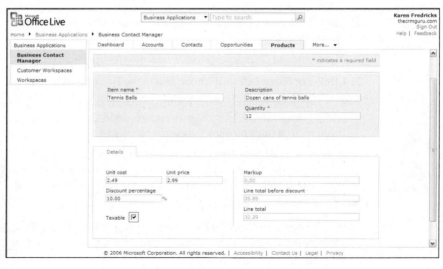

Figure 8-13:
Adding a
new
product.

Documenting Your Documents

Probably one of the first things you learned to do after you mastered the art of turning on your computer was to organize the documents you created. Presumably you discovered the My Documents folder and learned how to subdivide it into smaller folders, in much the same way that you create paper folders to help keep your paperwork in order.

Sharing documents with users in other locations presents a whole new set of challenges. First of all, you'll have to have some method of transmitting your documents to other people; after all, they can't see documents that you continue to store on your *own* computer. You might try e-mailing documents to people; however, in this day of spam and viruses you're likely to find it difficult to send and receive files — especially the larger ones. And then you have to find a way of keeping those files updated so that all users have the latest and greatest version of a document. Whew! What a nightmare.

Business Contact Manager and Office Live make it so easy to share documents that you might just think you're dreaming. You can either upload a bunch of documents directly to the Business Documents list, or you can create folders and upload documents directly into each folder.

Of course, if you've been following along through this book, by now you're an old pro at adding items to a Business Contact Manager list. But adding a document has a few extra twists. Here's what you need to know:

1. **Click Business Contact Manager from the Office Live Home page Navigation bar.**

   The Business Contact Manager dashboard opens.

2. **Click the More tab and chose Business Documents.**

   The Documents list opens. You might want to dive right in and start adding documents, but I highly recommend that you first give some thought to which folders you want to create.

   After you add a document to the Documents list, you can't move it to another folder. If you anticipate having a lot of documents in the Documents list, create folders before you upload documents.

3. **Choose New⇨New Folder.**

   You'll have a choice of New Folder or, well, New Folder. I recommend picking the New Folder option — especially considering that it's your *only* option!

The New Folder: Business Documents page opens.

4. **Fill in the Folder name and click OK to save your changes and return to the Documents list.**

   Your new folder is now proudly displayed on the Documents list; see Figure 8-14. To open the folder, all you have to do is click it.

5. **Click the Upload button and choose the documents you want to upload.**

   You have two options, depending on how many documents you want to upload:

   - *Upload Document:* This option allows you to browse to one file on your computer, select it, and click OK to add it to the current folder or Document list.

   - *Upload Multiple Documents:* The Upload Document page opens as shown in Figure 8-15. Click the plus sign next to the folder that contains your documents from the left pane, place a check mark next to the documents you want to upload in the right pane, and then click OK.

   Your documents now appear either in the current folder or directly on the Business Documents list.

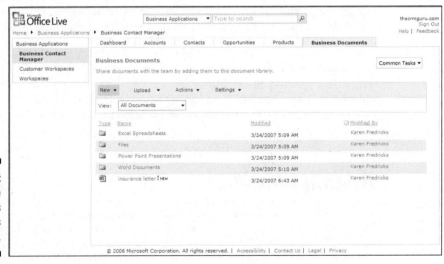

Figure 8-14:
The
Business
Documents
list.

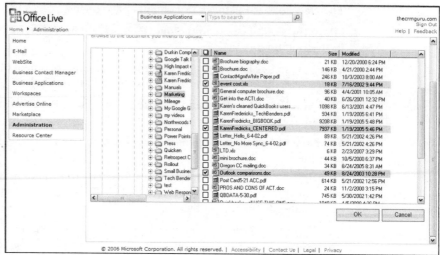

Figure 8-15:
Uploading
multiple
documents
to the
Business
Documents
list.

Receiving Change Alerts for a BCM Item

What's great about Office Live is that you can be completely mobile. You can work from home, an auxiliary office, or even on the road — all the while sharing your information with the folks back in the main office. However, all that mobility comes with a price: If you're not around when important changes are taking place, how do you find out about them?

Business Contact Manager has a nifty feature that sends you an e-mail alert every time specific information changes. For example, you can receive an alert when a new contact is added, or when an Opportunity hits a crucial sales stage. You can receive alerts for changes to a list or for changes to items within the list.

Adding an alert

You can receive an alert when account, contact, opportunity, or product information changes. You can create alerts for changes to any of your lists, or specifically for any item within a list. For example, you might receive one notice if a new Product is added to the Product list, or if the price of an already-existing Product changes.

Here's all you need to do to set it up:

1. **Click Business Contact Manager from the Navigation bar on the Office Live Home page.**

   The Business Contact Manager dashboard opens.

2. **Click the tab that contains the list you want to receive alerts for.**

3. **Choose Alert Me from the Actions drop-down menu.**

   The New Alert page springs open (see Figure 8-16).

4. **Fill in the fields to configure the alert:**

   - *Alert Title:* This information appears in the subject line of the e-mail alert.

   - *Send Alerts To:* Specify the user who is to receive the notice by clicking the book icon and selecting the name of an Office Live user.

   - *Change Type:* You can specify to receive notification about changes to items or all changes.

   - *Send Alerts for These Changes:* Filters your alerts based on the criteria you used in the current list view.

   - *When to Send Alerts:* Specify whether you want to be notified of changes immediately or as part of a daily or weekly summary.

5. **Click OK to return to the list view.**

Figure 8-16:
Configuring
an alert.

Removing alerts

If you decide that you no longer want to be alerted about a change, you'll have to go to a slightly different area of Business Contact Manager. Here's how to get there and what to do:

1. **Click Business Contact Manager from the Office Live Home page Navigation bar.**

   The Business Contact Manager dashboard opens.

2. **Choose Modify This Application or Workspace from the Common Tasks drop-down menu.**

   The Site Settings page opens.

3. **Click Go to Top Level Site Settings in the Site Collection Administration section.**

   The second page of Site Settings opens.

4. **Click User Alerts in the View section.**

   The User Alerts page opens, as shown in Figure 8-17.

5. **Select the name of the user from the Display Alerts For drop-down list and click Update.**

   You see a list of the alerts created for that particular user.

6. **Select the check boxes next to the alerts you want to remove, and then click Delete Selected Alerts.**

7. **Click OK to the warning message.**

   You no longer receive the alert notifications for the selected items.

Figure 8-17:
Deleting
e-mail
alerts from
Business
Contact
Manager.

Working with Existing Record Information

When you have a bunch of records, you can view them all at once, or you can view them in a more detailed form format. If you're looking at a list you can sort them to your heart's content, using existing views or your own views. For example, you can sort and view accounts by location, by payment status, or by assigned sales representative. If you decide that some of your information is incorrect or no longer needed, you can edit or delete an item.

The following sections show how to edit individual records. If you need to add, edit, or delete lots of records in one fell swoop, see the "Working with Datasheets" section later in this chapter.

Viewing your lists

All the lists work in essentially the same way. For simplicity, I use the Accounts list. Feel free to substitute *contact*, *opportunity*, or *product* anywhere.

Follow these steps to view your Accounts list:

1. **Click Business Contact Manager from the Office Live Home page Navigation bar.**

   The Business Contact Manager dashboard opens.

2. **Click the Accounts tab.**

   Your Accounts list appears in its full glory.

3. **Click on one of the Account names.**

   You can view your accounts in two ways: individually with a lot of detail or in a list with just a few of the most pertinent details. Clicking the Account name allows you to examine the Account in minute detail. You can click on any of the Account tabs to see even more information. The only thing you *can't* do is change your information.

4. **Click your browser's Back button to return to the Accounts list.**

   At this point, you might be finished snooping around in your accounts. If not, you can click another account name to get the 411 on that particular account. If you decide to stick around in the Accounts list for a while, you'll want to continue with the next steps.

5. **Click a column heading to sort your information by that field.**

   Want to see your Accounts sorted by city? No problemo — just click the City header. Bet you've already guessed how to sort your accounts according to their zip code; that's right, click on the Zip/Postal code header.

6. **Click the View drop-down and select one of the view options.**

   There are lots of ways to view your data. Figure 8-18 shows the choices on the Account View drop-down menu. If you look at the Opportunities list, you'll see choices such as By Sales Stage and By Account.

7. **(Optional) Chose Modify This View and customize the current view.**

   The Edit View: Accounts page opens. Just in case you're not happy with the default views you can always modify an existing one or create a brand-new view. You have several ways to change the view; make sure you scroll all the way down to the bottom of the page so you can see them all. You can change the Name of the view, the columns that show and their order, create a filter, and even decide how you'd like to see Accounts grouped.

   The width of your columns is directly proportional to the number of columns you have showing in a list. As you add more columns, your information starts to scroll to the next line, making your data harder to read.

8. **Click OK to save your changes.**

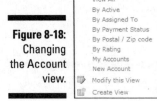

Figure 8-18: Changing the Account view.

View All
By Active
By Assigned To
By Payment Status
By Postal / Zip code
By Rating
My Accounts
New Account
Modify this View
Create View

My info, it is a changing

People move, things change, and you'll need to change your Business Contact Manager information. Of all the records you'll need to edit in Business Contact Manager, you'll probably find that Opportunities require the most editing. First of all, you'll want to change the sales stage — and corresponding probability of closing — as the opportunity marches its way through the sales process. If you didn't have a product in your Products list when you added the Opportunity, you need to add it to the Products list. Even if you added products, you might need to adjust their prices and/or quantities.

The thought of all that volatile information might have you running for cover. Relax! You'll find editing the Opportunity information just as easy as it was to enter in the first place.

Here's what you need to know to edit an existing Opportunity:

1. **Click Business Contact Manager from the Office Live Home page Navigation bar.**

   The Business Contact Manager dashboard opens.

2. **Click the Opportunities tab.**

   The Opportunities list opens in all its glory.

   If you'd just like to view the Opportunity in its entirety without editing it, just click the Opportunity name.

3. **Click the drop-down arrow next to the Opportunity that you want to edit and choose Edit Item.**

   The Opportunity opens in edit mode (see Figure 8-19).

4. **Make any changes you need on any Opportunity tab.**

   When you add an existing product to an opportunity, you create a copy of the product in the opportunity. Any changes you make to the product from within that opportunity are specific to the opportunity. Those changes do not automatically appear in the Products list.

5. **Click OK to save your changes and return back to the Opportunity list.**

Figure 8-19:
Editing an Opportunity record.

Deleting a record

If you no longer need a record, you can delete it. When you delete a record all the tracking items (phone logs, notes, and such) are deleted right along with the record.

If you added a contact to an account, the contact remains in the Contacts list even if you delete the account. When you delete an Account, Contact, or Opportunity record, however, you're also deleting all tracking items linked to them — such as phone logs and notes — and it will not be possible to restore those items. Proceed with caution!

Opportunities must be associated with either a Contact or an Account. If you want to continue tracking an existing Opportunity with a different Contact or Account, associate the Opportunity with a *different* Account or Contact before you delete the existing Account or Contact.

Deleting a Product from an Opportunity deletes only that copy of the Product. If the Product also appears in the Products list, it will remain there safely.

Here's all you need to do to delete a record:

1. **Click Business Contact Manager from the Office Live Home page Navigation bar.**

   The Business Contact Manager dashboard opens.

2. **Click the appropriate tab to access the list.**

3. **Click the drop-down list next to the record you'd like to delete, and then click Delete Item.**

4. **Click OK to the warning.**

   Your contact is now gone — but not forgotten. When you delete a record in Business Contact Manager, Office Live sends it off to the Recycle Bin — just in case! If you're not sure how the Office Live Recycle Bin works, turn to Chapter 11.

Working with Datasheets

So far this chapter has discussed various ways in which Business Contact Manager can help you become more efficient and organized. You're probably raring to go. You've started to enter Accounts, Contacts — but wait. Your work has suddenly come screeching to a halt. Entering a bunch of records one at a time is tedious — and takes an exorbitant amount of time. Inquiring minds want to know — there *must* be an easier way!

Fret not, dear reader. There is another method for entering data — and for editing and/or deleting it again for that matter. If you already have a list of your Contacts, Accounts, Opportunities, or Products, you can paste them into a datasheet. All at once. In the blink of an eye. And, should you need to delete them, you can zap those records en masse, rather than having to deal with them one at a time.

Quite simply, a datasheet is like a spreadsheet, consisting of rows and columns.

 Are you an Excel aficionado? If so you can add, delete, sort, or reorder the columns and rows of a datasheet exactly like you would with a spreadsheet. You can even using the mouse cursor to move information from cell to cell, or to fill down information.

Viewing data in a datasheet

One of the coolest things about viewing your data in a datasheet is how easy your data is to sort and filter. You do that by creating views — changing the filters and columns that you see in a list view — but the datasheet takes filter and sorting to the next level.

Here are some of the cool party tricks you can perform with a datasheet:

- **Widen or narrow a column:** Place your cursor on the right edge of a column header, hold down your left mouse button and drag to the left or right.

- **Change the column order:** Place your cursor on the column header, hold down your left button and drag the column header to the left or right.

- **Sort a column:** Click the header row drop-down list and choose Sort Ascending or Sort Descending.

- **Filter to show only blank (or only non-blank) entries:** Click the header row drop-down list, scroll to the bottom of the list, and choose (Blanks) or (Non-Blanks).

- **Filter by one criterion:** Click the header row drop-down list and select the criterion.

Adding data to a datasheet

Even if you are brand new to contact management and have to start building a database from scratch, you'll probably find entering multiple records is easier in a datasheet rather than through individual forms.

To open a datasheet, follow these steps:

1. **Click Business Contact Manager from the Navigation bar on the Office Live Home page.**

   The Business Contact Manager dashboard opens.

2. **Click the tab that contains the list you want to enter data for.**

3. **Select the view you want to work with.**

   The datasheet that opens reflects your current view. If you are using a view that contains only the name, city and phone number — those are the only columns that appear in your datasheet.

4. **Choose Edit in Datasheet from the Actions drop-down menu.**

   A datasheet appears (see Figure 8-20).

5. **Scroll to the bottom of the list and start to enter your data in the bottom row of the datasheet.**

   Business Contact Manager makes this task pretty easy. The column headers stay in sight, no matter how far down you scroll in the list. You can also press Tab to advance from one field to the next. When you get to the end of a record, your cursor immediately jumps to the next row, which is blank and just waiting for your data. You'll also see that if you start to type something that is already in the datasheet — for example *Chicago* or *United States* — the word autocompletes and you can move on to the next field.

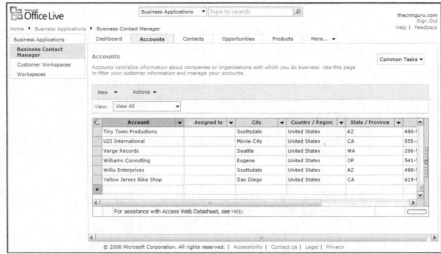

Figure 8-20:
A Business
Contact
Manager
datasheet.

6. **Celebrate when you're finished entering data.**

   Okay, I know that sounds like a strange instruction, but the one thing that's missing from the datasheet is an OK or Save button. Just move on to another spot in Office Live or go back to your list — your changes are saved.

I can think of few chores that are more boring than contact entry. Although Office Live doesn't allow for the ability to import data, you can copy the information from a spreadsheet and paste existing information into a datasheet. If the order of your datasheet column headings match those of the spreadsheet, just place your cursor in the first empty row and paste away. If your columns don't match, you can still paste in your information one column at a time.

Editing data

You might find your information easier to edit in a datasheet than in a record form. You can add, delete, edit, sort, and filter list items while working in a datasheet. You'll probably also find it easier to scroll through your information; the inaccuracies and missing data jump right out at you.

To edit data using the datasheet, follow these steps:

1. **Click Business Contact Manager from the Navigation bar on the Office Live Home page.**

   The Business Contact Manager dashboard opens.

2. **Click the tab that contains the list you want to enter data for.**

3. **Select the view you want to work with.**

4. **Choose Edit in Datasheet from the Actions drop-down menu.**

   The datasheet opens.

5. **Edit the cell you want to change.**

   You can even select a range of cells and hit your Delete key to clear the contents of several continuous cells.

6. **(Optional) If others are making changes as well, choose Refresh Data from the Actions drop-down menu to ensure that you're viewing the most current copy of the data.**

   Talk about things changing in front of your eyes! Often there's no sense changing data if someone else has already beaten you to the punch.

Deleting data in a datasheet

If you have lots of records that you want to delete from a list, using a datasheet is definitely the way to go. Here's the drill:

- ✔ **A single record:** Select a row by clicking the gray box to the left of the record, and then press your Delete key.

- ✔ **A contiguous list of records:** Select several rows by clicking the gray box to the left of the first record, holding down the Shift key while clicking the gray box to the left of the last record in the series, and then press your Delete key.

Don't forget that combining features can make your editing double-fast. For example, if you are no longer doing business in Boston and want to delete all your Boston contacts, you can filter the list to Boston by clicking the City header drop-down and choosing Boston. When your Boston contacts appear, select the first row, and then hold down your Shift key while selecting the last row. Press the Delete key and say Bye-bye Bean Town.

Chapter 9

Working with Workspaces

*I*f you subscribe to Office Live Essentials, or Office Live Premium, you can create a *Workspace*. A Workspace is a place where people can collaborate and exchange business documents and project information. Workspaces are separate-but-related sites on the Internet. Employees, vendors, business partners, or other groups can share information online and from any location, provided they have Internet access.

You might want to think of a Workspace as a private club because only those who are invited to attend can access a Workspace.

In much the same way a club manager checks your credentials before allowing you access, a Workspace requires that you present a password to access it. You can use a Workspace to collaborate with others in your organization. In addition, you can grant permission to people *outside* of your organization to access a Workspace.

If you need to upgrade your account to Office Live Essentials or Office Live Premium, see Chapter 2.

Setting Up a Workspace

Office Live comes with a variety of Workspace templates that you can use, or you can design a Workspace by scratch. Each Workspace you create can include several tabs or pages. Each page includes a corresponding list of information. For example, you might decide to set up a customer Workspace for three of your most important clients. You might include a Shared Documents page; this page would contain all of the documents pertaining to the client that you had uploaded to the customer's Workspace. The customer Workspace could also include a Calendar page on which you could list all the future meetings that you've scheduled with the customer.

The whole idea of a Workspace is to share it with others so that you have an easy way to collaborate — even if the collaborators are scattered hither and yon.

Creating the Workspace

Creating a new Workspace or two is ridiculously easy. Follow these steps to get you on your way.

1. **Click Workspaces on the Navigation bar of your Office Live Home page.**

   The Workspaces page opens; see Figure 9-1.

Figure 9-1:
The Workspaces page.

2. **Select Create New from the Common Tasks drop-down list.**

   The Business Applications – Create page opens, as shown in Figure 9-2.

Figure 9-2:
The
Business
Applications –
Create
page.

3. **Click Applications and Workspaces in the Web Pages section.**

   The Create New Application or Workspace page opens.

4. **Select Workspaces from the Select a Category drop-down list.**

5. **Choose a template from the Select a Template drop-down list.**

   There are many Workspace templates from which to choose (see Figure 9-3). With the exception of the Blank Meeting Workspace and the Blank Workspace templates, each template comes equipped with additional tabs that hold lists of data pertinent to the Workspace:

   • *Basic Meeting Workspace:* Includes sections for an agenda, attendees, a document library, and objectives.

   • *Blog:* Includes sections for posts, photos, other blogs, links, comments, and categories.

   • *Customer Workspace:* Includes sections for announcements, a calendar, links, and shared documents.

   • *Decision Meeting Workspace:* Includes sections for an agenda, attendees, decisions, a document library, objectives, and tasks. Figure 9-4 shows a Decision Meeting Workspace.

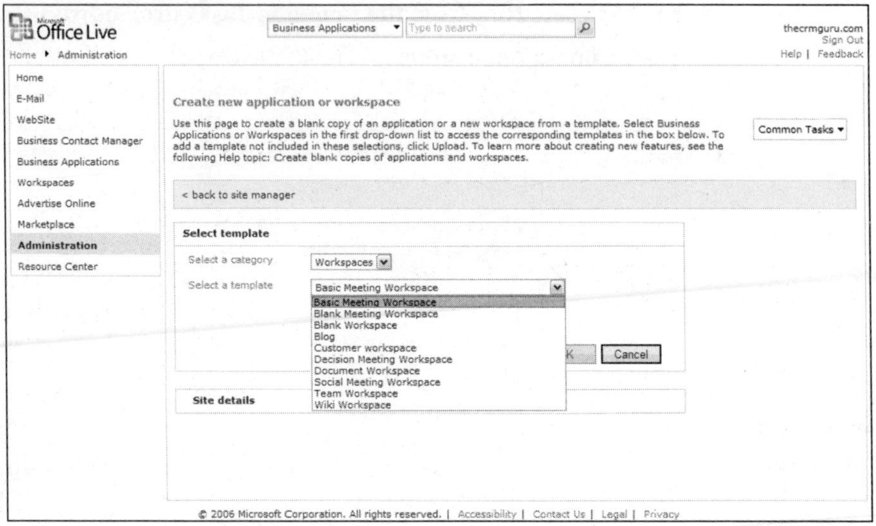

Figure 9-3:
Creating
a new
Workspace.

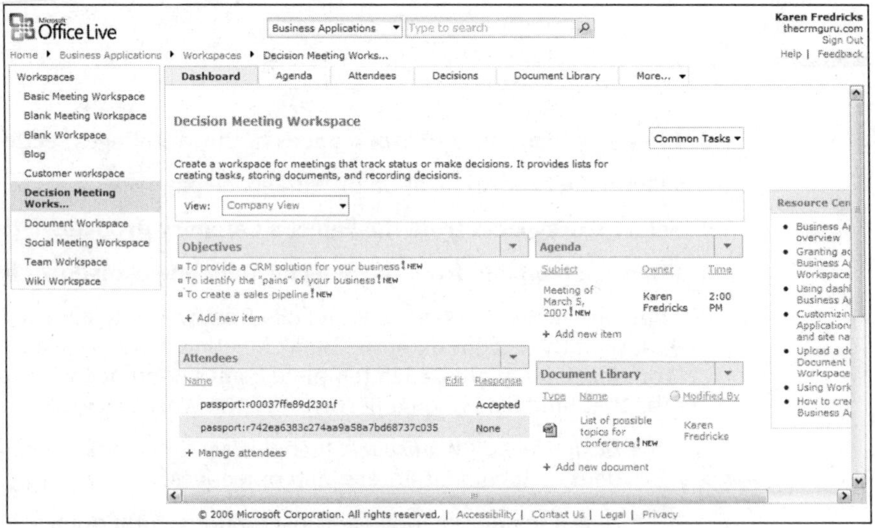

Figure 9-4:
A Decision
Meeting
Workspace.

- *Document Workspace:* Includes sections for announcements, a calendar, links, shared documents, tasks, and team discussions.

- *Social Meeting Workspace:* Includes sections for attendees, Directions, a discussion board, picture library, and things to bring.

- *Team Workspace:* Includes sections for Announcements, Calendar, links, shared documents, tasks, and a team discussion board.

- *Wiki Workspace: Wiki* means *quick* in Hawaiian. A wiki is an easy and quick place to gather information. Here's where you can set up pages for contributors to add links to other Web sites or add their own personal comments.

One of the neat features of Service as a Software (SaaS) is that the manufacturer can deliver new enhancements directly to your door. As Office Live becomes more popular, you'll start to see a proliferation of templates by third-party vendors. If you click the Find More Applications on Our Marketplace link, you can find those templates as they become available.

6. **Click OK to continue.**

   The Site Detail page opens.

7. **Fill in the required information and then click OK to create your new Workspace and return to the Workspaces page.**

   Don't panic if the words "fill in the required information" send chills down your back. Office Live has already done much of the work for you by filling in some of the information and providing you with a whole bunch of clues (see Figure 9-5). If you're unhappy with the Office Live suggestions, feel free to tweak them.

Figure 9-5:
Creating a
Shared
Workspace.

- *Title:* Office Live suggests a title for your Workspace page, basing the suggestion on the template you choose in Step 5. If you've set up several of the same templates (for example, you've set up Customer Workspaces for more than one customer) you'll want to change that title to something cool and interesting like "ABC Company" or "My Great-Paying Client."

  The Workspace title appears in the Navigation bar so avoid using titles such as "PITA Client" or "High-Maintenance Pest."

- *URL:* This is the URL that folks will use to access the Workspace. Avoid using spaces or symbols here.

- *Description:* Here's where you can state what you're trying to accomplish with this Workspace. You might include something like "To share information with my valued customer, ABC."

- *Display:* Here's where you can determine whether or not the Workspace shows up in the Navigation bar.

When Office Live finishes creating the new Workspace, the title of the Workspace appears in the Workspaces Navigation bar.

How safe is your information?

When you use Office Live to create Workspaces for your data and documents, Microsoft Office Live uses the security measures built into Microsoft Windows SharePoint Services to help protect your data against unauthorized access of your data and documents. Windows SharePoint Services employs a set of physical, technical, and administrative safeguards to help protect your documents and data against unauthorized access. In addition, the data and documents are encrypted.

However, even the best-laid (security) plans of mice, men, and Microsoft can go astray. As an additional security measure, you might want to follow these guidelines when creating Office Live Workspaces that others might post to:

✔ **Never post sensitive information on public Web pages.** Sensitive information isn't limited to items like Social Security numbers, bank-account numbers, and credit-card information. Sensitive information includes phone numbers, health information, as well as any other information that can be used to identify, contact, or locate a person (including an e-mail address).

✔ **Do not put personal information on Web pages that you think the public doesn't know about.** You never know when a page might be "opened" to the public, or stumbled upon accidentally.

✔ **Upload confidential documents with caution.** If you do need to upload a document that contains confidential information, make sure you give it a password.

Inviting others to join in

Creating a basic Workspace is only half the fun. The other half comes when you invite other people to visit the Workspace for a mutual sharing of information. When you create the Workspace initially, you are the only one who sees the Workspace listed in the Navigation bar. After you share the Workspace, those users also see the Workspace in the Navigation bar (that is, if you opted to show it on the Navigation bar when setting up the Workspace). If you opted not to include the Workspace on the Navigation bar, users can access it by going to the URL that you designated.

As the administrator, you get to control who accesses the information in the Workspace. For example, you can have one Workspace that is available just to your employees, and another Workspace that is available only to the employees of one of your customers.

You can also control the users' access rights. You can assign users different levels of access for each Workspace. For example, you might allow a user to just view the information in one Workspace, change the information in another Workspace, and be the administrator of another Workspace.

You can only grant Workspace permission to existing Office Live users. Check out Chapter 3 if you're not sure how to create user accounts.

Follow these steps to allow a user access to a Workspace:

1. **Click Workspaces on the Navigation bar of the Office Live home page.**

   The Office Live Workspaces page opens.

2. **Select Set permissions from the Common Tasks drop-down menu.**

   The User Permissions page opens, which provides you with a list of all your Office Live users; see Figure 9-6.

   Only the users that you set up in Office Live can access your Workspaces. If you'd like to open a Workspace to one of your clients, you have to add that client as a user.

   Your Office Live Essentials or Premium account comes with the capability to add (respectively) 10 or 20 users. If you start to add more company Workspaces, you might need to add more user accounts. You can add those user accounts in increments of five at a time for an additional $11.95/month. The User Permissions page includes a Users Usage area that indicates the number of active user accounts you currently have. Click the Buy More Users link if you want to buy more user accounts.

Figure 9-6:
Allowing an
Office Live
user
permission
to access a
Workspace.

3. **Click Edit next to the name of the user to whom you'd like to grant access to the Workspace.**

   The Edit User Information page opens.

4. **Expand the Workspaces list by clicking the plus sign.**

   Just in case you're wondering where your Workspaces are — they're hiding! An expanded list appears, as shown in Figure 9-7.

5. **Click the No Access drop-down list next to the Workspace you want to allow the user to access and choose an access level.**

   You have four levels of access rights from which to choose:

   - *No Access:* The user isn't allowed to access the Workspace.

   - *Administrator:* The user has full access to the Workspace and can set permissions for other users.

   - *Editor:* The user has full access to the Workspace but can't set permissions for other users.

   - *Reader:* The user can view the Workspace but can't make any changes to it.

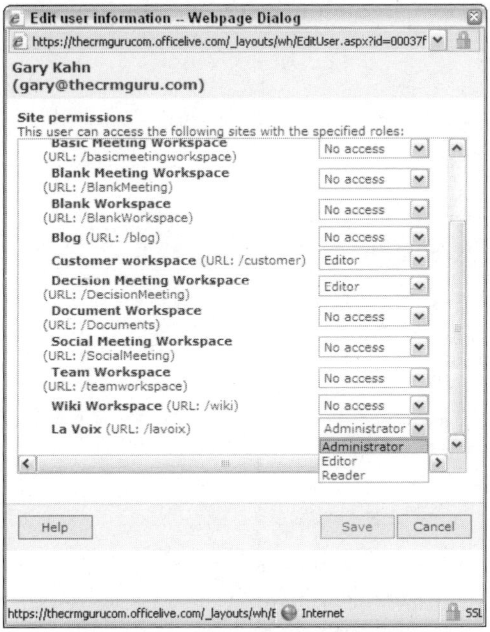

Figure 9-7:
The Edit
User
Information
page.

6. **Click Save to save your changes.**

   The Invite User page opens, as shown in Figure 9-8. Office Live thinks of just about everything. This page allows you to compose an e-mail to the new Workspace user.

7. **Fill in a brief message and click Send.**

   Your message hurtles through cyberspace and lands in the user's inbox. You're treated to a summary screen, which congratulates you on a job well done. (Gee. Makes you want to print it to hang on your refrigerator.)

8. **Click Finish to close the congratulatory window.**

   You end up back on the User Permissions page.

Your user is now ready to access the Workspace. If you'd like, you can pick up the phone and give the user a buzz just to make sure the e-mail got there and that he or she can access the Workspace without a hitch.

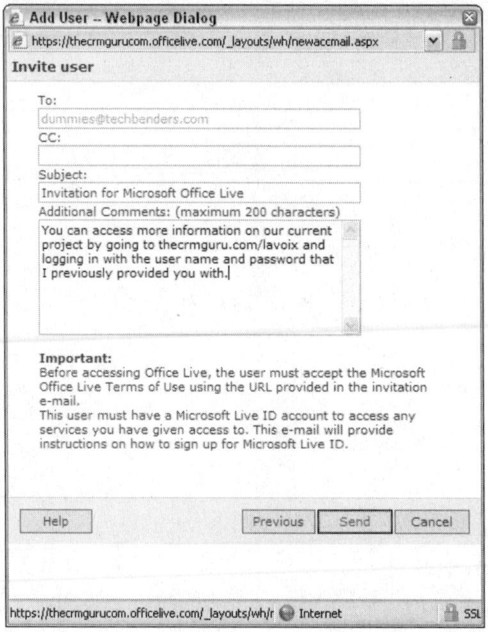

Figure 9-8:
Composing
an e-mail
inviting a
user to
access a
Workspace.

Administrative Workspace Tweaking 101

After you set up a Workspace you're free to start using it. However, the whole purpose of Office Live is to share so you'll probably want to share the Workspace with a user or two (or three or four!) You might find that the template you used to create the Workspace is perfect for your needs. However, some of you might want to be adventurous and add components to your Workspace. As a Workspace administrator, you have a number of ways to modify a Workspace.

Deleting a Workspace

The great thing about Office Live is that it's so easy to customize; the changes you make are immediately evident to all your Office Live users. The bad thing about Office Live is that if you make a mistake, all your users see it immediately. If you create a Workspace but then decide it was just not what you had in mind, it's easy to get rid of. Or, if just want to drive your users crazy, create a bunch of Workspaces and then delete them — leaving everybody to wonder if the Workspace ever existed in the first place. (Just kidding!)

Here's how you can delete a Workspace that you no longer want:

1. **Click Workspaces from the Navigation bar.**

   The Workspace page appears, treating you to a list of all your Workspaces.

2. **Choose Manage Applications and Workspaces from the Common Tasks drop-down list.**

   The Site Manager page opens.

3. **Locate the Workspace that you want to delete from the list, and then click Delete.**

4. **Click OK in response to the warning that appears.**

   Your Workspace is now gone — but is it forgotten? You be the judge!

Customizing the Navigation bar

The owner of the Office Live subscription is the only Microsoft Office Live user who can customize the display of links to applications that appear on the Navigation bar. You can display the links to the Workspaces that your users can access and hide the ones they don't use.

Only the Workspaces that a user has access to appear in the Navigation bar.

Add your Workspaces to the Navigation bar by following these steps:

1. **Click Workspaces from the Navigation bar.**

   Like clockwork, the Workspaces page opens.

2. **Choose Customize Left Navigation Bar from the Common Task drop-down list.**

   The Customize the Left Navigation Bar page opens; see Figure 9-9.

3. **Click the plus sign to the left of Workspaces to show the Workspaces that currently appear on the Navigation bar.**

   By default, Office Live's Navigation bar has a Workspace item; clicking it uncovers all the Workspaces that you've added to Office Live. If you decide you'd like to create additional Workspace groupings, you can.

4. **(Optional) Click New Group, fill in a new Group Name and corresponding URL and then click OK.**

   Figure 9-10 shows a group of Workspaces geared to clients.

Figure 9-9:
The Customize the Left Navigation bar page.

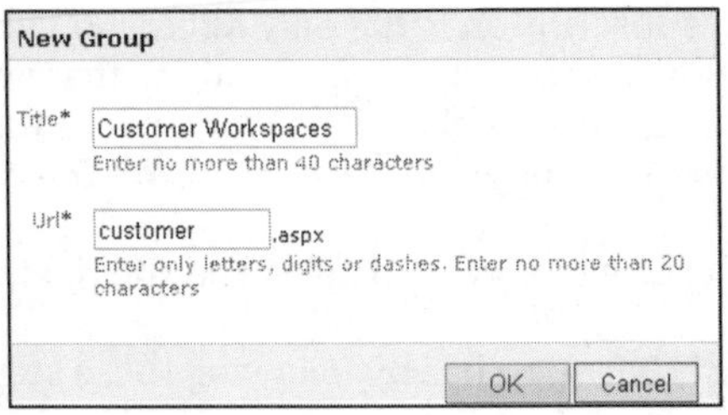

Figure 9-10:
Creating a new group of Workspaces.

5. **Click a Group or Workspace to select it on the Customize the Left Navigation Bar page and then choose one of the toolbar options:**

   • *Hide:* Hides a Workspace or group.

   • *Show:* Once you hide an object you can make it magically reappear.

   • *Move Up:* Moves a link up on the Navigation bar.

   • *Move Down:* Moves a link down on the Navigation bar.

   • *Move Into:* Moves a Workspace into another Group.

   • *Edit:* Changes the text of the link that appears on the Navigation bar.

   • *Delete:* Deletes any group that you've created.

   Your changes go into immediate effect; your users see them the next time they access the Office Live site.

Adding a page to a Workspace

You might want to think of a Workspace as a miniature Web page that you target for a specific group of users. Just like Web sites that come in both small and large varieties, your Workspaces can expand to fit your needs. Each page of your Workspace is actually a list of items. Therefore, when you add a new page to your Workspace, you are (in essence) creating another list of information.

You must first create an item before you can add it to a Workspace. It isn't possible to add a list or library from another application or Workspace, although you can import information from an external source into one of your Office Live lists.

Here's what you need to do in order to expand your Workspace:

1. **Click Workspaces on the home page Navigation bar.**

   As you would suspect, the Workspaces page cranks open.

2. **Click the Workspace that you want to modify.**

   For example, click Customer Workspace if that's the one you'd like to modify, tweak, or change in some other way.

3. **Choose Create New from the Common Tasks drop-down list.**

   The Create page opens, showing you various lists you can add to the Workspace. If you hover your mouse pointer over any of the options, a box magically appears, explaining the option in greater detail (see Figure 9-11).

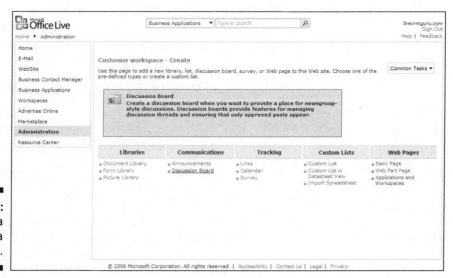

Figure 9-11:
Adding a
list to a
Workspace.

4. **Click the item that you want to add.**

   The New Web page opens, as shown in Figure 9-12.

5. **Fill in the name and description for the item, and whether you want it to appear on the Navigation bar.**

6. **Click Create to create your new page.**

   When you've finished, the item appears as a tab in the Workspace.

Deleting a page from a Workspace

The purpose of creating Workspaces is to share information. The purpose of adding pages to a Workspace is to share even more information. It only stands to reason that the more information you have, the larger — and more used — your Workspace is. After setting up all those great Workspaces, however, you might find that no one is using them. Okay, that might be because your users aren't doing their jobs — or it might be because the pages you added aren't pertinent to the task at hand.

You'll find that removing a page from a Workspace is easy; follow these steps:

1. **Click Workspaces on the Home page Navigation bar.**

   Once again, the Workspaces page opens.

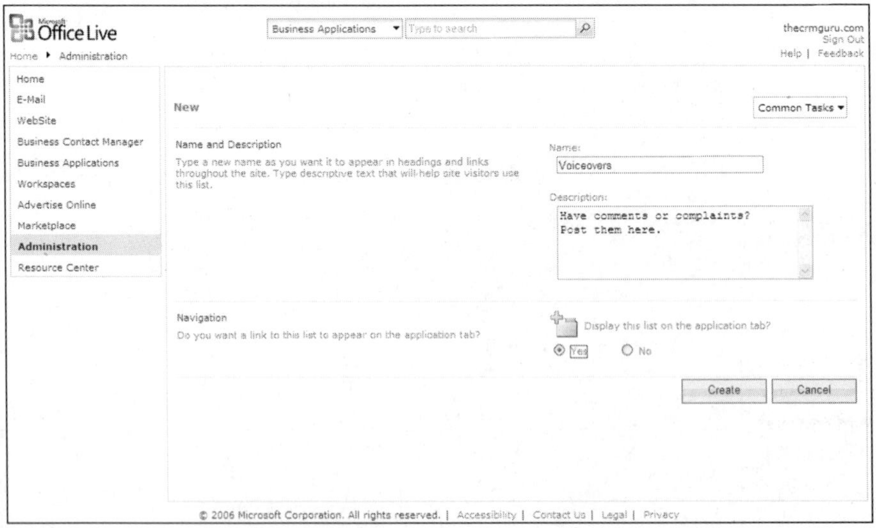

Figure 9-12:
Giving the 411 for a new Workspace page.

2. **Click the Workspace that you want to modify.**

3. **Click the tab for the item that you want to delete.**

   The appropriate page of your Workspace appears.

   If you don't see the tab you're looking for, you may have added so many tabs that they all can't all appear on-screen at the same time. Click the More tab and you find a drop-down list of all your other tabs.

4. **Click Settings on the toolbar and choose the appropriate settings command.**

   This step is a bit confusing because what you get on the Settings drop-down list depends on what page you're changing. If you're deleting a discussion board, the option reads *Discussion Board Settings* (see Figure 9-13). If you're deleting an announcement page, then the option would read *Announcement Settings*.

   At any rate the Customize page opens.

5. **Click Delete in the Permissions and Management section.**

   Again, the option depends on the type of page you're deleting from your Workspace. If you're deleting a discussion board, the option reads Delete This Discussion Board, as shown in Figure 9-14.

Figure 9-13:
The Settings option for a Workspace page.

Figure 9-14:
The
Customize
page.

6. **Click OK to the warning message that appears.**

   Say sayonara to the page!

Renaming a Workspace page

Some of you might have dabbled in programming somewhere along the line.
If you did, you know that even the smallest change to a program could require
lines and lines of additional coding. Such is not the case in Office Live. You've
already seen how easy it is to create — and delete — a Workspace. Other
changes are every bit as easy. A case in point is renaming a Workspace page;
you might find creating a Workspace easier than deciding on the best name
for it.

Don't fret — if you're not happy with the moniker you gave the Workspace,
it's easy enough to change it by following these steps:

1. **Click Workspaces on the home page Navigation bar.**

   By this time it should come as no surprise to you that the Workspaces
   page opens.

2. **Click the Workspace that you want to rename.**

   You're now in the Dashboard area of the Workspace page.

3. **Click the tab for the page that you want to rename.**

   You go to the appropriate page of the Workspace.

4. **Click Settings on the toolbar and choose the appropriate settings command.**

   For example, if you're renaming a list, you'd click List Settings.

5. **Click Title, Description, and Navigation in the General Settings section.**

   The General Settings page opens (refer to Figure 9-12).

6. **Type a new name in the Name field, and then click Save to save your changes.**

Dabbling with the Dashboards

When an Office Live user accesses a Workspace, he lands in the Dashboard area of the Workspace. Each Workspace has its own Dashboard. The Dashboard provides a snapshot of the various pages within the Workspace. You might think of the Dashboard as the Workspace's home page.

You can add additional sections to the Dashboard to include more information. If (for example) you added a new Special Announcements page to your Workspace, you can in turn add a Special Announcements section to the Dashboard.

In addition to adding recaps of your Workspace pages to the Dashboard, Office Live includes a couple of special sections called *Web Parts*. You can add a What's New Web Part to highlight all the latest and greatest changes that users have made, no matter what page they changed.

Follow these steps to add a Web Part:

1. **Click Workspaces on the Navigation bar.**

   Right on schedule, the Workspaces page opens.

2. **Click the Workspace whose Dashboard you'd like to customize.**

   You land with a virtual plunk in the Dashboard of the selected Workspace.

3. **Choose Customize Dashboard from the Common Tasks drop-down menu.**

   The Dashboard is now in editing mode; a yellow bar runs across the top of the Dashboard. The Dashboard is divided into sections on the top, left and right sides, as shown in Figure 9-15. Each one contains an Add a Web Part link.

Figure 9-15:
Editing a
Workspace
Dashboard.

4. **Click Add a Web Part on the section of the Dashboard where you want a Web Part to appear.**

   The Add Web Parts page opens (see Figure 9-16). The page is divided into two sections:

   - *Lists and Libraries:* Lists all the pages contained in your Workspace.

   - *All Web Parts:* Includes several cool tools to help you customize your Dashboard. For example, the Content Editor Web Part allows you to change the wording that appears in your Dashboard; the What's New Web Part adds a section to include all new items that have been added to any of your pages.

5. **Place a check mark next to the items you want to add, and then click the Add button.**

   The new section now appears in the Dashboard.

6. **(Optional) To remove an item, click the X next to the item.**

7. **Click Exit Edit Mode when you've finished customizing the Dashboard.**

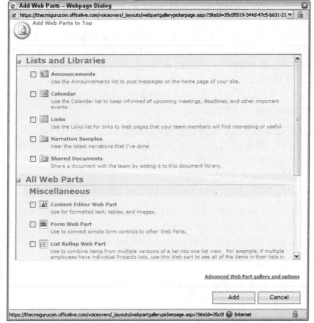

Figure 9-16:
Adding Web
Parts to the
Dashboard.

End User Tweaking 202

So far this chapter has been devoted to all the administrative tasks that are associated with creating a Workspace. The rest of this chapter is devoted to the features that any user can use.

Accessing a Workspace

After you set up permission for a user to access a Workspace, users can access it in a number of ways. All methods lead to the exact same results. In addition, all methods require that the user log into Office Live using the Office Live e-mail address and password that was assigned to them. After they log in, users can access the various Workspaces and make changes based on the permissions that the Office Live administrator assigned to them.

Here are three ways a user can log in to the Workspace:

- ✔ **Go to** www.officelive.com **and click the Sign In link.** By using this method, you don't have to worry about remembering the Office Live Web site URL. A window opens asking for your e-mail address and password. Fill it in and you end up in the home page of the Office Live account. Click Workspaces and you see only those Workspaces that you have permission to access.

- ✔ **Access the home page directly by going to** https://yourwebsitecom. officelive. The *yourwebsitecom* part is the name of the domain you registered when you created your Office Live account. Remember to use https (rather than the more typical http) because of the extra level of security that surrounds an Office Live account.

- ✔ **Enter** https://yourwebsitecom.officelive/Workspace **to go directly to the Workspace.** The *yourwebsite.com* part is your domain and *Workspace* is the URL you used when creating the Workspace.

Using the user's view

The cool thing about Office Live is that an administrator can configure the Workspaces, Navigation bar, and Dashboards, so the user can focus on adding data to the Workspace rather than having to learn all the minute customization capabilities of the program. However, each user has the ability to use — and customize — personal Dashboards. For example, a Workspace might contain six pages but the user might only need to work with three of them. By modifying the Dashboard, the user can focus on those three without having to view information that isn't relevant. Only the user who created the Personal Dashboard can view it — and can switch back and forth between the company Dashboard that the administrator created and the personalized Dashboard.

Only the site owner or Workspace administrator can allow a user to access a Workspace. Without that permission, a user cannot create a personalized Dashboard for a Workspace or add pages to an existing one.

Until you customize the Personal View, it's identical to the Company View.

Follow these steps to customize the Personal View of a Dashboard:

1. **Click Workspaces from the Navigation bar.**

   The Workspaces page opens.

2. **Click the Workspace for which you'd like to customize the Dashboard.**

   You land in the Dashboard of the selected Workspace.

3. **Select Personal View from the View drop-down list.**

4. **Choose Customize Dashboard from the Common Tasks drop-down list.**

   The Dashboard is now in editing mode (refer to Figure 9-15).

5. **Click Add a Web Part on the section of the Dashboard where you want a Web Part to appear.**

6. **Place a check mark next to each item you want to add, and then click the Add button.**

   The new section now appears in the Dashboard.

7. **Click the X in the upper-right corner of each area of the Dashboard that you don't want to appear.**

8. **Click Exit Edit Mode to save your changes.**

Adding data

The whole point of a Workspace is to enter and store data that other users can access and share. Some users only use the Workspace to see data that has been entered by other users. If you're one of those people, you can put down this book, flip on the tube, and take a snooze. However, if you plan to enter data into a Workspace, you'll have to postpone your nap for a minute or two.

A Workspace is nothing more than a list of data. Even if you create more and more complex Workspaces by adding additional pages, each page is still nothing more than a list of data. You can edit list items by using either a form or a datasheet.

Adding information using a form

Using a form is the most common way that you'll probably add information into a Workspace. The good news is that a form leaves little to your imagination; you'll stick to the necessary facts — and just the facts. The bad news is that using a form can be somewhat time-consuming because you have to type in your information one item at a time.

To input information into Office Live using a form follow these steps:

1. **Click Workspaces from the Navigation bar.**

   The Workspaces page opens.

2. **Click the Workspace that you want to work with.**

   You're on the Dashboard of the Workspace in question.

3. **Click the tab of the page you want to work with.**

   Depending on the Workspace you're using, you might have a bunch of choices here. You can choose to add new documents, appointments, or even Web-site links.

4. **Click New on the Workspace page toolbar.**

   The form that opens depends on the type of data you're entering.

5. **Fill in all the important information and click OK to save your changes.**

   Some forms, such as those used to schedule an appointment, have lots of fields to fill out. Other forms, such as ones that add links to the workspace, only have three fields that require information (see Figure 9-17).

   Your item(s) now appear on the Workspace page.

Editing list items using a datasheet

If you have a whole bunch of data to add at one time, you'll probably want to use a datasheet to make your changes. A *datasheet* is a view of your information that looks like a spreadsheet or table. You can add, delete, sort, and filter list items while you're working in a datasheet.

Here's how you can add information into a datasheet:

1. **Click Workspaces from the Navigation bar.**

   The Workspaces page opens.

2. **Click the Workspace that you want to work with.**

   You're on the Dashboard of the Workspace. (By now you're probably familiar with the drill!)

3. **Click the tab of the page you want to work with.**

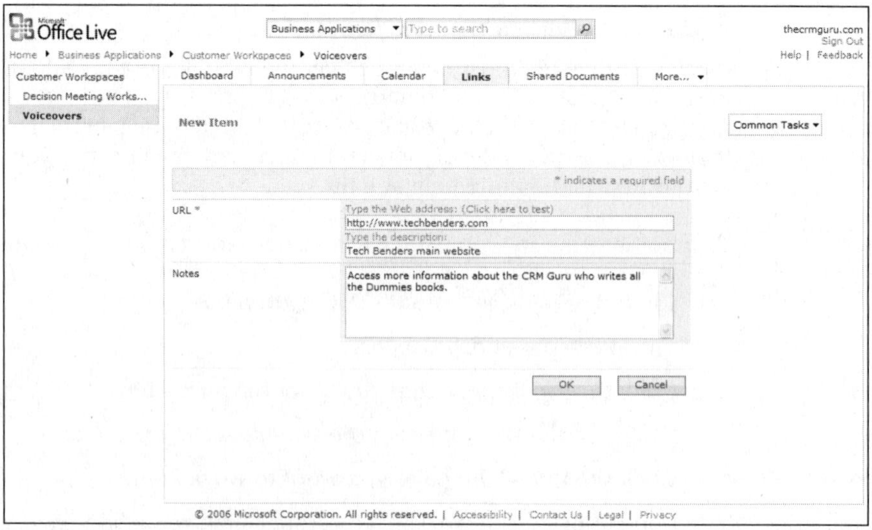

Figure 9-17:
Adding information into a form.

4. **Click Actions on the Workspace page toolbar and choose Edit in Datasheet.**

   The datasheet that appears depends (once again) on the information that you're adding to the Workspace page. Figure 9-18 shows an example of the datasheet used to add links to a Workspace.

5. **Click any cell and type your information.**

   Any information that users have entered previously appears in the top rows of the datasheet. To add to the list, just click on the first empty row and start typing away.

6. **(Optional) Click Settings from the datasheet toolbar and choose one of the following options:**

   - *Create a Column:* Adds a new column to include additional information.

   - *Create View:* Allows you to determine which columns appear in the data sheet.

   - *List Settings:* Manages settings such as permissions, columns, and views.

   - *Share Data:* Create a form that you can put on a public Web site to collect data.

   Press Tab to progress your way through the various columns and/or to create another row for additional data.

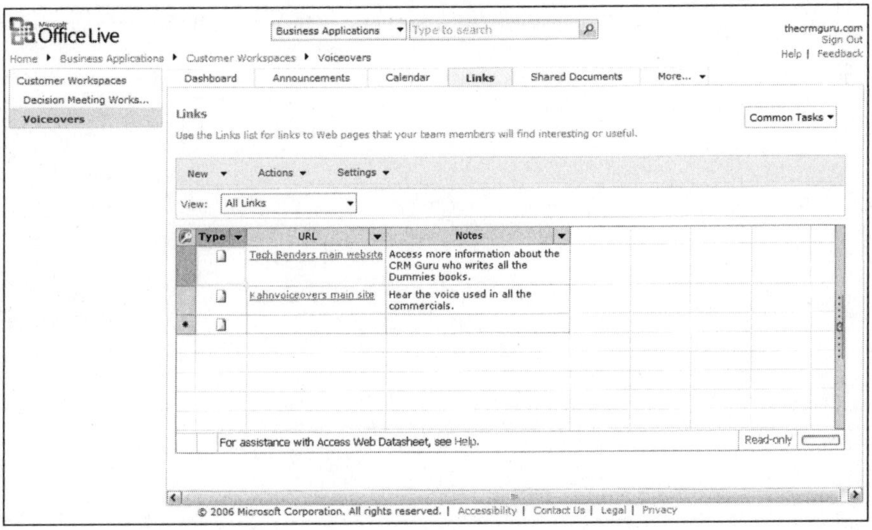

Figure 9-18:
Adding
information
to a
Workspace
using a
datasheet.

7. **Click Actions from the toolbar and select Show in Standard View when you've finished making your changes.**

   You return to the appropriate Workspace page where you can see all the new information.

Deleting or changing an item

As the saying goes, easy come, easy go. You might need to change — or remove — data after you've entered it into Office Live. Here's all you need to know to do exactly that:

1. **Click Workspaces from the Navigation bar.**

   The Workspaces page opens.

2. **Click the Workspace that you want to work with.**

   You're on the Dashboard of the Workspace.

3. **Click the tab of the page you want to work.**

   You see all the fruits of your labor — or, better yet, the fruits of *other people's* labor — sitting right there.

4. **Click Edit next to the item that you want to change.**

   A form containing your data appears. At this juncture you have one of two options:

   • Make any needed changes in the form that appears, and then click OK to save your changes and return to the Workspace page.

   • Click Delete Item and click OK when the warning appears.

Chapter 10

Taking the Show on the Road

· ·

· ·

*O*ffice Live is all about mobility and accessing your data no matter where your travels take you. However, there will be times when you'll want to look at all your Office Live data in your desktop edition of Outlook. And, if you're using the Office Live edition of Business Contact Manager, you'll want all of that material to appear magically in your desktop version of Business Contact Manager as well. Finally, if you have a hunger for the instant gratification of sharing information in real time, read on to find out how you can use Office Live to send your messages instantly.

Connecting Office Live Mail and Outlook

Many of you are using both Office Live and Outlook. You might use Outlook when you're in the office and Office Live when you're on the road. Or, you might use Outlook for your personal data and your company uses Office Live. You'll probably want to access some of the same data from either Office Live or Outlook. Obviously, you could enter the same information into both programs; however, if I know you, you'll want to synchronize the two to avoid all that double-entry drudgery. (Call it an educated guess.)

Microsoft has designed a nifty tool — the Microsoft Office Outlook Connector — and included it as part of the Office Live Essentials and Premium subscription. The tool allows you to *synchronize* basic elements, so you can update them using either Office Live or Outlook. You'll find that using the Office Outlook Connector is beneficial in a number of ways:

✔ You can access, send, and receive e-mail messages from multiple Microsoft Office Live Mail accounts, and view the corresponding calendars and contacts, from within Microsoft Outlook.

✔ You can also schedule meetings, or share calendars with other Microsoft Office Live subscribers, by viewing your various Office Live calendars all in one area of Outlook.

✔ When you make updates in Outlook such as deleting messages, adding new contacts, scheduling meetings or creating new tasks your changes are automatically synchronized and reflected in your Microsoft Office Live Mail account.

✔ Offline changes synchronize to Office Live as soon as you connect to the Internet.

You can synchronize the following items between Office Live and Outlook:

✔ Personal Calendar

✔ E-mail Contacts

✔ Deleted Items

✔ Drafts

✔ Inbox

✔ Notes

✔ Tasks

After you connect Office Live to Outlook, the information automatically synchronizes every time you hit Outlook's Send/Receive button — or every time Outlook does an automatic Send and Receive. Think of what a great time-saver this is. For example, you might be working on a new e-mail message in Office Live but have to wait for some more information before you can complete it. You save the e-mail as a draft. Later, you open Outlook and see your draft just waiting to be finished. You finish the e-mail, and send it from Outlook using your Office Live account. The recipient replies to the message — which you can now view in either Office Live or Outlook.

In order to use the Outlook Connector, you must have either a paid Microsoft Office Live Essentials or Microsoft Office Live Premium subscription. The Outlook Connector is not available with Microsoft Office Live Basics subscriptions, although it is available with a fee-based Hotmail account.

Connecting with the Outlook Connector

The first thing you need to do is to download the Outlook Connector from the Microsoft Download Center. Probably the easiest way to do this is to go to the Microsoft Web site and type **Outlook Connector** in the search box. Here's what you have to do:

1. **Find the download on the Microsoft site.**

2. **Save the file to a spot on your computer.**

3. **When the download is complete, navigate to the site where you saved the file and give it a double-click.**

   The Installation Wizard starts. You'll be clicking Next a few times to advance through it.

4. **Open Outlook.**

   The Outlook menu now contains Outlook Connector (see Figure 10-1).

Figure 10-1: The addition of Outlook Connector to the Outlook toolbar.

Setting up your Office Live accounts in Outlook

Configuring Outlook with your Office Live accounts is just about as easy as it was to install the Outlook Connector in the first place. If you have multiple Office Live accounts, you can connect each one of them to Outlook. Sound complicated? It's not — if you follow these steps:

1. **In Outlook, choose Outlook Connector⇨Add a New Account.**

   The Microsoft Office Outlook Connector dialog box opens; see Figure 10-2.

```
Microsoft Office Outlook Connector                                      ☒

Set up Outlook Connector to automatically synchronize your Web-based accounts in Outlook.

    Type your e-mail address and password.                         Help

        E-mail address:  karen@outlookdiva.com
        Password:        ********
                         Forgot your password?

    Type the name that you want to appear in the receiver's Inbox.

        Name:            Outlook Diva


                    ┌──────────┐   ┌──────────┐
                    │    OK    │   │  Cancel  │
                    └──────────┘   └──────────┘
                    ☑ Remember my password

    🔑 Microsoft Passport Network
    Account Services        Privacy Policy        Terms of Use

    © 1999-2006 Microsoft Corporation. All rights reserved.
```

Figure 10-2:
Adding your
Office Live
account to
Outlook.

2. Fill in the following pieces of information:

- *E-mail address:* Use your Office Live e-mail address.

- *Password:* Use your Office Live e-mail address password.

- *Name:* This is the name that your recipients see if you send e-mail in Outlook from one of your Office Live accounts.

3. Click OK to create the Office Live account in Outlook.

You're prompted to restart Outlook.

4. Restart Outlook.

Upon opening, Outlook performs a Send/Receive.

5. Scroll toward the bottom of the Outlook folder list.

At this point, if you're tempted to jump up and down in excitement when you see your Office Live account(s) listed in the folder list, restrain yourself. There's even more good stuff yet to come.

6. Select your Office Live Mail account.

7. Click the plus sign (+) next to your e-mail address.

Now you can really get excited because you'll see all your Office Live items listed there filled with all of your Office Live information, as shown in Figure 10-3. If you've set up folders for your Office Live Inbox, then the folders appear as well.

For the very lazy — or very smart — readers who might have a bunch of contacts lurking in their main Outlook Contacts folder, you might consider dragging them down to the Office Live contacts folder so they'll synchronize with

Office Live. You can also drag appointments, tasks, and notes from one Office Live account to another. It sure beats the heck out of adding all that information to Office Live, one item at a time!

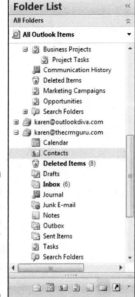

Figure 10-3:
Office Live folders as they appear in the Outlook folder list.

The Contacts form in Outlook contains more fields than the Contacts form in Office Live. If you create a new contact in Outlook, and then synchronize it to Office Live, you see only the Office Live fields. When you open the same contact in Outlook, however, all the available fields — and their information — appear.

Deleting an Office Live account in Outlook

As cool as the synchronization is between Office Live and Outlook, all good things must come to an end. The time may come when you no longer use an Office Live account. You can delete an Office Live account from Outlook exactly as you delete any other Outlook e-mail account. If you're not sure how to do it, follow these steps:

1. **In Outlook, choose Tools⇨Account Settings.**

   The Account Settings dialog box opens, as shown in Figure 10-4.

2. **Select the account that you want to delete and click Remove.**

3. **Click Close to close the Account settings dialog box.**

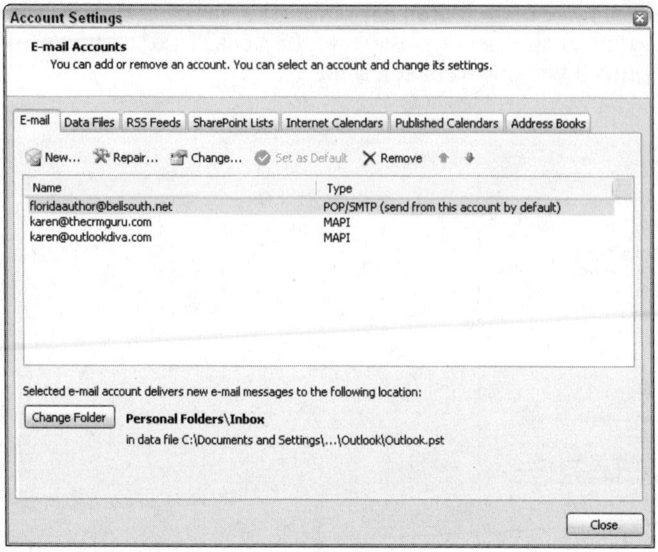

Account Settings

E-mail Accounts
You can add or remove an account. You can select an account and change its settings.

E-mail | Data Files | RSS Feeds | SharePoint Lists | Internet Calendars | Published Calendars | Address Books

New... | Repair... | Change... | Set as Default | Remove | ↑ | ↓

Name	Type
floridaauthor@bellsouth.net	POP/SMTP (send from this account by default)
karen@thecrmguru.com	MAPI
karen@outlookdiva.com	MAPI

Selected e-mail account delivers new e-mail messages to the following location:

Change Folder | **Personal Folders\Inbox**
in data file C:\Documents and Settings\...\Outlook\Outlook.pst

Close

Figure 10-4:
Deleting an
Office Live
e-mail
account
from
Outlook.

Sending e-mail from your Office Live Mail account

After you connect Outlook to Office Live, you may want to try a few other party tricks. Because your Office Live e-mail contacts now synchronize to Outlook, you can address an e-mail to any one of them with a click of a button. In addition, you can easily send e-mail messages in Outlook using any of your Office Live e-mail accounts.

Here's all you have to do:

1. **In Outlook, select any one of your Inbox folders and then click the New button.**

   You don't need to select any specific Inbox folder — you just want to have the New E-Mail Message page appears.

2. **Click the Account button and select the e-mail account that you want to send the e-mail.**

   You can use your default Outlook e-mail account — or choose one of your Office Live e-mail accounts. You can see a list of Accounts in Figure 10-5.

3. **Click the To button.**

   The Select Names: Contacts page appears.

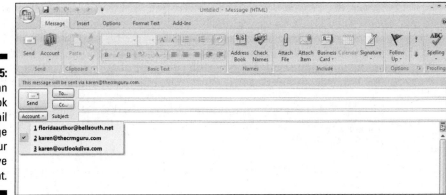

Figure 10-5:
Sending an
Outlook
e-mail
message
using your
Office Live
account.

4. **Click the Address Book drop-down list and choose the name of the Office Live account that contains the contact you want to e-mail.**

   You can select more than one contact if you want to send mail to more than one recipient.

5. **Click OK to return to the New E-Mail Message page.**

6. **Click the Send button.**

   Zoom! Your e-mail hurtles through cyberspace to its intended destination. Your recipient can recognize that the e-mail is from you because it carries the name you selected when you set up your Office Live account in Outlook.

Exporting a List to Office Outlook 2007

Before the advent of Office Live, companies used to spend $5,000 or more to implement the infrastructure that would allow remote users access to key information. They purchased a fairly robust server — and then called in an IT specialist to configure it. They were forced to make decisions about confusing technologies — VPN, IIS, Terminal Services — which, frankly, they didn't fully understand. The server required routine maintenance — and of course the business owner was responsible for any costs incurred when something "went wrong." For smaller companies, remote access was a luxury they simply couldn't afford.

With Office Live, you can easily select various lists and libraries and *export* them to Outlook so that you can view your Office Live information even if you don't have Internet connectivity. When you export a library or list, a link is created between the list or library and Outlook and the items appear in Outlook in a folder called SharePoint Lists. Any additions or changes that you make to the lists or libraries in either Office Live or Outlook are automatically reflected in both.

When you connected your Office Live e-mail account, personal calendar, notes and contacts to Outlook, you did so by configuring Outlook. You can export your Business Contact Manager Contacts, Employees lists, and items in an Office Live document or picture library to Outlook. However, you do so with some simple tweaking in Office Live. So simple, in fact, that you won't have to call in your IT guru — or break open your checking account!

Although exporting a list or library from Office Live to Outlook — and then synchronizing it as changes occur — is a powerful feature, it's surprisingly simple to set up:

1. **Select the list or library in Office Live that you want to export to Outlook.**

   For example, if you're exporting a Contacts list, click Business Applications in the Navigation bar and then choose Business Contact Manager.

2. **Select Connect to Outlook from the Actions drop-down menu.**

   The Microsoft Office Outlook dialog box appears.

   You can't export any list you may have — just the Business Contact Manager Contacts, the Employee List, and document and picture libraries. If you don't see the Connect to Outlook item on the Action menu you can't export the list into Outlook!

3. **Click Yes.**

   Depending on the size of the document in the library list, you might see the Outlook Send/Receive flash in front of you as the documents are synchronized to your Outlook account.

4. **Scroll down Outlook's folder list to SharePoint Lists.**

   If necessary, click the plus sign to expand the SharePoint Lists folders. The Office Live folders are now safely nestled in Outlook (see Figure 10-6). And you can feel safe knowing that you can change a document from either Office Live or Outlook — and still access the latest version in either program.

Messaging Instantly with Windows Live Messenger

As a CRM consultant, my clients range from "Mom and Pop" organizations running businesses from tree houses in backyards to Fortune 100 companies with multiple locations. Ironically, no matter how large organizations may get, they all have the same requirements regarding technology: Keep it simple, mobile, cheap, and integrated.

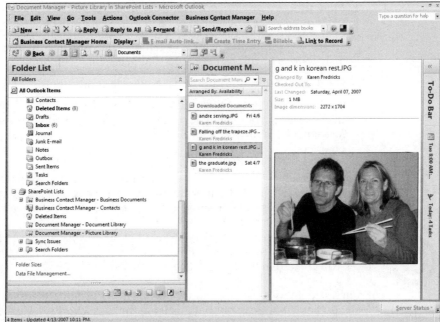

Figure 10-6:
Seeing your
Office Live
folders in
Outlook's
SharePoint
Lists.

No one is looking for a complicated, expensive solution if they can avoid it. Office Live covers all the technology bases. In fact, some people actually shy away from Office Live because they view it as just too good to be true. (Hey, that's their loss.)

Office Live Mail gives you the opportunity to download and use Windows Live Messenger. You can use it from within Microsoft Office Live Mail to communicate with employees and clients through instant messaging or PC-to-mobile phone text messaging. And, after you install Windows Live Messenger, your e-mail contacts automatically appear in Windows Live Messenger.

Here's all you need to do to get started:

1. **Click E-Mail on the Navigation bar of the Office Live Home page.**

2. **Click Download Now in the Instant Message section.**

   You land on Microsoft's Windows Live Messenger page.

3. **Click the Download button.**

   You might not actually see a download button; realize that Microsoft can change this page on a whim. You might see a button that says something like "Get It Free" or "Give It to Me!"

   A file download page appears.

4. Click Run.

After a moment or two of whirring, a new program appears on your screen — Windows Live Messenger. Another Web site opens, giving you instructions on all the cool stuff that Messenger can do.

5. Gasp in wonder at Windows Live Messenger.

Okay, you don't have to gasp, but you might look slightly impressed because all of your Office Live contacts have magically appeared in Messenger. Figure 10-7 shows Windows Live Messenger with Office Live contacts.

As an extra added attraction, if you make a change to your Web site, anyone who has included you in their Windows Live Messenger account sees a yellow asterisk next to your name if you're logged in to Messenger.

Your Messenger contacts are organized in groups. Wondering where those groups came from — or how to create a few more? The groups reflect the ones you created in your Office Live Contacts.

From this point on, any new contacts you add — or update — using your Live Mail contact list appears automatically in the Windows Live Messenger.

Figure 10-7:
Windows
Live
Messenger.

Chapter 11

A Few Other Tricks of the Trade

*Y*ou're probably already familiar with the concept of a Recycle Bin; in this chapter, you find out how the Office Live version of the Recycle Bin works. If you rely on Office Live, you'll need to know how to create a backup. And (more importantly) if a disaster occurs, you need to know how to restore your information from that backup. If you use Office Accounting 2007 and an accountant, you can take advantage of other features; you can use your Office Live account to send data back and forth via a secure environment.

Protecting Your Data

The thought of losing data is universally scary. In fact, for most folks who are used to standalone systems, the specter of data loss inspires anxiety — and is directly proportional to the amount of data they've stored in Office Live. And if they've spent oodles of money on an IT Department and extra software to guard against data loss — and the unthinkable happens anyway — the next stage is Panicky Despair.

Well, fear not. Microsoft uses *redundant* systems to guard against hardware failures. Redundancy means that Microsoft uses several computers to perform the same tasks. If one of those computers goes up in smoke, another computer stands ready to take its place. Redundancy ensures that your Office Live site continues to be up and running, and that you don't lose any of your data.

Microsoft Office Live also maintains a backup copy of your data to guard against data loss. The backup contains all your Office Live data — including your Web site, Business Applications, and Workspaces. Microsoft creates a new backup at least once a day, so your data is one day old at most. Should a disaster occur from your end — for example, a user accidentally deletes a large portion of your contacts — you can rest easier in the knowledge that a prior copy of your data exists. An Office Live Administrator can restore the backup in a heartbeat — hopefully saving you a heart attack!

Checking the status of your backup

If you're from Kansas (or is that Missouri?) — or you possess the doubting gene — you might want to see for yourself that a backup copy of your data exists. Here's how you check it out:

1. **Click the Business Applications link from the Office Live Home page.**

   The Business Applications page opens.

2. **Select Modify This Application or Workspace from the Common Tasks drop-down menu.**

   The Site Settings page opens.

3. **Click the Restore Site link in the Recycle and Restore area of the Site Settings page.**

   The Restore Your Site page opens, as shown in Figure 11-1, where you find the date and time of your last backup.

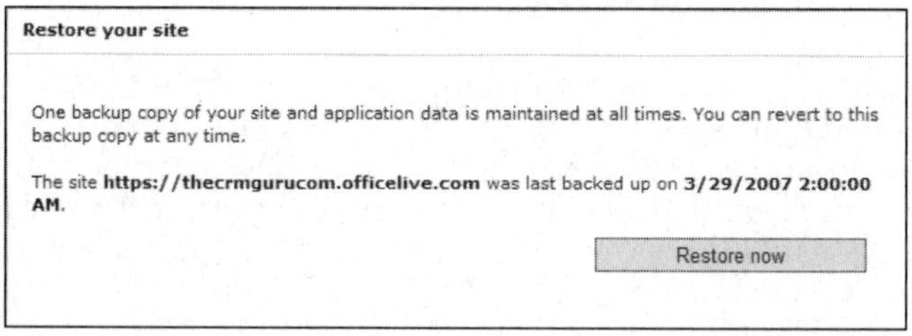

Figure 11-1:
Checking out the date and time of your last backup.

> **Restore your site**
>
> One backup copy of your site and application data is maintained at all times. You can revert to this backup copy at any time.
>
> The site **https://thecrmgurucom.officelive.com** was last backed up on **3/29/2007 2:00:00 AM.**
>
> Restore now

Restoring a backup copy of your data

You can restore your Microsoft Office Live data at any time. Your subscription is backed up at least once a day, and you can revert to the most recently saved version.

Here's what you need to know about restoring your backup file:

1. **Click the Business Applications link from the Office Live Home page.**

   The Business Applications page opens.

2. **Select Modify This Application or Workspace from the Common Tasks drop-down menu.**

   The Site Settings page opens.

3. **Click the Restore Site link in the Recycle and Restore area of the Site Settings page.**

   The Restore Your Site page opens.

4. **Click the Restore Now button.**

   A warning box, as shown in Figure 11-2, opens — informing you that any changes you've made since your last backup will be lost.

Figure 11-2:
The very
clear
warning you
receive
before
restoring a
backup.

> **Windows Internet Explorer**
>
> (?) Are you sure you want to restore your site?
>
> If you revert your site, all changes made since 3/29/2007 2:00:00 AM will be lost. If you are sure you want to continue, click OK.
>
> [OK]   [Cancel]

5. **Click OK to continue.**

6. **Click your browser's Refresh button.**

   You might have to hit the Refresh button several times. The restoration may take anywhere from minutes to over an hour depending on the amount of data that you have. Eventually, when your restoration is finished, you see a Restore Completed page; then you're free to roam about the cabin — or start entering data you may have lost.

Do not make any changes to your Office Live account until you receive the Restore Completed message. Any changes made between the time you start your backup and the time the message appears will be lost.

If the restoration fails for some reason, you'll receive an error message. Click the Contact Us for Assistance link to send an SOS to Microsoft. Your data remains as it was before you attempted to restore it to an earlier version and you won't be able to use the restore option again until it's fixed.

Restoring from the Recycle Bin

You can't delete lists that are part of the business applications included with your Office Live subscription. However, you can delete any lists that you have added to your subscription. You can also delete items that are stored within a list. When you delete lists or items, they fly off to the Office Live Recycle Bin where only an Office Live Administrator can restore them.

Deleted list items and lists only stay in the Recycle Bin for 30 days. During that time, an Administrator can restore them to the location from which they were deleted. If the deleted list items or lists aren't restored within 30 days, they are automatically deleted permanently.

Follow these steps to restore items and lists from the Office Live Recycle Bin:

1. **Click the Business Applications link from the Office Live home page.**

   The Business Applications page opens.

2. **Select Modify This Application or Workspace from the Common Tasks drop-down menu.**

   The Site Settings page opens.

3. **Click the Deleted Items link in the Recycle and Restore Area of the Site Settings page.**

   The Administrator Recycle Bin opens as shown in Figure 11-3.

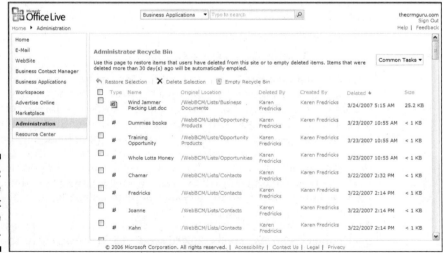

Figure 11-3:
The Administrator Recycle Bin.

4. Select the check boxes next to the items that you want to restore.

All the items you deleted are listed in column format. You can click on any of the column headers to sort the items in a different fashion. You can even see the name of the culprit who deleted the item in the first place. You might want to keep track of that information — it comes in handy at bonus time!

5. Click Restore Selection, and then click Yes.

You'll be so happy that all your previously deleted items are restored that (no doubt) you'll want to race over to the appropriate spots in Office Live to check it out for yourself. It should come as no shock to find them there — right where you originally put them.

Getting Your Books in Order

Traditionally, QuickBooks has dominated the small-business accounting arena; Peachtree Accounting was the somewhat dismal second-place finisher. Microsoft's Office Accounting 2007 replaces the older Small Business Accounting program; guess Microsoft is hoping that a name change will attract a few more customers. Office Accounting has much the same look and feel of its competitors but with a much smaller price tag.

But wait — there's more! To further encourage mass exodus from its rivals' camps, Microsoft is offering a couple of great incentives to switch to Office Accounting 2007:

- ✔ Integration with the Business Contact Manager portion of Outlook
- ✔ Integration with Office Live
- ✔ A free, Express version of Office Accounting 2007
- ✔ A free Accountant View utility that allows your accountant to access your books both manually and online

Microsoft is offering a basic version of Office Accounting 2007, called Office Accounting Express 2007, for *free* (as in no extra charge) simply by downloading it from the Microsoft Web site. So what's the catch? Needless to say, you'll receive messages from time to time encouraging you to buy the full-blown version of Office Accounting 2007. And Microsoft is (of course) hoping that once you purchase Office Accounting, you'll buy additional services such as credit-card-and-payroll processing.

Office Accounting Express 2007 contains all the features you'd expect to find in your accounting software — including the capability to track vendor payments, record invoices, and make life generally easier for your accountant. You don't need an IT department to install Office Accounting Express 2007. The Startup Wizard helps to set up your company books, and you can easily import data from other programs such as QuickBooks, Microsoft Money, and Excel so you don't have to start from scratch.

Now comes the fun part. By uploading and storing your files on an Office Live Workspace, you can access the information from any place where you have Internet access. You can take care of accounting tasks while on the road, and share information with your accountant.

Office Accounting Express 2007 includes a feature that integrates with eBay. You can list items, upload and manage pictures, and track activity in real time. Further integration with Outlook lets you send invoices in an e-mail message and include a direct link to your PayPal account.

If you don't plan on using Office Accounting Express 2007, feel free to skip the rest of this chapter.

Sharing information with your accountant

Getting your tax information to your accountant can be a nightmare. You can try e-mailing the file but the file may be too large. You can burn it to a CD but you may find that process confusing. You can copy it to a USB drive and hope that the accountant returns it. If you still have a Zip drive, you might create your backup on one of those relics — although it's doubtful that your accountant will even be able to use it. However, Office Accounting Express 2007 combined with Office Live makes the job seem almost *too* easy.

If you signed up for an Office Live Essentials or Premium account, you have the option to upload a copy of your Office Accounting Express 2007 backup to a Workspace. Your accountant can then access the information online and import it into his or her system.

After you complete the initial setup, it's a snap to send your data back and forth. However, there are several steps involved:

1. You transfer a manual copy of your books to your accountant.

2. The accountant enables you as a client with manual sharing rights, and sends you an invitation to start online sharing.

3. You accept the invitation from the accountant and start sharing your books online.

In addition, both you and the accountant must have Microsoft Passport accounts.

Transferring a review file to your accountant

The online option for Accountant Transfer allows you and your accountant to have a quick and secure method of transmitting your financial data back and forth during review. To use the online option, both you and your accountant must follow certain steps to enable this capability.

The steps you need to start with are very simple:

1. **Open Office Accounting Express 2007 and choose Company⇨ Company Information.**

   The Company Information dialog box, as shown in Figure 11-4.

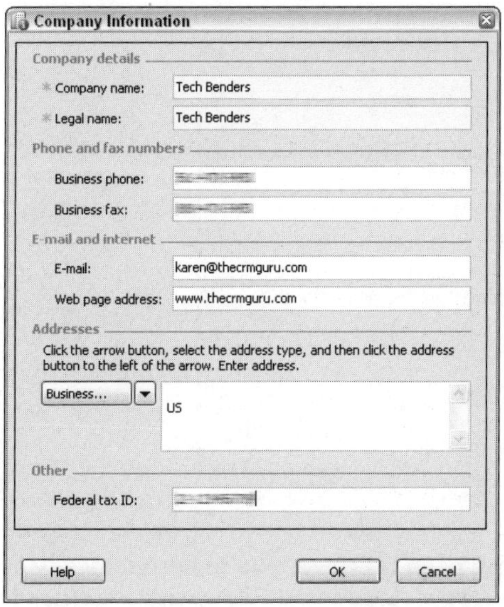

Figure 11-4: The Office Accounting 2007 Company Information dialog box.

2. **Fill in your Microsoft passport e-mail address in the E-Mail box and click OK.**

   Microsoft is enhancing your security by making you use one of their approved e-mail addresses.

3. **Choose File⇨Accountant Transfer⇨Send Books.**

   The Accountant Transfer: Send Wizard opens.

4. **Choose the Send Books Manually option and then click Next.**

   Before the online option can be enabled, you must send a backup of your financial data to your accountant manually. Office Accounting 2007 very nicely provides you with a wizard to help you out with this.

5. **Select a cutoff date and click Next.**

   After you set a cutoff date, you can't make any changes prior to that date. This ensures that the information your accountant is using is correct — thus saving you lots of money in professional accounting services down the line!

6. **Select who will run the payroll while the books are being reviewed (you or your accountant), and then click Next.**

7. **Indicate where you will be saving the backup file, and then click Next.**

   You'll need to indicate both the filename and location (see Figure 11-5).

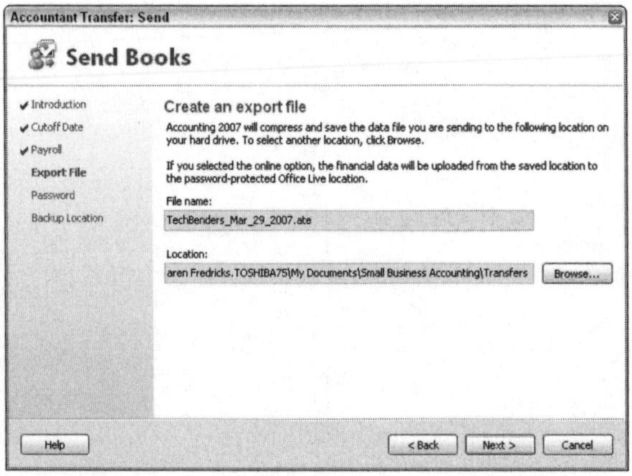

Figure 11-5:
Creating an Accountant's copy of your Office Accounting 2007 data file.

When the data file has been received, you're automatically added to the My Clients table on the Accountant View with a status of `Manual sharing`.

8. **(Optional) Give your file a password and then click Next.**

9. **Click Export, wait a minute or two, and then click OK.**

   You'll have to wait while your computer grunts and groans its way through preparing your backup file.

10. **Send the backup file to your accountant.**

    You're kind of on your own here. Just get the file to your accountant this time — the next time will be much easier!

Accounting for the accountant's part

Your part of the transfer process is pretty much over. Now the accountant comes in to play. Knowing that he or she is probably charging you by the hour, Microsoft made the accountant's part very easy — so easy that they're hoping everyone's accountants will start requiring *all* their clients to use Office Accounting 2007.

If your accountant is a little puzzled by Office Live, offer a copy of this book with this section highlighted:

1. **Sign up for an Office Live Essentials or Premium account.**

   Think of all the postage you'll save by being able to send all your client files online. Think of the Web site you'll have. Think of how cool you'll look to your clients when they realize you're using the latest technology. Think of the increase in your bottom line!

   Not sure how to sign up for an Office Live account? Chapter 2 shows you how!

2. **Open the Accountant View.**

   When you install Office Accounting 2007 a folder appears on your Start menu, containing some Office Accounting 2007 tools; the Accountant View (see Figure 11-6) is one of them.

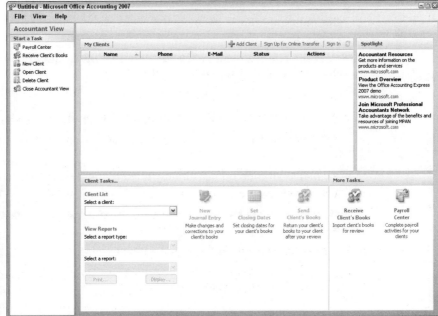

Figure 11-6:
The Accountant View of Office Accounting 2007.

The Accountant View tool is one of the elements of Office Accounting 2007 Express, which is a free product download from the Microsoft Web site.

3. **Click Sign Up for Online Transfer on the My Clients toolbar.**

   If you haven't signed in to your Windows Live account, you're prompted to do so. Use the e-mail address you used when you created your Office Live account.

4. **Choose File⇨New Client to set up the client with whom you wish to communicate.**

   Don't sweat the details here — a company name and e-mail address are all you need. The rest of the import info shows up with the client's backup file.

   You must use the e-mail address that is associated with your client's Microsoft passport account. If this procedure doesn't work — well, don't say I didn't warn you!

5. **Click the Receive Client's Books icon in the Client Tasks area of the Accountant View and restore the backup file that your client has so nicely provided.**

   At this point you're asked to navigate to the spot where you saved the client's backup. Go get a cup of coffee and *voilá* — the information is uploaded to the client's file.

6. **Select the client's name in the My Clients table, click the down arrow in the Actions column, select *Enable online sharing*, and then click Go.**

   After online sharing is enabled, the client Status changes to `Online enabled`.

7. **Select the client's name, click the down arrow in the Actions column, select Send Invitation, and then click Go.**

   The Select E-Mail Template dialog box opens.

8. **Select the Invite for Online Sharing text file, and then click Open.**

   The Online Sharing text file is a great choice — in fact, it's your *only* choice.

   An e-mail invitation opens, already filled out and ready to send (see Figure 11-7).

9. **Feel free to tweak the e-mail slightly, or keep it as is. Send the e-mail on its way.**

   After you've sent the invitation, the client status changes to `Invite Sent`.

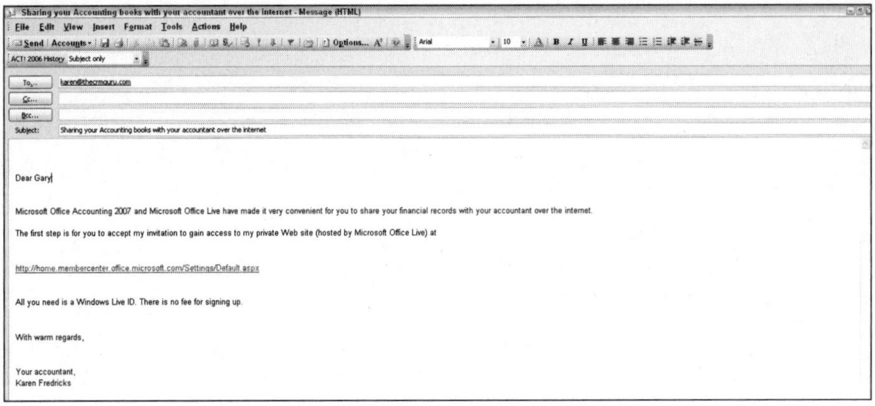

Figure 11-7:
Sending an
e-invitation
to the client.

Accepting the accountant's invitation

A few more steps must take place after the accountant sets you up as a client, receives your backup file and sends you an invitation. Don't worry — the worst part is over!

Follow these steps to finish getting Office Live and Office Account Express 2007 working together:

1. **Open the e-mail from the Accountant and click the link on the invitation to accept.**

   The accountant's Office Live Web site opens. Feel free to close it.

2. **In Office Accounting Express, choose File⇨Accountant Transfer⇨ Sign In.**

   You're prompted for your passport e-mail and password.

3. **Choose File⇨Accountant Transfer⇨Receive Books.**

   You now have the file back from the accountant.

After online transfer has been enabled, your accountant can use the Accountant View to request that you send your books for review. Making a request in this manner allows the accountant to indicate the cutoff date to be used. Your status changes to Books Requested. After the accountant receives the books, the Status changes to Books Received by Accountant.

Accountants must use the Accountant View to send and receive client files.

Part IV
Getting Premium Service

The 5th Wave   By Rich Tennant

"The odd thing is he always insists on using
the latest Premium version of Office Live."

In this part . . .

As your business grows, Office Live grows right along with it. With the Premium version, you can track large projects and initiate sales campaigns. Office Live takes the pain out of managing your employees by providing you with a whole arsenal of human-resources tools. You can keep your finger on the pulse of your company by accessing everything from informational dashboards to lists of your company–owned assets.

Chapter 12

Minding Your Business with Business Applications

*T*his chapter focuses on Business Applications — a Premium Office Live feature, consisting of mini-applications designed to help you organize every aspect of your business. You find out about the various Business Applications that come with Office Live, as well as the templates you can use for creating your own customized Business Applications.

Before digging into the chapter, check out Chapter 8 (about Business Contact Manager) and Chapter 9 (about Workspaces); those chapters provide you with the basic concepts used in Business Applications.

Getting Down to Business Applications

A Business Application is nothing more than a fancy Workspace. The Essentials account provides you with the capability to create Workspaces; it also gives you (as a taste of Premium features) the use of a Business Application — Business Contact Manager.

The Office Live Premium account supplies you with a number of Business Applications to help you organize, manage, and share business information with others. Business Applications come in three flavors:

> ✔ **Default out-of-the-box Business Applications:** These are designed to be useful just as they are, and most users won't have to tweak them. (See the section "Knowing the Default Business Applications.")

✔ **Out-of-the-box Business Applications that you modify:** If you don't find a Business Application among the Office Live applications that suits you, you can build one by modifying an existing application. For example, you might add a new list that contains customers of only a specific product. (See the section "Modifying an Existing Business Application.")

✔ **Business Applications that you create using an Office Live Business Application template:** See the section "Using the Business Application Templates."

Knowing the Default Business Applications

Before you learn *how* to use a Business Application, you'll need to know *where* to find them. Finding them is easy — Business Applications is a top-level item in the Home page Navigation bar. Click the Business Applications link and the default Business Applications appear in the Navigation bar (as shown in Figure 12-1).

How Business Applications are similar to Workspaces

Workspaces and Business Applications have a lot of similarities:

✔ The Business Application opens to a customizable dashboard.

✔ A Business Application is list-based; when you open the application, you see a list of records pertaining to that application.

✔ A Business Application consists of several pages; each page is represented by a tab on the Application's Home page.

✔ You add items to, or edit, the list by opening a form that contains all the fields available to that item. Alternatively, you can open a Datasheet to enter or edit information.

✔ You can customize, filter, and sort the various lists as much as you like. Then you can save your customized view and print the list.

✔ The subscription owner of the Office Live site is the person who is in charge of setting up the Business Applications. The owner can then assign rights to other users to determine what users get to access which applications.

If you've recently upgraded your Office Live account from Essentials to Premium, make sure all your Office Live users have access rights to the various Business Applications. You'll find all the information you need to assign rights in Chapter 9.

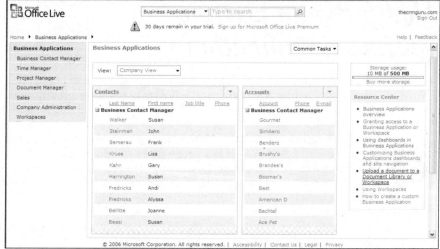

Figure 12-1:
The
Business
Applications.

When you open the Business Applications dashboard, you see the seven default Business Applications (there's more detailed information about them throughout this book):

- **Business Contact Manager:** Organizes the sales part of your business by organizing your Accounts, Contacts, Opportunities, Products, and Documents (see Chapter 8). Business Contact Manager is available in both the Essentials and Premium Office Live accounts.

- **Time Manager:** Contains personal and company scheduling information. Think of it as your Personal Calendar on steroids (see Chapter 17).

- **Project Manager:** Contains information about your company's projects. Helps you plan, track, and update your projects' progress and issues — and share that information with others (see Chapter 14).

- **Document Manager:** Contains all the documents and pictures you upload (see Chapter 17).

- **Sales:** Includes three applications rolled into one — the Competition Tracker, Customer Support, and Estimates — which helps take you (and your business) through all the steps of the sales process (see Chapter 15).

- **Company Administration:** Contains five applications — Company Assets, Employee Directory, Expenses, Jobs and Hiring, and Training — all of which help keep you, your company, and your employees organized (see Chapter 16).

- **Workspaces:** You might think of Workspaces as simplified Business Applications. Workspaces are available in both the Essentials and Premium Office Live accounts (see Chapter 9).

Modifying an Existing Business Application

The possibilities for creating and customizing lists and applications are almost limitless. Chapter 9 shows you the basics of entering, editing, and deleting items from a list. But who says you can't teach an old dog new tricks?

If you are already familiar with the concept of a database, you're probably familiar with fields. A *field* is a single piece of information and is the term that most software programs use. However, Office Live uses the word *column*, which becomes a bit confusing (most of us associate a column with a spreadsheet or a list view).

Confusion aside, think of how nicely this could play out using an Office Live Business Application:

1. You define a need.
2. You add a new page to an existing application.
3. You add new field(s).

Probably the hardest part of tweaking an application isn't *how* to tweak it but *what* to tweak. Do your homework: Decide whether a page will prove important enough to justify the time it takes to create it and fill it with data.

You might think, for example, that the Employee Directory section of the Company Administration application is the next best thing to sliced sourdough bread. But then you start to think that you need to add just a few more things to an employee record. Before you know it, you're jamming all sorts of extra information into the Notes section: maybe a commission rate or a spouse's mobile phone number. And you're not only *jamming* — you're also *forgetting* when you jammed in all that information. Suddenly you have an inspiration: How about adding a Personal Contact information tab to the Employee Directory?

Adding a new application tab

Adding a tab to an existing application — and populating it with a field or two — is surprisingly easy, considering what a powerful tool it is. When you've defined a need that is not being met by an existing Office Live Business Application, you can start embellishing an application by following these steps:

1. **Click Business Applications on the Navigation bar on the Office Live Home page.**

   The Business Applications dashboard opens.

2. **Click the Business Application you'd like to modify.**

3. **Choose Create New from the Common Tasks drop-down list.**

   Here I've chosen to modify the Employee Directory, so the Employee Directory — Create page opens (see Figure 12-2).

Figure 12-2:
Customizing an existing application.

You can add a lot of different tabs to an existing application. To save you a bit of time, here's a brief rundown.

You can add three types of libraries:

- *Document:* Here's where you can add documents so that you can collaborate on, share, and monitor the versions of documents in a shared location.

- *Form:* For the more technically oriented folks in the crowd, you can create a form library where you store XML-based business forms (such as status reports or purchase orders).

- *Picture:* Here's where you can create an online album of the pictures you want to share.

There are two types of Communications tabs:

- *Announcements:* Create an announcements list when you want a place to share news, status, and other short bits of information.

- *Discussion Board:* Create a discussion board to provide a place for newsgroup-style discussions. Discussion boards provide features for managing discussion threads and ensuring that only approved posts appear.

There are two type of Tracking tabs:

- *Links:* You can create a links list to include links to Web pages or other resources that you want to share.

- *Survey:* If someone has told you that if they want your opinion they'll ask for it — here's the place where they're asking. You can create a survey to find out how the other members of your organization feel about various issues and concerns.

4. **Choose the type of tab you want to add or if none suit your purposes, choose Custom List to create your own tab.**

   The New Page window opens.

5. **Give the page a name and then click Create.**

   Faster than you can say Holy Guacamole, you return to the application — where your new page now sits in all its glory.

6. **Choose Create a Column from the Settings drop-down list.**

   Office Live calls the field a column because theoretically it can appear as a column in a list view. At this point, there is only one field on your new tab — so you'll want to add a few more (see Figure 12-3).

7. **Start creating the new field.**

   Office Live offers a few cool field options you can use:

   - *Column Name:* Give the field a name.

   - *Type:* Select the type for the field; there are many types from which to choose. The type of field determines the type of information that you can enter into it. The Single Line of Text option means that you can only type one line of information whereas the Multiple Lines of Text option means you can write a book. Choosing Choice is not only hard to say; it also allows you to build a customized drop-down list. The Lookup field allows you to add fields from an existing list so that the two lists are linked together. For example, if you are adding a Personal Information tab you create a Lookup field based on the Employee Directory and include one of the Employee Directory fields such as Employee Name.

     Proceed with caution and choose the field type carefully! As of this writing, you can't change the field type after you select and save it.

   - *Description:* Give further clues about the field, or describe the type of information you're looking for.

   - *Require That This Field Contains Information:* You can make this field a required one by selecting the Yes radio button.

   - *Add to Default View:* Check this option if you'd like to add the new field to the default list view.

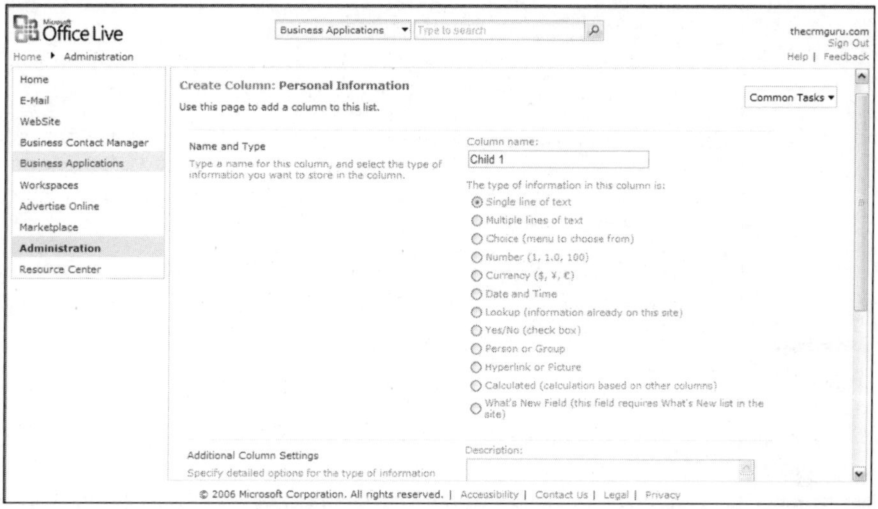

Figure 12-3:
Creating a
new field.

8. **Click OK to save your field and return to your new tab.**

   At this point, you'll probably need to repeat Steps 6 and 7 quite a few times — at least once for each new field you'd like to add.

9. **If you'd like to change the name of your tab, click Title, Description, and Navigation on the Customize tab.**

   The List General Settings page opens, as shown in Figure 12-4.

10. **Fill in the new tab name and click Save to save your changes.**

You can change the name of just about any Business Application tab, except for the tabs that you see in Business Contact Manager. In addition, you can add new fields to any of those tabs — again, with the exception of those in Business Contact Manager.

You can change any part of a Business Application by clicking the Settings icon and choosing Create Column. If you don't see the Settings icon, you can't make a change to that section.

Adding a whole lot of columns

The previous section shows you how easy it is to create another tab for a Business Application and then populate it with new fields (okay, "columns"). You even see how to add an existing field to the new tab so that when the value changes on one list, the other list updates itself automatically. Unfortunately, you have to add those fields to the new tab one at a time — which can take a lot of your time, but at least you only have to do it once.

Figure 12-4:
Changing a
new tab
name.

You might find yourself in a situation where you'd like to see a lot of the same information on two different tabs. For example, you might have an Employee Directory that you allow all your Office Live users to access, but you'd also like to have a second, similar tab that only you can access (say, one that includes private information, including personal-contact information and pay rates). So you create the new tab — and realize you'll want to include all the employee contact information that already exists in the Employee Directory.

You could cancel your golf game and spend an hour adding all those fields to your new tab — or you could follow these steps:

1. **Click Business Applications on the Navigation bar on the Office Live Home page.**

   The Business Applications dashboard opens.

2. **Click the Business Application you'd like to modify, and then select the tab that contains the field you'd like to change.**

   At this point, you're looking at the new tab you created.

3. **Choose List Settings from the Settings drop-down list.**

   The Customize page opens.

4. **Click Add from Existing Site Columns in the Columns section.**

   If you've already added a whole bunch of new columns, you might have trouble locating that option — it's buried all the way at the bottom of the list.

   The Add Columns from Site Columns page opens, as shown in Figure 12-5.

5. **Select an option from the Select Site Columns From drop-down list.**

   This area is a tad confusing. It would be easier if you were given choices like Employee Directory or Business Contact Manager. The choices you are given are a bit more generic — so you'll see things like Core Contact and Calendar Columns and Customer Support Fields. Don't worry about it too much; as you make selections, the corresponding fields appear in the Available Site Columns box.

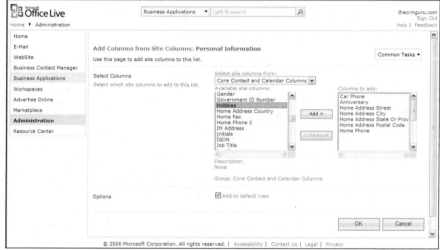

Figure 12-5:
Adding existing fields to a new tab.

6. **Select the field(s) you'd like to add to your new tab and then click the Add button.**

   Each field disappears from the left side and makes a magical reappearance in the Columns to Add box. If a field appears there by mistake, select it and then click the Remove button.

7. **Click OK when you finish adding fields.**

   Voilá — you now have numerous fields available to you on the new tab.

Making a few changes to your fields

In the previous section, I stress the importance of doing your homework before adding a bunch of new pages and fields to your Office Live applications. However, it's pretty certain that after you create them, you'll want to change things around a bit.

Should you decide to modify one of the fields, here's what you need to know:

1. **Click Business Applications on the Navigation bar on the Office Live Home page.**

   The Business Applications dashboard opens.

2. **Click the Business Application you'd like to modify, and then select the tab that contains the field you'd like to change.**

   At this point, you're looking at the tab you'd like to modify.

3. **Choose List Settings from the Settings drop-down list.**

   The Customize page opens.

4. **Click the name of the field you want to change in the Column section.**

5. **Make your changes to the fields.**

   You don't have as many field options as you did when you created the field originally (see Figure 12-6). However, you can change the field name and description, and make the field a required one.

6. **Click OK to save your field changes.**

   You end up on the Customize page. When you open the tab, it shows the changes you made to the field.

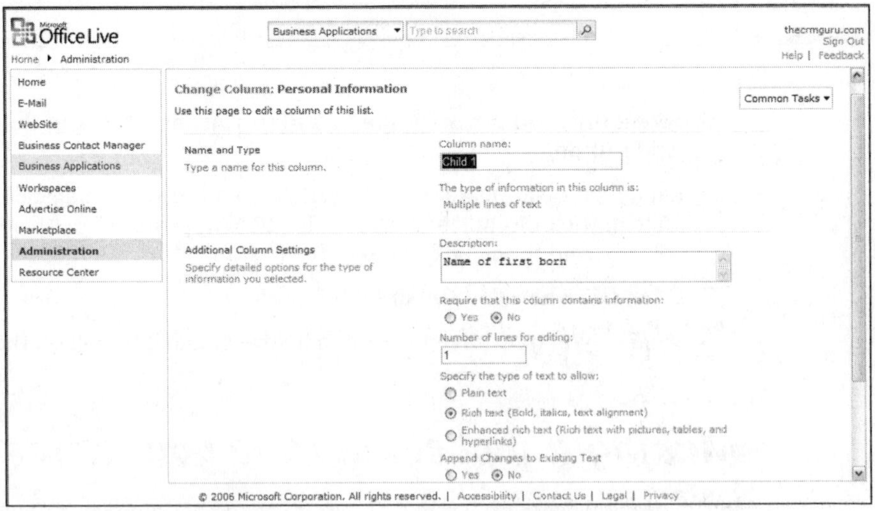

Figure 12-6:
Making changes to new tabs and fields.

Using the Business Application Templates

If you're one of those people who just have to have things their own way, you might be a bit disappointed with the Business Applications templates. The templates are basically clones of the default Office Live Business Applications. However, if you manage two companies — or have several totally separate areas of your business — you might want to use one of those templates to help organize the various parts of your business. Using templates gives you the flexibility to mold Office Live as your business grows and/or a new need arises.

Follow these steps to open a Business Application template:

1. **Click Business Applications on the Navigation bar on the Office Live Home page.**

2. **Select Create New from the Common Tasks drop-down list.**

   The Business Applications – Create page opens.

3. **Click the Applications and Workspaces link.**

   The Create New Application or Workspace page opens.

4. **Select Business Applications from the Category drop-down list.**

   At last! This is the first distinction between an Essentials and a Premium account. If you had an Essentials account, you'd have only one available category — Workspaces.

5. **Select a template from the drop-down list.**

   Life is full of choices — and you'll certainly find a bunch of them here. However, you might want to look at the originals first before using one of these clones:

   - Company Assets
   - Competition Tracker
   - Customer Support
   - Document Manager
   - Employee Directory
   - Estimates

- Expenses
- Jobs and Hiring
- Project Manager
- Time Manager
- Training

You'll notice another option — the Find More Applications on Our Marketplace link. Give it a click to view some of the applications that various third-party vendors have developed. Many of these applications are industry-specific. Microsoft anticipates that the number of applications listed on the Marketplace will increase steadily.

The Create New Application or Workspace page opens.

6. **Give the new Application a name, URL, and description; indicate whether it should appear in the Navigation bar.**

7. **Click OK to save the new application.**

The new application now appears in the Navigation bar (if that's what you indicated while creating it). At this point you can add, modify, or delete fields and tabs to your heart's content.

Chapter 13

Time (Manager) Is on Your Side

In This Chapter

▶ Understanding Time Manager

▶ Scheduling and reservations

▶ Managing your To-Dos

▶ Working with shared resources

▶ Planning for the holidays

Time Manager helps conquer four mundane — but important — parts of your business day. You have a Scheduling and Reservations system so that you can view everyone's schedule — including your own — in one easy place. You have an easy-to-access To-Do list so that none of your important follow-ups fall through the cracks. As your company expands you might need to keep track of the various company resources (such as a delivery truck or a conference room) so your staff isn't forced to fight over them. Finally, even though most holidays come around once a year, you don't want to be caught off-guard when you come in to work — and find that your entire staff is at home eating Thanksgiving dinner.

Time Manager is designed to help larger organizations with scheduling. Chapter 7 discusses the Personal Calendar that is available with all Office Live subscriptions; this chapter focuses on the Time Manager Business Application, which is only available with Premium accounts.

Managing Your Time with Time Manager

Office Live designed Time Manager to help you manage your schedule. As your business grows, so do your responsibilities. Adding employees is a mixed blessing: They help you run your business but also represent one more area of responsibility. It seems like everyone has too much to do — and not enough time to do it with. Although Office Live can't add another hour or two to your day, it can help you stay better organized by giving you the use of the Time Manager Business Application.

You can find Time Manager by clicking Business Applications from the Navigation bar of the Office Live Home page and then choosing Time Manager.

Time Manager consists of five tabs:

- **Dashboard:** The customizable dashboard provides a comprehensive, personalized view of the information stored in Time Manager. It gives you an easy way to view your most important data at a glance. Figure 13-1 shows the Time Manager Dashboard.

- **Schedule and Reservations:** View your schedule — as well as those of the other Office Live users — in a calendar list format.

- **To-Do:** See a list of all your important tasks.

- **Resources:** Keep track of shared assets such as conference room and presentation equipment so that users can reserve them — see them listed in the Schedule and Reservations tab.

- **Manage Resources:** Group individual resources together into a single unit. For example, you can group a shared laptop and projector into a single "Presentations Equipment" item.

Business Applications works just like Workspaces. If you're not sure how to customize a list or dashboard, flip to Chapter 9 to find out how.

Figure 13-1:
The Time
Manager
dashboard.

Creating a Company Calendar

The Schedule and Reservations calendar in the Time Manager allows you to keep track of your calendar and your resource reservations. You can also view the calendars of others on your team. By viewing the current schedule, you get a list of scheduled appointments as well as reserved resources.

You can create custom views of the information to best meet your business needs. You can also add this list to the Time Manager dashboard so you can review it side-by-side with any other information on the dashboard. You can even see a calendar showing when your resources are being used.

Follow these steps to access the company calendar — and add a new activity:

1. **Click Business Applications on the Navigation bar and then Time Manager.**

   The Time Manager dashboard opens (refer to Figure 13-1). This is the place where you can view snapshots of the various Time Manager elements in one centralized location.

2. **Click the Schedule and Reservations tab.**

   As expected, the Schedule and Reservations tab opens. Figure 13-2 shows the Calendar view of the tab.

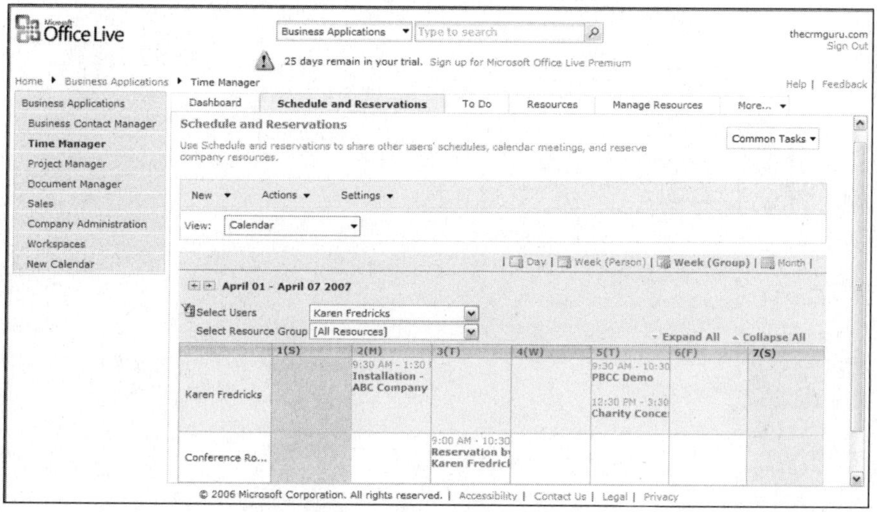

Figure 13-2: The Schedule and Reservations tab.

You might want to change views by selecting a different option from the View drop-down list; the other views rely on list format rather than calendar format.

- To change to a different week, click the up (right) or down (left) arrows next to the Date.

- To change to the Day, Week (Person), Week (Group), or Month calendars, click the appropriate links. The boldface link indicates your current calendar.

3. Click the arrow next to New, and choose Schedule.

The New Appointment page opens, as shown in Figure 13-3.

If you are reserving one of the shared resources, you have the option of selecting Reservations from the New drop-down list. Alternatively, you can schedule the appointment and include the resource(s) that you need in the Resource field.

4. Type all the appointment information.

The Appointment Name is the only mandatory field. The remaining fields are optional but nonetheless important:

- *Title:* Identify the appointment with a word or phrase; the title appears on your calendar.

- *Participants:* Select a name from the users listed on the left and then click Add to include users in the appointment. The appointment appears on the selected user's calendar.

Figure 13-3:
Creating
a new
appointment.

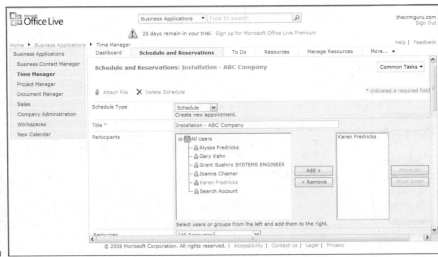

- *Resources:* Select a resource from the list of resources on the left, and then click Add to commandeer the resource for this appointment. The rest of the people in your company can now see that the resource is unavailable for the selected time period.

- *Free/Busy:* Allows you to view the availability of each invitee.

- *Begin:* Select starting date and time of your meeting.

- *End:* Select the ending date and time of your meeting.

- *All Day Event:* Check the Make This an All-Day Activity that doesn't start or end at a specific hour if you are scheduling an all-day event.

- *Recurrence:* Check the Make This a Repeating Event option if you are scheduling a recurring event. The Recurrence field expands before your eyes to include the additional options (see Figure 13-4).

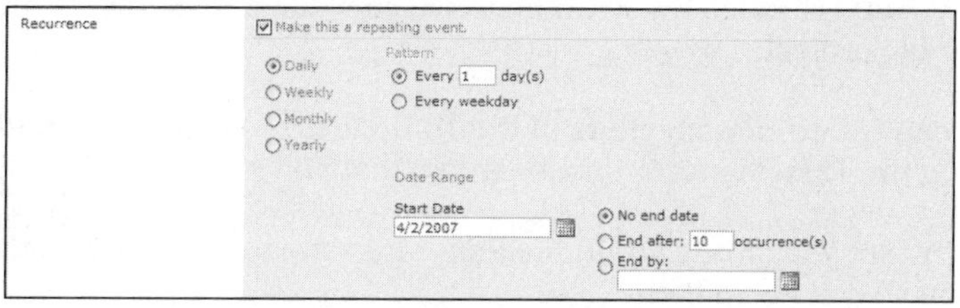

Figure 13-4: Scheduling a recurring event.

- *Check Double Booking:* Click the Check icon to make sure this appointment is viable for all invitees. If there is a conflict, the Check Double Booking area expands to show you a warning.

- *Location:* There are three rules that govern appointments: location, location, location. Knowing *when* an appointment occurs does you absolutely no good if you don't also know *where* the appointment is to take place.

- *Category:* Select the category that this scheduled event falls under, or click the Specify radio button and create your own category.

- *Description:* Type a description of the event. You can also use this area to include other important tidbits of information such as "remember to bring brochures" or "it's his turn to buy lunch."

- *Meeting Workspace:* Check the Use a Meeting Workspace to organize attendees, agendas, documents, minutes, and other details for this event option if you'd like to create a new Workspace for the meeting. Talk about cool: A New Meeting Workspace page opens — already filled in with the pertinent details. Click OK and the Workspace is added to Office Live and you return to the New Appointment page.

5. **Click OK to save the appointment and return to the Schedule and Reservations tab.**

   As you might have already guessed, your new appointment is now included on your already-busy schedule.

Much To-Do About Nothing

Most contact management programs have a Task List that holds the myriad tasks that you need to remember not to forget. Office Live has its own version of the Task List, which is called the To-Do list. The To-Do list enables you to keep track of simple tasks or *To-Dos* that you and your team need to complete.

Chapter 14 talks about projects, which are major undertakings that have so many To-Dos associated with them that they have to be tied together in one great big project.

You can create custom views of the To-Do list. You can also include the To-Do list on the Time Manager dashboard so that you can review it.

So why are you sitting around reading? It's time to take a few of the To-Dos you have and get *to* them:

1. **Click Business Applications on the Navigation bar, and then click Time Manager.**

   The Time Manager dashboard opens.

2. **Click the To-Do tab.**

   As expected, the To-Do tab opens with a loud Ta-da (just kidding), as shown in Figure 13-5.

3. **Click the New icon.**

   The To-Do – New Item page opens. Because To-Dos are short little tasks, this is a relatively short little form.

4. **Fill in the desired pieces of information.**

   There is only one required field — the Task Name. Here's a rundown of the various To-Do fields:

   - *Title:* Add a word or phrase that identifies the task.

   - *Priority:* Choose a priority of High, Medium, or Low.

   - *To-Do Status:* Set the current status as Not Started, In Progress, Completed, Deferred, or Waiting on Someone Else. You'll want to go back and edit the To-Do at a later date; hopefully you'll be changing the status to Completed.

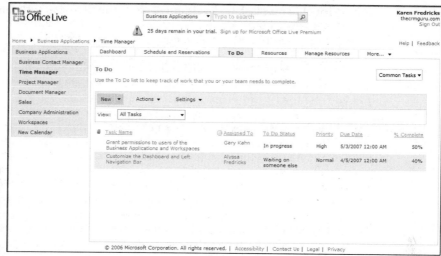

Figure 13-5:
Ta-da —
it's the
To-Do tab.

- *% Complete:* Give your best guesstimate of how far along you are toward completing the task.

- *Assigned To:* Select the Office Live user that you've assigned to the task. Once assigned, the user sees the To-Do on his or her To-Do list. (Of course, you can always assign the To-Do to yourself — but it's so much more fun to share the wealth!)

- *Description:* If the task title isn't enough to jar your memory, feel free to add an expanded version of the task here.

- *Start Date:* Select a start date for the task from the calendar.

- *Due Date:* Select an end date for the task from the calendar.

5. **Click OK to save the To-Do.**

   You return to the To-Do tab, where you'll see yet another something that you have to do.

Can I Borrow the Keys to the Conference Room?

Picture this scenario: Your biggest client is coming to your office for a visit. He's mentioned that he has some really exciting news for you — and you interpret that to mean he's going to double the amount of money he's currently spending with your company. You knock yourself out making sure the meeting will be perfect to the *n*th degree. You've arranged for the caterer to come at noon; your assistant was up all night collating your great new sales presentation. You usher Mr. Client into your conference room — only to find it devoid of furniture and the floor covered in drop-cloths.

Hopefully you've never experienced this kind of nightmare. But if you work in a large organization — or at least large enough to share resources — then you've probably run into resource-scheduling conflicts.

Two of the Time Manager tabs — Resources and Manage Resource — help you keep tabs on your resources so you don't end up having employees grappling on the floor for the keys to the conference room.

You actually schedule the resource on the Schedule and Reservations tab; as I mentioned earlier, you can either add a resource to an appointment as you schedule it or just schedule the resource itself. The Resource tab lists all the resources your business has; the Manage Resource tab lets you group those resources together. For example, you might have a projector, laptop, and conference room that are shared among your various employees. Rather than scheduling each item separately, you can group them together as one item — Sales Conference — on the Manage Resources tab; that way you have just one item to schedule.

Follow these steps to add a new resource:

1. **Click Business Applications on the Navigation bar, and then click Time Manager.**

   The Time Manager dashboard opens.

2. **Click the Resources tab.**

   As expected, the Resources tab opens, as shown in Figure 13-6.

Figure 13-6:
Keeping track of your shared resources.

3. Click the New icon.

The Resources – New Resource page opens; see Figure 13-7.

4. Fill in some information about the resource.

There's not a whole lot to input here. Give the resource a good name; if that doesn't do the trick, add a more detailed description.

5. Click OK to save the Resource and return to the Resource list.

At this point, you can sit back and calm down, knowing you're never going to run into a scheduling conflict (okay, never say *never*, but relax). If two or more of your resources are commonly lumped together in a larger unit, however, continue with the rest of these steps.

6. Click the Manager Resources tab.

The Manage Resources tab opens.

7. Click the New icon.

The Manage Resources: New Resources Group page opens, as shown in Figure 13-8.

8. Fill in the pertinent information.

- *Group Name:* Assign a name to the group.

- *Resources:* Select two or more of your resources from the left column and then click the Add button.

- *Comment:* Just in case you don't think the other employees will understand which resources belong to the group, you can spell it out for them here.

9. Click OK to save the group and return to the Manage Resources tab.

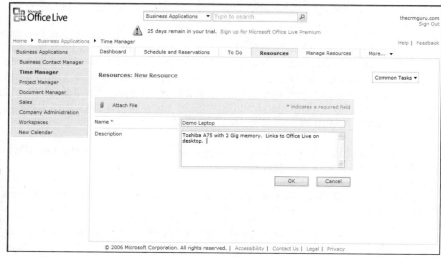

Figure 13-7:
Creating a
new shared
resource.

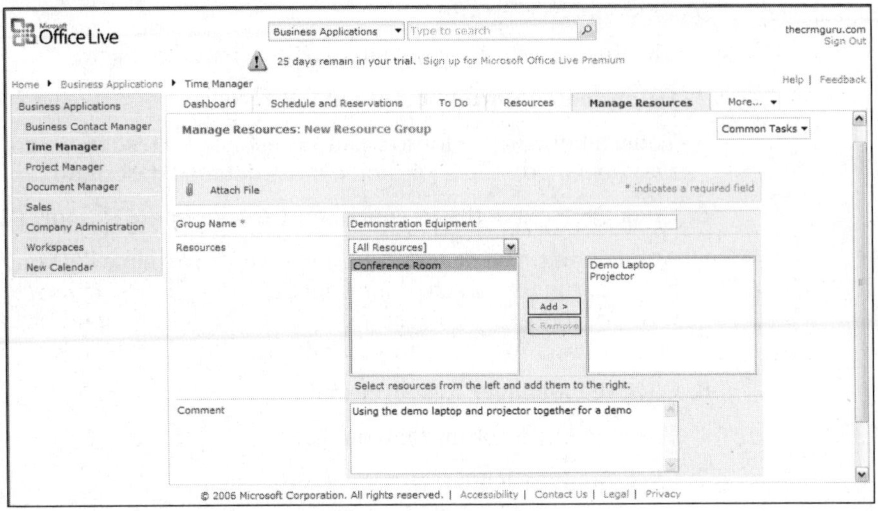

© 2006 Microsoft Corporation. All rights reserved. | Accessibility | Contact Us | Legal | Privacy

Figure 13-8:
Creating a
group of
resources.

Celebrating the Holidays

As likely as not, your employees have already committed a list of national holidays to memory — and can give you an exact countdown until the next occurrence. As the owner of the business, however, you might get so busy that you have to schedule yourself a coffee break.

Holidays are further complicated by the fact that they are just so darned inconsistent. Thanksgiving always fall on a Thursday — but is it the third or fourth Thursday in November? You need an abacus to calculate religion holidays such as Easter and Passover. Thank heavens that Office Live comes equipped with a handy dandy list of the most common holidays.

In addition to including a list of the common holidays, you can create new holidays on the Holiday list. You might be scratching your head and wondering whether you missed the Act of Congress that declared your birthday a national holiday. However, maybe you want to include your employees' birthdays on the Holiday list — even if you still make them work that day. Your employees will also find it useful to know which days they have off if (say) the Fourth of July falls on a Tuesday.

Adding a new holiday to the Holiday list is easy — wrapping all those presents is the hard part:

1. **Click Business Applications on the Navigation bar and then click Time Manager.**

   The Time Manager dashboard opens.

2. **Click the Holiday tab.**

   The Holiday tab, shown in Figure 13-9, appears.

3. **Click the New icon.**

   The Holidays – New Holiday page opens.

4. **Fill in the pertinent details.**

   A new Office Live holiday consists of four fields; Holiday Name and Date are required ones.

   - *Holiday Name:* Give the holiday a name; for example, you might call your birthday "Give a Present to the Boss Day."

   - *Date:* It's hard to celebrate a holiday without a date; here's where you fill one in. You have to use the *yyyy/mm/dd* format; there is no clever little calendar to help you.

   - *Category:* The categories consist of Japan, United States, Germany, France, and United Kingdom. Optionally, you can create your own category, which is a good idea unless you've decided to start celebrating Bastille Day.

   - *Non-Working Day:* Office Live assumes that you have to work on all new holidays — boy, do I hate *that* assumption! However, if that assumption is inaccurate, check the Mark as Non-Working day option to give yourself — and the rest of the company — the day off.

5. **Click OK to save the holiday and return to the holiday list.**

   You might want to linger for a moment or two, dreaming of the upcoming holidays.

Figure 13-9:
The Holiday tab.

Chapter 14

Managing Your Projects with Project Manager

*I*n this chapter, you find out how to achieve your major goals through the use of another Office Live Premium Business Application called Project Manager. When you've identified a project, you can then set milestones — and assign tasks that help you reach those milestones. And, should you be faced with a major obstacle that keeps you from reaching your goal, you can identify it so you can find a solution.

Using Project Manager to Manage Your Business

Chapter 7 shows how to create a calendar of activities and tasks — and even share it with others if necessary. This chapter concentrates on super-size activities that require several steps — and possibly several people — to complete.

Project Manager consists of four parts:

✔ The project

✔ Project tasks

✔ Project milestones

✔ Project issues

Each of these parts is represented by a separate tab on the Project Manager Home page. In keeping with the rest of Office Live, the Project Manager contains a dashboard that gives you a bird's-eye view of all your ongoing projects.

You can access Project Manager by following these steps:

1. **Click Business Applications in the Navigation bar of the Office Live Home page.**

   The Business Applications page springs to attention. It provides you with a list of the Business Applications in the Navigation bar.

2. **Click Project Manager.**

   The Project Manager dashboard, shown in Figure 14-1, opens. By default, the various dashboard items are sorted by status. To see all your projects by a certain status, click the tiny plus sign to expand the status category.

   From here you can click on any of the tabs (Projects, Project Tasks, Project Milestones, and Project Issues) to delve further into Project Management.

3. **Click on any item to view it in its entirety.**

   Once clicked, the item will open into its own, detailed window where you can view the smaller details that might not appear on the tab list.

4. **(Optional) Click Edit Item, make your changes, and then click OK.**

   You can change any aspect that your little heart desires. For example, if you finished a task you might want to change the status to Complete.

5. **(Optional) Click Delete Item and click OK to send an item packing.**

   You can delete an item if you no longer need it.

Figure 14-1:
The Project Manager dashboard.

Creating a New Project

When using Office Live, the first step in project management is to identify the project and create a record of the project details. Once created, you can associate milestones, tasks, and issues to the project to help you track the project from start to finish. All your projects appear in a list on the Projects tab of the Project Manager. You can customize the list to best suit your business needs. You can also add the project list to the Project Manager dashboard so you can view a recap of your projects, along with any outstanding milestones, tasks, and issues.

Not sure how to customize the Projects list view and or add it to the dashboard? Flip to Chapter 9, where I tell you how to do it.

Follow these steps to create a new project:

1. **Click Business Applications on the Navigation bar of your Office Live home page and then choose Project Manager.**

   The Project Manager dashboard opens.

2. **Click the Projects tab.**

   Figure 14-2 shows the Projects tab.

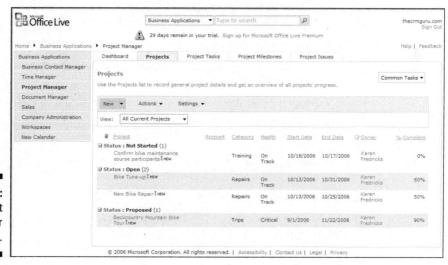

Figure 14-2:
The Project Manager Projects tab.

3. **Click the New icon.**

   The Projects – New Item page opens (see Figure 14-3). If you're feeling a sense of déjà vu, you might be having a flashback to the '60s — or to Chapter 9. Business Application looks, feels, and acts pretty much like Workspaces.

4. **Fill in the Project details.**

   Only three of the fields — Project, Status, and Health — are required fields. You can edit the project at a later date to fill in more details — or change the existing ones — if necessary.

   - *Project:* Name the project with a word or phrase to help you identify it.

   - *Account:* Select an account from the drop-down list to associate the project with one of your Business Contact Manager Accounts.

   - *Category:* You can categorize the project type as Create, Analyze, Manage, or Improve.

   - *Status:* You must assign a status of Open, Proposed, Not Started, or Closed.

   - *Start Date:* The date on which the project is scheduled to begin.

   - *End Date:* The date on which the project is due.

   - *Health:* You must assign a project health assessment of Critical, At Risk, or On Track.

   - *Owner:* Select an Office Live user as Project Manager.

   - *% Complete:* Fill in your best guesstimate of how far along the project is in its overall progress.

   - *Budget:* Enter the dollar amount you're allotting to this project.

   - *Budget in Days:* Enter the number of days you're allotting to this project.

   - *Comments:* Add a comment if you need to add a longer explanation of the project.

5. **Click OK to save your project.**

   You return to the Project tab where your new project is now included with the other projects in the Project List.

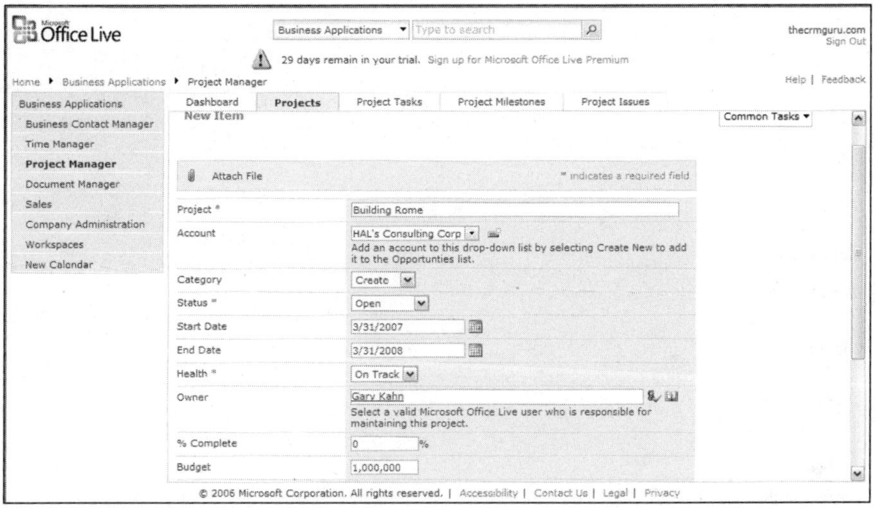

Figure 14-3: A Project form.

Getting Mileage out of Your Project Milestones

Project Milestones is a list in the Project Manager in which you can record and track the progress of major dates and stages. When you create a new milestone, you specify the project that it belongs to. This association allows you to see the entire picture when viewing a Project record. You'll also see the Milestone list on the Project Management dashboard.

By definition, a milestone is a significant event or stage. Rome wasn't built in a day — or so I'm told. The Romans probably had milestones along the way: get zoning approval, find a large rock quarry, arrange for slave labor. They probably had a large toga party every time they achieved one of those milestones; if they were using Office Live, the project manager would indicate that the milestone had been reached so other users could celebrate silently in their cubicles. (Ah, progress.)

Follow the bouncing ball to set Project Milestones:

1. **Click Business Applications on the Navigation bar of your Office Live Home page and then click Project Manager.**

   The Project Manager dashboard opens.

2. **Click the Project Milestones tab.**

   The Project Milestones tab opens according to plan; see Figure 14-4.

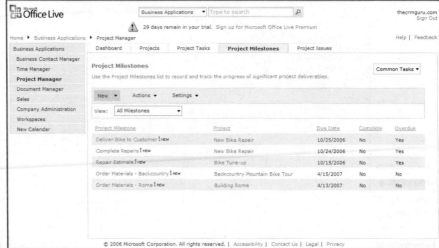

© 2006 Microsoft Corporation. All rights reserved. | Accessibility | Contact Us | Legal | Privacy

Figure 14-4:
Project Milestones tab of the Office Live Project Manager.

3. **Click the New icon.**

   The Project Milestones – New Item page opens (see Figure 14-5).

4. **Fill in the necessary information.**

   Okay, stop complaining. You only have four things to add here, and only one — the Project Milestone name — is mandatory.

   - *Project Milestone:* Name the Milestone with a word or phrase to help you identify it. You might use something along the lines of "Materials Ordered" or "Carthaginian Slaves Arrived."

   You might find it a good idea to use a standard naming convention for your Project Milestone. You can sort the various Project Milestones on the Project Milestones tab by name; it might prove useful so see all your Material Orders grouped together on the list.

   - *Project:* Although this field is not required, it's an important one. This field ties the milestone to an existing project. You'll find all the Office Live projects by clicking the drop-down arrow.

   - *Due Date:* The date on which the milestone is due.

   - *Complete:* Indicates whether the milestone is completed, regardless of due date.

   - *Comments:* Comments about the milestone.

5. **Click OK to save your changes and return to the Project Milestones tab.**

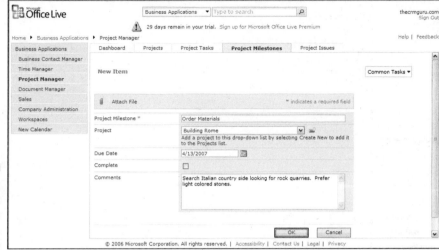

Figure 14-5:
The Project
Milestones
form.

Tracking Your Project Tasks

It's always easier to work on a large project one piece at a time. Dividing a project into a series of smaller tasks helps ensure that your project is moving along as scheduled. This works even better if you assign the tasks to other slaves — er, employees — so you can track their progress. The tasks help you to reach your milestones, which lead to a completed project.

When creating a new task, you can associate it with an existing project. This association provides the flexibility for you to categorize tasks by project.

Follow these steps to create a new Project Task:

1. **Click Business Applications on the Navigation bar of your Office Live home page and then click Project Manager.**

   The Project Manager dashboard opens.

2. **Click the Project Tasks tab.**

   The Project Tasks tab opens, as shown in Figure 14-6. The Project Tasks tab looks a bit different from the other Office Live Workspace and Business Application pages. The Project Tasks tab contains a Gantt chart at the top of the page and a list of your tasks beneath it. A *Gantt chart* depicts tasks in relation to time, and is often used in planning and tracking a project.

Figure 14-6:
The Project
Tasks tab of
the Office
Live Project
Manager.

The Gantt chart only appears in the Project Tasks view on the Project Tasks tab. However, you can add a Gantt chart to any of the other Project Tasks views. Not sure how to do it? Chapter 9 shows you how to change the elements on a tab.

3. **Click the New icon.**

The Project Tasks – New Item page opens as shown in Figure 14-7.

Figure 14-7:
Adding a
new Project
Task.

4. **Fill in the Project Task information.**

You only have to include the information for the Project Task field; the rest of the fields are optional. Okay, it may be a hassle to fill them in, but chin up: Like most everything else in life, no pain, no gain.

- *Project Task:* Name the task with a word or phrase to help you identify it.

- *Project:* Click the drop-down list to associate the task with an existing project.

- *Milestone:* Click the drop-down list to associate the task with an existing milestone.

- *Priority:* Set a priority level of High, Normal, or Low.

- *Task Status:* Choose Not Started, In Progress, Completed, Deferred, or Waiting on Someone Else as the status of the task.

- *% Complete:* Fill in your best guesstimate of how far along the project is in its overall progress.

- *Assigned To:* Select the Office Live user who is supposed to get the job done. (You might think of this as the Passing the Buck field.)

- *Description:* Here's where you can write a mini-novel that includes all the task details.

- *Start Date:* The date on which the task is scheduled to begin.

- *Due Date:* The date on which the task is due.

- *Cost:* Enter the dollar amount that you are allotting to this task.

- *Cost in Days:* Enter the number of days that you are allotting to this task.

5. **Click OK to save your changes and return to the Project Tasks tab.**

Dealing with Project Issues

The best-laid plans of mice and men can often run into obstacles. Someone gets sick, something else breaks — things happen. It's one thing to face an obstacle — it's another one to let someone know about it and get the problem resolved.

The Project Issues tab contains a list of the issues and concerns that are keeping you from achieving your goal. Once these are created, management can view the various issues and deal with them accordingly. For example, if the project is in jeopardy of being delayed because a vendor has not provided materials on a timely basis, management can withhold payment to the vendor — or seek the services of a *new* vendor.

You might think of Project Issues as the final piece of the project puzzle. You've set up a project and created tasks to help you reach your milestones — yet your project has come to a screeching halt. Project Issues help you identify the culprit(s) by you associating specific problems with a project.

Here's how you can create the issues to be solved — hopefully you'll be able to rectify them later:

1. **Click Business Applications on the Navigation bar of your Office Live Home page and then click Project Manager.**

   The Project Manager dashboard opens.

2. **Click the Project Issues tab.**

   The Project Issues tab opens, as shown in Figure 14-8.

3. **Click the New icon.**

   The Project Issues – New Item page opens, as shown in Figure 14-9.

Figure 14-8:
The Project
Issues tab
of the Office
Live Project
Manager.

4. **Fill in the Project Issue information.**

   You only have one required field here — the name of the Project Issue. As usual, what goes around, comes around; the more details you add, the quicker (ideally) the problem will be resolved.

   - *Project Issue:* Name the issue with a word or phrase to help you identify it.

   - *Project:* Click the drop-down list to associate the task with an existing project.

- *Assigned To:* Select the Office Live user who is supposed to get the issue resolved.

- *Owner:* Select an Office Live user who is ultimately responsible for the project.

- *Issue Status:* Choose Active, Resolved, or Closed as the status of the issue.

- *Priority:* Choose High, Normal, or Low as the priority of the issue.

- *Description:* Fill in a few more details, if you have them, about the issue. With any luck, this won't be the beginning of a horror novel!

- *Category:* Assign the issue to Category 1, Category 2, or Category 3. This helps you to sort and filter your issues later. As of this writing you are pretty much stuck with those categories but hopefully later editions of Office Live will allow you to create new, more useful categories.

- *Due Date:* The date by which the issue must be resolved. You might think of this as a deadline because your chances of staying in your current position might be dead if you can't get the issue resolved.

- *Related Issues:* Talk about having issues! If you find that your other issues have snowballed into this one, large, scary issue, here's where you can attach any existing issues that haven't yet joined the pile.

- *Comments:* Guess Microsoft is thinking that having issues means you'll spend a lot of time on the psychiatrist's couch — and have lots to say. If you didn't complete your novelette in the Description field, feel free to finish it here.

5. **Click OK to save your issue and return to the Project Issues tab.**

   Hopefully you'll also save your little rear end by solving all these issues!

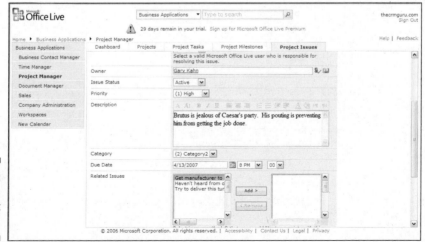

Figure 14-9:
Identify a
new project
issue.

Chapter 15

Selling Your Heart Out

· ·

· ·

Chapter 8 discusses Business Contact Manager, the business application that you can use to track potential sales opportunities; this chapter focuses on what goes into making an actual sale. You start by creating quotes and fulfilling orders. Then, once you have the customer's dollar in your hot little fist, you find various ways to keep your customer happy — and (hopefully) coming back for more! Finally, as much as you'd probably like to ignore them, your competitors are often lurking in the background, just dying to take one — or all — of your customers away from you. This chapter helps you deal with those demons as well.

Selling with the Sales Business Application

Office Live designed the Sales application to give you the tools you need to make sales to new customers — and to make sure they stay your customers.

You can get to the Sales application by following these steps:

1. **Click Business Applications in the Navigation bar of the Office Live Home page.**

   The Business Applications page opens, featuring the sales dashboard. All the Office Live Business Applications are listed in the Navigation bar.

2. **Click Sales from the Navigation bar.**

   The Sales application opens. In addition to a dashboard, the Sales application features three components in the Navigation bar: Competition Tracker, Customer Support, and Estimates.

You might feel compelled to change the content of the Sales dashboard. If that urge strikes you at any time, flip to Chapter 9 to find out how.

Estimating Your Estimates

Creating an estimate is an important part of the sales process. After all, no one wants to purchase a product now and ask the *price* later. The Estimates portion of the Sales application divides this into two pieces: creating a quote and then ordering the product.

You'll find the Estimates section easy to navigate if you follow these steps:

1. **Click Business Applications in the Navigation bar of the Office Live Home page, and then click Sales from the Business Applications Navigation bar.**

   The Sales page opens.

2. **Click Estimates from the Navigation bar.**

   The Estimates portion of the Sales application opens to the Quotations tab. Estimates consist of two tabs: Quotations and Order Information (see Figure 15-1).

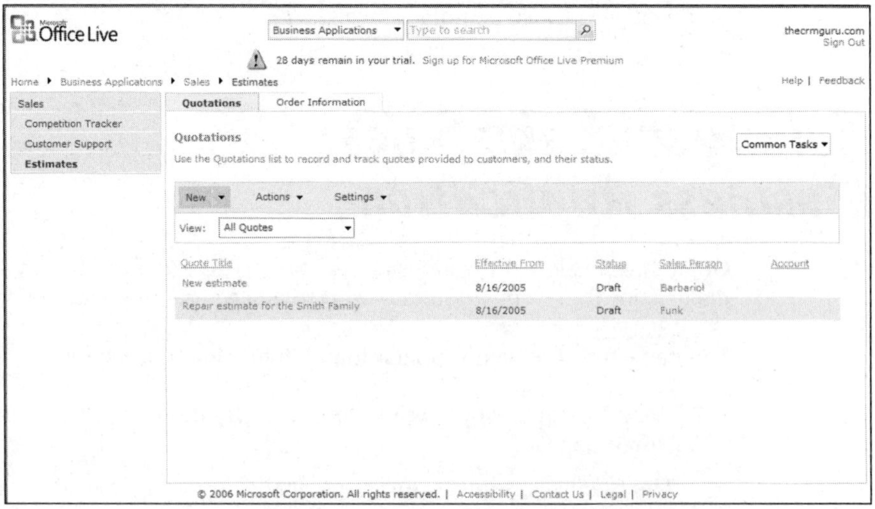

Figure 15-1:
The Office Live Quotations tab.

Can I quote you on that?

The Quotation list provides you with a list of your currently outstanding quotes. After you create a quote, you can update its status and track it through the sales process by checking its status in the Quotation list.

Providing a quote to a customer is useful in two ways. Obviously, the customer needs to know what he or she should expect to pay for your product or service. In addition, when you use Office Live, any of your employees can access the quote. That way, if you're tied up with any one of the millions of details that consume your time as a business owner, any one of your employees can step in and help close the deal.

Follow these steps to create a new quote:

1. **Click Business Applications in the Navigation bar of the Office Live Home page; then click Sales, and then Estimates.**

   You have now landed smack dab in the middle of the Quotations tab — which is exactly where you want to be.

2. **Click the New icon.**

   The New Quotation page opens, as shown in Figure 15-2.

3. **Fill in the juicy details.**

   The only required fields are Title, Account, and Effective From. Here's a rundown:

   - *Quote Title:* Supply a name or brief description for the quote so you can identify it later.

   - *Account:* You can't have a quote if you don't have a customer. Choose one of your Business Contact Manager Account records from the drop-down list.

   - *Contact:* From among the Business Contact Manager contacts, choose a specific person you're dealing with.

   - *Sales Person:* Unless your company consists of a one-person sales force — you — you'll find it helpful to choose the name of one of your employees from the drop-down list.

   - *Effective From:* The day that the offer goes into effect.

   - *Valid Through:* The last day for which the offer is valid.

   - *Status:* Choose a status of Draft, Submitted, Rejected, Accepted, or Closed.

   - *Notes:* If you have a few other things on your mind regarding the quote, here's where you can put them.

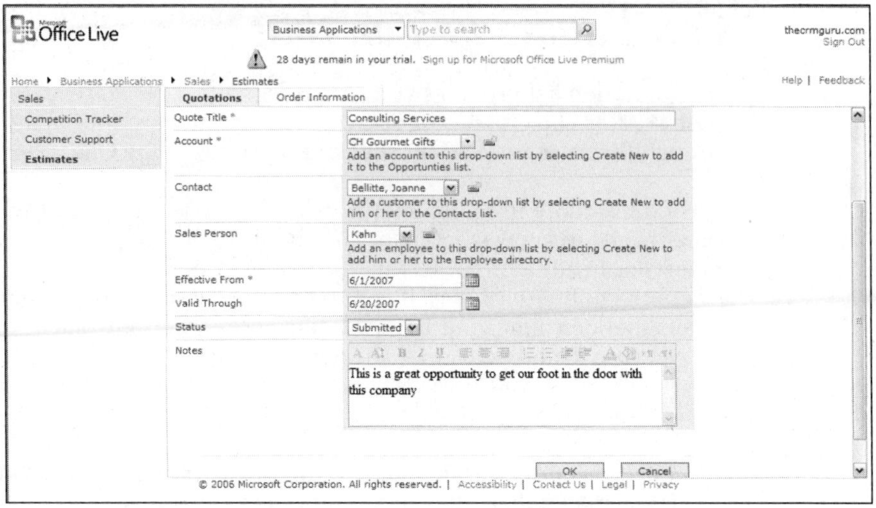

Figure 15-2:
Creating an
Office Live
quote.

4. **Click OK.**

You immediately return to the Quotation tab where you can note with pride the addition of your newly created quote in the Quotations list.

May I take your order, please?

Not everything follows along as smoothly as we hope, but you can certainly hope that your quotes will progress to a full-blown order — and help nudge it in that direction.

Typically, here's the way your business progresses:

- You do a bit of advertising to attract new business.

- You receive a call from another business that is interested in using your products or services.

- You provide the other business with a quote — which you add to the Sales application's Quotations list.

- A few days later, the other company calls back to accept the estimated costs in the quote.

Of course, a bit of price haggling occurs somewhere in the process until you and the other company see eye to eye on the negotiated price. At this point, you can celebrate your new sale — or panic about what comes next.

Inputting information into the Order Information list helps ease the transition from quote to fulfillment. You or one of your employees can view the basic quote details in the Quotations list, and then complete the sale and document the order in the Order Information list.

Here's how to add the Order Information into the scheme of things:

1. **Click Business Applications in the Navigation bar of the Office Live Home page; then click Sales, and finally Estimates.**

   The Estimates portion of the Sales application opens.

2. **Click the Order Information tab.**

   Your existing orders are in the Order Information list, as shown in Figure 15-3.

3. **Click the New icon.**

   The New Order Information page opens, as shown in Figure 15-4.

4. **Fill in the pertinent information.**

   Here's a rundown of the Order Information fields; only the Title and Product fields are required.

   - *Quote Title:* Select an existing quote from the drop-down list.

   - *Product:* Fill in the name of the product or service you are selling.

   - *Cost per Unit:* Fill in the dollar cost per unit that you are selling.

   - *Quantity:* Fill in the quantity of the items that are being ordered.

   - *Description:* Here's where you can include other important ordering information such as how you're delivering the order.

Figure 15-3:
The Order
Information
tab.

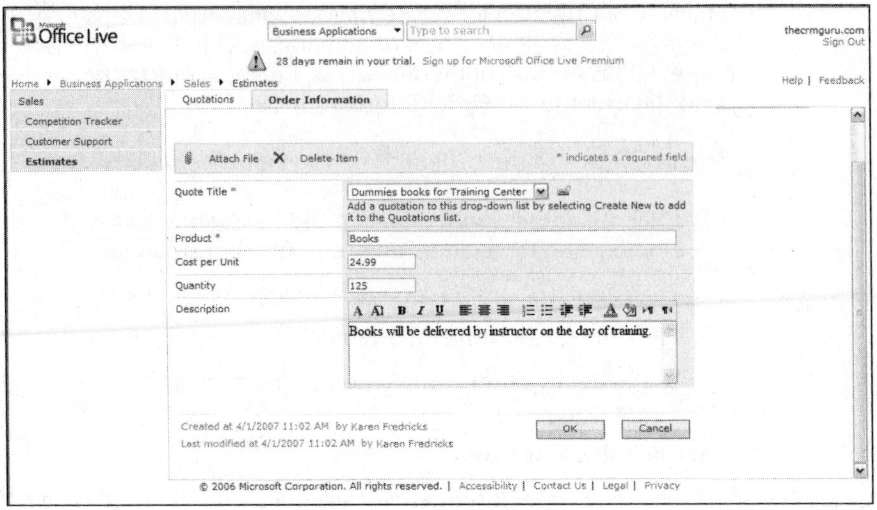

Figure 15-4:
Filling out
the Order
Information
form.

5. **Click OK to save the Order Information and return to the Order Information list.**

   When you return to the Order Information list, the total of your order shows up loud and clear in the Total Order column — even though you didn't enter any information into that field. Office Live calculates this field by multiplying the cost per unit by the quantity of units.

   To ensure that you're not spinning anyone's wheels, you'll want to go back to the original quotation and change the quote status to Accepted.

Supporting Your Customers

You received a request for one of your products, you issued a quote, and it was accepted. You then created an order and the customer received it right on schedule. But wait — why does that phone keep ringing? Uh-oh. A strident voice on the other end of the phone is breaking into your idyllic daydreams.

Sound familiar? All too often products break — and you need to fix the problem immediately. No worries, mate. Office Live is up to the challenge.

Service requests

Sometimes you can fix a customer's woes with a little patience — "That's right, Mr. Big, the product works *much* better when it's plugged in." Other times, however, you'll have to wait to resolve the problem — and the customer is going have to wait right along with you.

You can use the Service Requests list in the Customer Support application to record service requests, track resolutions, and even associate a request with a Knowledge Base article so that other people in your organization won't have to hunt for an answer should the same problem arise in the future.

Keeping track of Service Requests helps you to stay on top of any problems that arise. It also helps ensure that your employees are aware of those problems — and can help resolve them as quickly as possible.

Here's all you need to do to create a new Service Request:

1. **Click Business Applications in the Navigation bar of the Office Live Home page and then click Sales.**

   The Sales page opens.

2. **Click Customer Support from the Navigation bar.**

   The Customer Support portion of the Sales application opens with the Service Requests tab showing (see Figure 15-5).

Figure 15-5: The Service Requests list.

3. **Click the New icon.**

   The New Service Request page opens, as shown in Figure 15-6.

4. **Fill in the necessary details.**

   Only three of the fields are required: the Service Request name, Customer, and Status.

   - *Service Request:* Give the Service Request a title that makes it stand out of the crowd.

   - *Details:* Fill in the details — no matter how terrible — of the request.

- *Customer:* Choose the name of a customer from the Business Contact Manager Contacts list.

- *Product:* Using the drop-down list, choose the product that the problem pertains to.

  Not sure how to add more products to the Product drop-down list? Go to Chapter 8, where you can add products using Business Contact Manager.

- *Status:* Assign a status of Initiated, Engaged, or Closed to the Service Request.

- *Assigned To:* Using the drop-down list, select the name of the employee who is going to fix the problem.

- *Remarks:* Fill in any additional comments or steps you've taken to resolve the issue.

5. **Click OK to save your changes and return to the Service Requests list.**

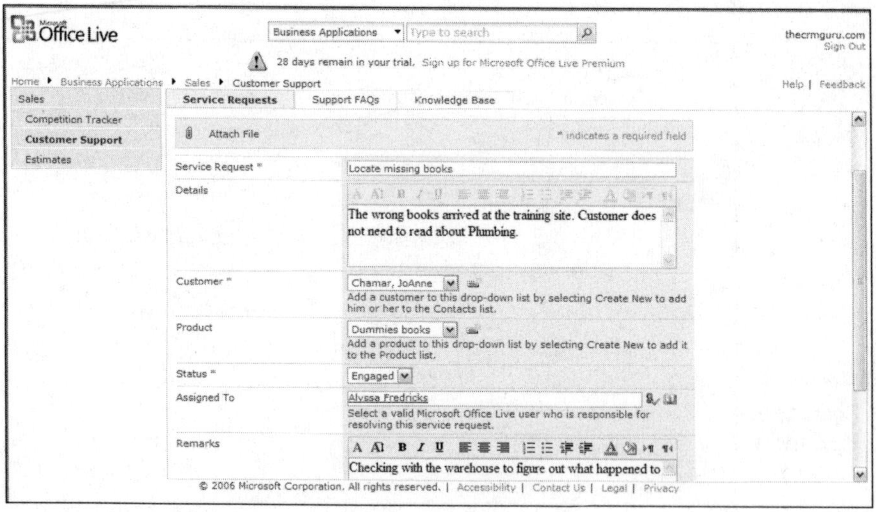

Figure 15-6:
The Service
Request
form.

The Service Request form screenshot

Just the FAQs, please

The only thing worse than working is having to do that body of work over again. Answering questions can be a case in point: The longer you remain in business and the more customers you have, the more you're going to hear the same questions — and find yourself repeating the same answers.

By creating a FAQ, the business owner (or other problem solver) can create suggested answers for typical questions so other employees can make appropriate suggestions to customers.

Follow these steps to create your very own FAQ page:

1. **Click Business Applications in the Navigation bar of the Office Live Home page; then click Sales.**

   The Sales page opens.

2. **Click Customer Support from the Navigation bar.**

   The Customer Support application opens to the Service Requests tab.

3. **Click the Support FAQs tab.**

   The Support FAQs tab opens, as shown in Figure 15-7.

4. **Click the New icon.**

   The New Support FAQ page opens; see Figure 15-8. The good news is that there are only three fields to fill in. The bad news is that you'll want to spend a lot of time with your wording so others can fully understand the questions — and, more importantly — the answers.

   - *Question:* Fill in the question; needless to say, this is a required field.

     Typically you'll want to sort your FAQs into a usable order. You might consider numbering your questions or starting all similar questions with the same phrase (such as "How do I" or "When ordering") so like items appear together.

   - *Question Details:* Here's where you can clarify the question by adding a few more details.

   - *Answer:* The answer that employees should provide to customers who inquire about the issue or service addressed in the FAQ.

5. **Click OK to save the Support FAQ and return to the Support FAQs list.**

Figure 15-7:
The Support
FAQ tab.

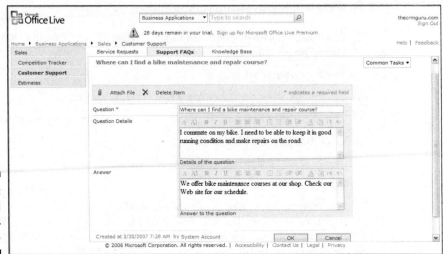

Figure 15-8:
A typical Support FAQ form.

Getting savvy with the Knowledge Base

You might think of a FAQ as a small answer to a little question, and a Knowledge Base article as a large solution to a big problem. A Knowledge Base is actually a library of articles designed to help you solve the larger support issues in your business.

For example, say that you manufacture the proverbial widget. Widgets are quite expensive, and you don't like them returned without first determining that your customer isn't causing the error. And, if the widget does need to be returned, you want to make sure that the customer packs it correctly — and sends it to the right place. By writing instructions, and then uploading them to a Knowledge Base article, you ensure that all your reps know exactly how to return those broken widgets.

Follow these steps to set up a Knowledge Base:

1. **Click Business Applications in the Navigation bar of the Office Live Home page; then click Sales.**

   The Sales page opens.

2. **Click Customer Support from the Navigation bar.**

   The Customer Support application opens to the Service Requests tab.

3. **Click the Knowledge Base tab.**

   The Knowledge Base list opens, as shown in Figure 15-9. The familiar Word and Web-page icons show in the Type Column. That's because you can either upload a document or create one online.

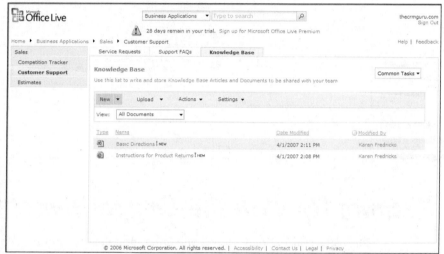

Figure 15-9:
The
Knowledge
Base list.

4. **Create the new Knowledge Base article using one of the following methods:**

   • *Click New to create an online article.* The New Wiki page (see Figure 15-10) opens. Give the article a name, type the contents of the article, and then click Create to save it and return to the Knowledge Base list. The Web icon (meaning it's a Web page) appears to the left of the new item.

   If you've already written the information in Word or another word processor, copy the contents of the article and then paste it into the Article Content area.

   • *Click Upload and then click the Browse button to navigate to the existing document.* Select the document, and click Open to upload the file to your Office Live site. The Knowledge Base form opens; give the article a name and then click OK to save it to the Knowledge Base list. A Word icon appears next to the article, indicating it's a Word documents users can download.

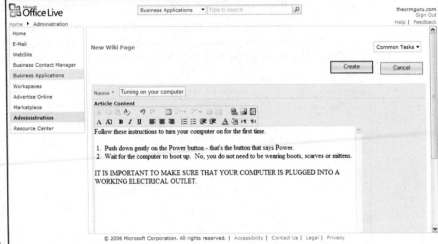

Figure 15-10:
Creating a
new
Knowledge
Base article.

Keeping Up with the Competition

The Sales application includes one other module: the Competition Tracker. The purpose of the Competition Tracker is to keep track of your competition by knowing who they are, what they sell, and any other information you can collect on them.

The Office Live Competition Tracker gives you so much information about your competition that you might start wondering whether Microsoft uses these methods to track *their* competition. If your competition consists of a Mom & Pop store down the street, you might find parts of the Competition Tracker to be overkill. However, if you want to keep up with the Joneses — or at least your competition — you'll find the Competition Tracker to be extremely useful.

Know thy competition

It's good to know who your competition is — and what they are up to. If your competition is selling a product you carry at rock-bottom prices, you might use the information to have your own sale. If your competition is running classes, you might want to start running a few of your own.

Think of the Competition tab of the Competition Tracker as the place you go for all the inside scoop on the enemy. You can tell at a glance who they are — and where to find out even more information if necessary. You can even rate them according to risk factor.

If you want to keep your eyes peeled for savvy moves by the competition, here's what you need to do:

1. **Click Business Applications in the Navigation bar of the Office Live Home page; then click Sales.**

   The Sales page opens.

2. **Click Competition Tracker from the Navigation bar.**

   The Competition Tracker application opens to the Competition tab (see Figure 15-11).

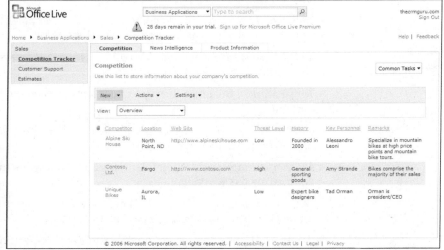

Figure 15-11: The Competition tab.

3. **Click the New icon.**

   The New Competition page appears as shown in Figure 15-12.

4. **Fill in the pertinent information.**

   Only one of the fields — Competitor — is mandatory. (A few of the fields might seem to require the hiring of some sleazy-looking guy in a dark raincoat and sunglasses to help you collect the information.)

   • *Threat Level:* Rate the competitor's as a High, Medium, or Low risk to your company.

   • *Competitor:* Supply the name of the competing company.

   • *Location:* Fill in the location of the competitor's offices.

   • *Web Site:* Jot down the competitor's Web site address.

   • *History:* Give a brief description of the competitor's history.

   • *Key Personnel:* Supply the names of the competitor's main people.

- *Remarks:* Here's where you can write a capsule summary about the competitor.

  Unless you can get your hands on the company's financial statements — or your competitor is a publicly traded company — the next three fields will probably remain blank:

- *Revenue (last year):* Fill in the company's total revenue for the last year.

- *Profit (last year):* Indicate the profit that the company showed for the last year.

- *Growth:* Give the percentage of growth that the company experienced during the last year.

- *Intellectual Properties:* If the competitor holds any patents or intellectual properties, you can write about them here.

- *R&D Focus:* Here's where you can add a synopsis of where the competitor is headed — if you know it.

- *Target Market:* Describe the type of consumers the competitor is targeting.

- *Market Shares:* Write a description based on your best guesstimate of the competitor's share of the market.

- *Number of employees:* Fill in the number of employees that the competitor has working.

- *Avg. Compensation (per month):* Fill in the average amount of money that the competitor is paying its employees.

5. **Click OK to save your changes and return to the Competition List.**

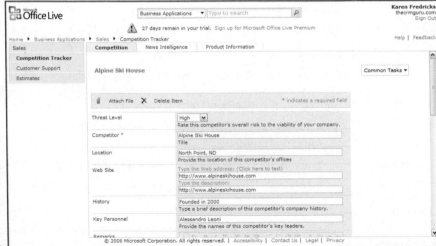

Figure 15-12: The Competition form.

Is there any intelligence in the news?

As the owner of a business, you're constantly being bombarded with information. You probably can't process all that information at once but would like to keep track of it for future reference. The purpose of the News Intelligence list in the Competition Tracker is to store news items about your competitors for exactly that purpose.

Imagine picking up the morning paper and seeing an article about one of your competitors. Maybe they've designed a new product, or maybe they're sponsoring a charity event. This might set the wheels in your head in motion because now you're thinking that now is the time to launch that new product, or to run that event you've been contemplating. Unfortunately, all too often those thoughts get buried in everyday details and hidden away — and are soon forgotten. By keeping track of them in the News Intelligence list, you can keep them handy to refer to later.

To store a piece of information on the News Intelligence list, follow these steps:

1. **Click Business Applications in the Navigation bar of the Office Live Home page; then click Sales.**

   The Sales page opens.

2. **Click Competition Tracker from the Navigation bar.**

   The Competition Tracker application opens.

3. **Click the News Intelligence tab.**

   The News Intelligence tab opens; see Figure 15-13.

Figure 15-13:
The News Intelligence tab.

4. **Click the New icon.**

   The New News Intelligence page opens (see Figure 15-14). You follow the usual drill; only the title of the News Item is required.

   - *New Item Title:* Typically, this is where you would type the headline that you read.

   - *Company:* Select the name of one of your competitors from the Competition list.

   - *Category:* Select Breaking News, Financial Info, Marketing, Product, or Other.

   - *Source:* Fill in the Web address associated with the item.

   - *Body:* You can type either the content of the news item or a summary of it.

   If an article about the news item appears on the Internet, copy the text from the Web and paste it here. Web sites — particularly those containing news items — are volatile; the article may no longer be available the next time you want to read it.

5. **Click OK to save the News Intelligence item and return to the News Intelligence list.**

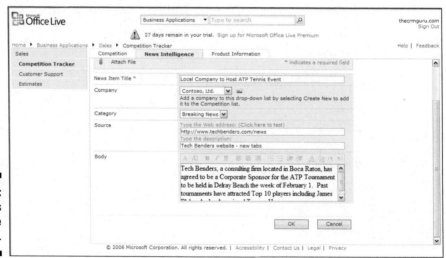

Figure 15-14: The News Intelligence form.

Keeping track of competing products

Whoever said that you can't learn from your competition never used Office Live — or at least not the Competition Tracker. There are times you'll find that your prospect purchased from one of your competitors. As painful as it might be, finding out what your competitor offered that you didn't can help you close the next deal — and the one after that and the one after that.

You can use the Product Information list in the Competition Tracker to compare your products with your competitors' products, and monitor their successes and failures.

Here's how you can start keeping track of all those competing products:

1. **Click Business Applications in the Navigation bar of the Office Live Home page; then click Sales.**

   The Sales page opens.

2. **Click Competition Tracker from the Navigation bar.**

   The Competition Tracker application opens.

3. **Click the Product Information tab.**

   The Product Information tab opens as shown in Figure 15-15.

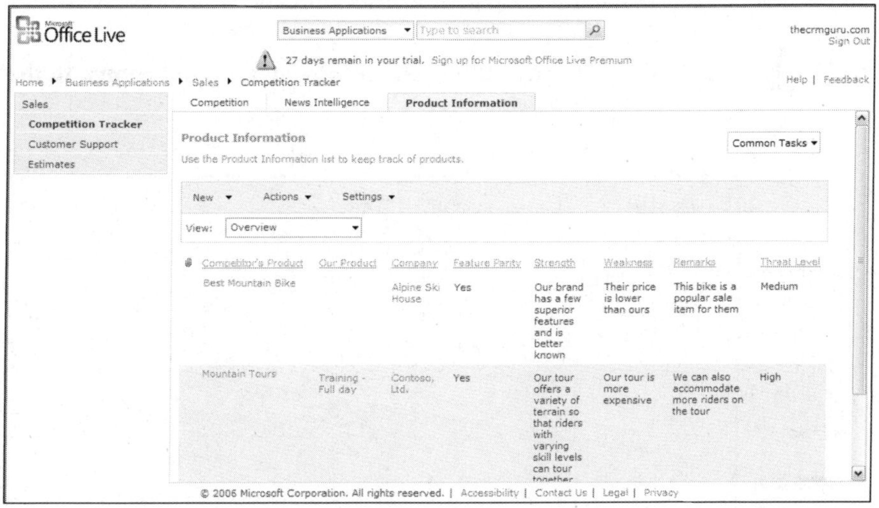

Figure 15-15: The Product Information tab.

4. **Click the New icon.**

   The New Product Information page opens, as shown in Figure 15-16. The only necessary field is the name of the competing product.

   - *Competitor's Product:* Give the name of the competitor's product.

   - *Threat Level:* Choose High, Medium, or Low.

   - *URL:* Fill in the Web site address where you can find additional product information.

   - *Price:* The price per unit of the competitor's product.

   - *Company:* Select a company from the Competition list.

   - *Our Product:* Choose your company's equivalent product from the Business Contact Manager product list.

   - *Feature Parity:* Describe how the competing product is similar to your product.

   - *Strength:* List the strengths of the competitor's product.

   - *Weakness:* List the weaknesses of the competitor's product.

   - *Marketing Strategy:* Discuss the strategy that your competitor uses to market its product.

   - *Customer Base:* Describe to whom your competitor is marketing the product.

   - *Remarks:* Fill in any other thoughts you might have about the competing product.

5. **Click OK to save the Product Information and return to the Product Information list.**

Figure 15-16:
Keeping an
eye on
competing
products.

Chapter 16

We're Going to the Library

The Document Manager is the Business Application you'll turn to when you want to share documents with the rest of your company. You can use Document Manager to store, share, and supervise the versions of your business documents. In addition, as with a traditional library, you can decide who is allowed to check out documents — and you can monitor what kind of shape they're in when they return.

Managing Your Documents with the Document Manager

If you've ever tried to e-mail a large attachment to a colleague, you know that a seemingly easy task can run into a whole bunch of snags. The file might be too big to get past your ISP — or, if you *can* send it out, it might be too big for your recipient's ISP. If the file is large, it might take a long time to transmit — during which you don't receive any other e-mail. Your recipient might have an aggressive spam blocker or company e-mail policies that prohibit receiving file attachments.

By using the Document Library you can create a library of documents and graphics that can be shared by all members of your staff. For example, you might be collaborating with a colleague who works from home on a brochure. Or perhaps you're building a custom-ordered widget for your best customer and want to show off the documentation on the specs, as well as some sketches of the final product. By placing documents and graphics in the Document Library, you — and anyone else you authorize — can view files *whenever* and *wherever* needed.

You can find the Document Manager — and add a few documents to it — by following these steps:

1. **Click Business Applications from the Navigation bar of the Office Live Home page.**

2. **Click Document Manager from the Business Applications Navigation bar.**

   The Document Manager opens to the Dashboard. The Document Manager consists of three tabs:

   • *Dashboard:* You can customize the dashboard to create a comprehensive overview of the information stored in Document Manager.

   • *Document Library:* This is where you store your documents.

   • *Picture Library:* This is where you store your graphics. See Figure 16-1.

3. **Click the tab to which you'd like to add a file.**

4. **Click the Upload drop-down arrow and choose whether to upload one or multiple documents or pictures.**

   • If you're in the Picture Library, click Upload Picture or Upload Multiple Pictures.

   • If you're in Document Library, click Upload Document or Upload Multiple Documents.

5. **Upload your file(s).**

   • If you chose to upload a single file, click the Browse button to navigate to the file location, select the file, and click Open.

   • If you chose to upload multiple files, the Upload Document page opens as shown in Figure 16-2. Use the pane on the left to navigate to the appropriate folder, check the files you want to upload in the right pane, and then click OK.

Figure 16-1: The Office Live Picture Library tab of the Document Manager.

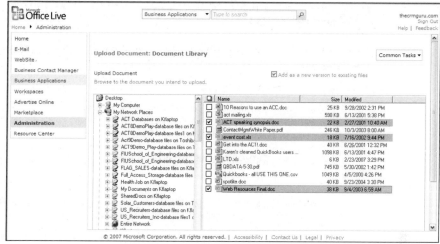

Figure 16-2:
Uploading
multiple
documents.

6. Click Check In when prompted to upload your file(s).

Like the local library, you can "check" documents in and out of Office Live so you can keep track of them if you have multiple people accessing the same document.

Depending on the size and number of files, you might have to wait a moment or two for the file(s) to upload. You end up back on the Library tab where your files now appear, ready to be accessed by the rest of your groupies.

You can add a Library page to any workspace or Business Application to hold lists of your documents, pictures and forms. Then, you can upload and download documents to and from your computer and the Document Library. Chapter 10 shows you how to synchronize those libraries with Outlook. Not sure how to add a new page to a workspace or application? Chapter 9 helps you add one quicker than you can say *open sesame*!

You can add graphic and document files to a Library page in the same way you add documents to the Document Manager tabs. However, unless you turn on the Version feature (see the "Verifying Your Versions" section later in this chapter), you're not prompted to check in the document.

Dealing with Your Documents

After you add documents and graphics to the Document Manager, you'll probably find it even more useful than the local library. You can view your files, save a copy to your own desktop, create new ones, and even send them out to your adoring masses of customers and fans.

Opening a document from the library

For your first trick, you'll want to access the files you've uploaded. If you're thinking that you'll have to paperclip this page for future reference, you're wrong — unless you just want to keep reminding yourself how easy it is to work with the Office Live libraries.

1. **Click Business Applications from the Navigation bar of the Office Live Home page; then click Document Manager.**

2. **Click the tab that contains the saved file.**

3. **Click the file you'd like to see.**

   - *Documents:* You're prompted to save or open the document. If you choose to open it, the document magically appears before your eyes.

   - *Graphics:* Right-click the graphic; choose Open to see it in an enlarged version, or Save Picture As to save it to your computer.

Creating new folders

You can create folders in any of the Office Live libraries to help you keep the contents organized in the same way you organize the files on your desktop computer. In addition, should you synchronize your Library to Outlook, the folders — and their contents — synchronize to Outlook.

After you save a document, you can't move it into another folder. Your only alternative is to open the file, save it to a new location, and then delete the original.

To create a new folder in an Office Live Library, follow these steps:

1. **Open the Library for which you want to create folders.**

   In addition to the Document Manager application, you can create folders in any of the other libraries you've created.

2. **Click the New drop-down list and select New Folder.**

   The New Folder page opens.

3. **Type the name of the folder and click OK.**

   Figure 16-3 shows several folders at the top of the Document Library.

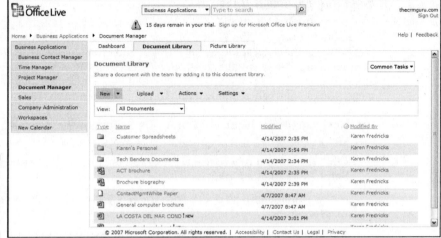

Figure 16-3:
The
Document
Library.

Sending your files via e-mail

Creating a library page has several benefits. Obviously, you can access a file when you want it — and where you want it. As a bonus, Office Live has also thrown in a couple of handy capabilities: You can send your e-mail recipients links to your documents and send graphic files directly from the library page.

Sending a graphic file

Here's all you have to do to send someone a graphics file directly from a picture library page:

1. **Navigate to the picture library that contains the graphics you want to send.**

   You'll find one in the Document Manager application. In addition, you'll find them lurking in any of the Business Applications and/or Workspaces that you might have added one to.

2. **Check the check boxes of the graphics you'd like to send.**

3. **Choose Send To from the Actions drop-down menu.**

   A new e-mail page appears — and the graphics that you had selected appear as attachments.

4. **Fill in the recipient's e-mail address, subject and add a message.**

5. **Click Send to send your e-mail — and the attached graphics — to their intended destination.**

E-mailing document links

You might find it a bit strange — at least I do anyway — that the graphics and documents libraries differ a bit. For example, the previous section showed you how to e-mail a graphic by selecting it and choosing Send To from the Actions menu. Therefore it seems only logical that the same procedure would apply for sending a document. Wrong! When you e-mail an Office Live document, you are actually sending a *link* to the document.

1. **Navigate to the document library that contains the document you want to send.**

2. **Click the drop-down to the right of the document name and select Send To⇨E-mail a Link.**

   A new e-mail message opens with the link you'd like to send in the message area.

3. **Fill in the recipient's e-mail address, add a subject, and add a message to the hyperlink.**

4. **Click Send to send your e-mail on its way.**

Verifying Your Versions

Sharing documents is a great time-saver, particularly for those of you who often work from remote locations. Often just being able to download and review a document is enough to make you a very happy — and productive — camper.

However, hosting shared documents in Office Live opens a whole other can of worms. For example, two of your employees are collaborating on new sales materials from separate, remote locations. They both download copies of the same document and make changes to it. The first employee uploads the document to the library when she is finished. An hour later, the second leader uploads his copy of the document to the library and overwrites the first employee's document. Yikes!

The folks at Microsoft must have run into the exact same problem because they came up with a great solution. *Versioning* enables you to track and manage multiple versions of the same document — and to view and recover earlier editions if necessary.

You can configure several settings that affect versioning, including which type and how many versions to retain. You can also configure settings that work hand in hand with versioning, such as requiring content approval or that users must formally check out files from the library.

This chapter focuses primarily on libraries. However, you can set up versioning for most of your lists as well. For example, you might set up a training program and want to know how often someone has tweaked the curriculum. You set up versioning for lists in exactly the same way you do for libraries. However, in lists, all versions are tracked in the same way; you won't have as many options available to you.

You can't tell your version without a number

When you enable your documents for versioning, Office Live supplies the versions numbers as you create them. In a list or in a library with simple versioning enabled, version 1 is the first version that you create or upload; each time you make a change the version number increases by increments of whole numbers, as in version 2, version 3, and so on.

When you track Major and Minor versions, the Major versions are whole numbers, and the Minor versions are decimals. For example, 1.0 is the first (and first Major) version of a file, 1.3 is the third Minor version of a file, 2.0 is the second Major version of a published file.

Sound confusing? It can be. However, you might consider creating a custom library view that includes the Version, Modified, and Modified By columns so that you — and the rest of your cronies — can see where the document stands at a glance.

Starting at the beginning is always a good thing, so start by enabling versioning:

1. **Open the list or library that contains the document(s) for which you'd like to enable versioning.**

   If this instruction sounds vague, it's because in addition to the Document Library, you might have library pages sprinkled throughout the various Office Live applications and workspaces.

2. **Choose Document Library Settings from the Settings drop-down menu.**

   The Customize page shown in Figure 16-4 opens.

   If you are setting up versioning for a list, choose List Settings from the Settings drop-down menu and a slightly modified version of this page opens.

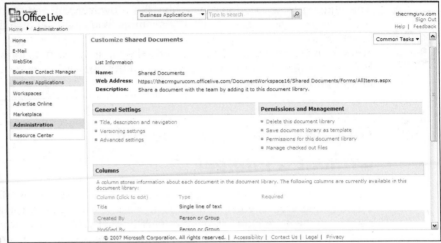

Figure 16-4:
Customizing
a Library.

3. **Click Versioning Settings in the General Settings area.**

   The Document Library Versioning Settings page opens; see Figure 16-5.

4. **Specify your Content Approval settings.**

   Select Yes for the Require Content Approval for Submitted Items option if you want to require content approval. When content approval is required, a list item or file remains in a Draft or Pending state until the head honcho/honcha approves or rejects it. If the file status is Approved, anyone with permissions to view the file can access it. If the file status is Rejected, it remains in a Pending state and is visible only to the people with permission to view drafts.

Figure 16-5:
The
Document
Library
Versioning
Settings
page.

5. Specify your Document Version History settings.

You have a couple of options here:

- *Create a version each time you edit a file in the document library:* Select No Versioning, Create Major Versions, or Create Major and Minor (Draft) Versions.

  Major versions label each new version with a whole number (1, 2, 3 . . .) and Minor changes label them with decimal numbers (0.1, 0.2, 1.1 . . .).

  When you turn on versioning for a document library, any new documents are automatically labeled as version 1.0.

- *Keep the following number of versions:* To help manage storage space — and avoid too much confusion — you can specify how many versions you want to store: Select this check box, and then type the number of versions you want to keep.

- *Keep drafts for the following number of Major versions:* Select the check box, and then type the number of drafts that you want to keep. By default, each Major version can have up to 511 drafts.

Wondering what a *draft* is? Office Live uses the term synonymously with *Minor version*.

If you limit the number of retained versions, you should make sure that contributors are aware that earlier versions are *permanently* and *automatically* deleted when the version limit is reached — as in: They're not even sent to the Recycle Bin. They're just trashed. And if you keep Minor versions, the Minor versions are deleted right along with the Major versions. For example, if you limit the versions to 20 — and your users manage to create 25 — only versions 6 through 25 are kept. Versions 1 through 5 get zapped — along with their children 1.1, 2.12, and 3.17.

6. Specify the Draft Item Security settings.

With a horde of Major and Minor versions wandering around, many of your users could end up in a major state of confusion. You might want to cut through that confusion by restricting access to Minor draft versions.

7. Indicate your Require Check Out preference.

Just like the local library requires you to have a valid library card in order to check out a book, Office Live can require you to check out documents before you can edit them. And with all those Major and Minor versions being passed around, it's probably a great idea.

8. Click OK.

Hey — check this out!

The Check-Out option prevents multiple people from making changes to the same document at the same time. When a document is subject to a lot of modification, this feature avoids the confusion that can lead to frustration and a lot of nasty words.

When you create a new file or add a new file to a library and you require check-out, you must check it in before other people can see it. Then whoever else wants to edit the document must check it out — at which point that person has sole access to the file.

When check-out is required, you cannot add files or change files (or change file properties) without first checking out the file. When you check in a file, you're prompted to provide comments about the changes you've made, which helps create a more meaningful version history.

When a file is checked out, no one can edit it except for the person who checked it out. The document's icon changes to include a green arrow, indicating that the file is checked out; when you rest your mouse pointer on it, the name of the person who checked out the file appears in a ScreenTip. Although you can still view the file, you can't change it or see the changes that someone else makes. The status of the file changes automatically to Draft.

Here's what you need to know about how to check out a document — and check it back in again:

1. **Find the library or list that contains the document, click the document's drop-down list, and choose Edit Document.**

    It's pretty easy to tell if a document requires check-out; when you try to open the document for editing, you receive the message shown in Figure 16-6.

Figure 16-6:
This
document
requires
check-out.

2. **Click OK at the prompt and begin to edit the document.**

    When you open the document for editing, it opens in the corresponding software. For example, a Word document opens in Word.

3. Save your changes.

You receive the prompt shown in Figure 16-7 asking you very nicely if you'd like to check the document back in.

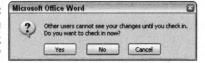

4. Click Yes at the prompt.

After you agree to check the file back in, you receive yet another prompt shown in Figure 16-8.

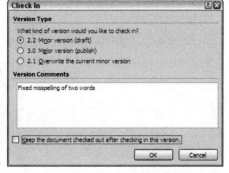

Figure 16-8:
Adding
additional
Check-In
information.

5. Fill in the Check In information and then click OK.

If a library tracks versions, you can indicate whether this is a Major or Minor revision; don't worry about the version number because Office Live handles that for you. You can also opt to overwrite the previous Minor revision, and add a comment if you'd like.

Getting the seal of approval

By default, when you check out a file it has a Pending status and is only visible to its creator and to people with permission to manage lists. When you check in a file with a Major version change, the file still has the Pending status. The file remains in a Pending state until approved or rejected by someone who has the needed permission to approve it. If the item or file is approved, the status is changed to Approved and other users can once again access the file. If the item or file is rejected, it remains in a Pending state and is visible only to its creator.

Minor versions are considered drafts that are still being developed, so they don't appear as pending items and don't require approval.

Here's how you can Approve — or Reject — a Pending document:

1. **Click the drop-down arrow of the document that requires approval and choose Approve/Reject.**

   Documents that require approval have Pending status.

   The Approve/Reject page opens, as shown in Figure 16-9.

2. **Indicate your approval status and an optional comment.**

   Here's where you can decide if the document is Approved, Rejected, or should remain in Pending mode.

3. **Click OK to save your changes.**

   The document now appears in the library with the new status, if you approved it.

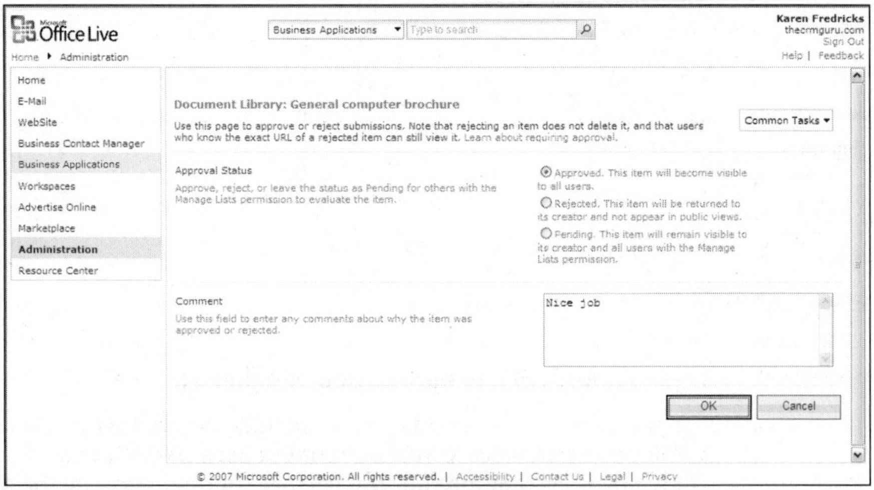

Figure 16-9:
Putting your
seal of
approval on
a pending
document.

Who says you can't change history?

The versioning process follows a very logical progression from start to finish — you create a document, check it out, make a few revisions, and then check it in. And, if you're not the head cheese, the person who is can wave the imperial magic wand and approve your document.

The main reasons to make use of versioning have to do with limiting the confusion that happens when a lot of folks put their spoons into the same dish. You can be pretty certain that somewhere along the line a conflict will occur.

Take this scenario, for example: You are working on the company brochure with another associate. You check out the brochure, make changes to it, and check the document back in. Your boss, Mr. Pinhead, approves the new brochure version — not realizing that you had inadvertently deleted the entire last page. Your associate calls that mistake to your collective attention. Needless to say, you'll want to restore a prior version — and Office Live lets you do just that.

Here's how you can view all the previous versions of a document:

1. **Click the drop-down arrow of the document for which you'd like to view the prior versions, and then choose Version History.**

   The Version History page opens (see Figure 16-10), showing you all existing versions of the document.

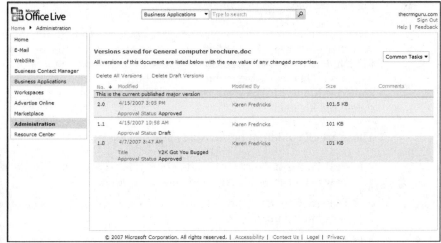

Figure 16-10:
Reviewing versions of a document.

2. **Click the version you'd like to review and click Open.**

   You can now view the prior version. But wait — there's more!

3. **Close the version you are currently viewing.**

4. **Hover your mouse pointer over the version name until the drop-down arrow appears, and then click the arrow.**

   You have a couple of choices here because you can choose to view, restore, or delete the version. If you choose to restore the version, you receive a warning telling you that you're replacing the latest version with the version you just selected.

5. **Click OK to replace the latest version, or Cancel if you'd like to think about it for a moment.**

   If you'd prefer not to wipe out the newest version, you can always view the earlier revision, copy the needed parts into it, and paste it into the newest version.

Issuing a library card

Versioning is a double-edged sword. It's a great feature because it allows multiple people to work on the same document without worrying that one user's revision will overwrite another's. However, having all those versions around can certainly confuse the masses. Typically, you'll use Major revisions to denote documents that have undergone Major changes. You typically create Minor revisions, or *drafts*, when making small modifications such as correcting misspellings and grammar.

Lists and libraries have permissions that correlate to both document versions and check-out status. An Office Live administrator can edit permission levels to include customized permission levels. Permissions help restore order to what could become a very chaotic procedure. For example, you may want someone to be able to delete *versions* of a file without having permission to delete the file itself.

These are the different permissions you can assign:

- ✔ **Full Control:** Can view and delete versions, override Check-Out, approve new and changed items, and change user access.
- ✔ **Design:** Can view and delete versions, override Check-Out, and approve new and changed items.
- ✔ **Contribute:** Can view and delete versions.
- ✔ **Read:** Can view versions.

You can specify which groups of people can view drafts of files. This setting can be different from the setting for the group of people who can view the rest of the items in your list or library (such as the Major versions of files or the approved files or list items).

When you track Major and Minor versions, you can specify whether people must have permission to edit files before they can view and read a Minor version. When this setting is applied, people who have permission to edit the file can work on the file, but those who only have permission to read the file can't see the Minor version. For example, you may not want everyone who has access to your library to see comments or revisions while a file is being edited. Here's a quick list of other major points to keep in mind about versions:

- ✔ If Major and Minor versions are being tracked and no one has published a Major version yet, the file is not visible for people who don't have permission to see draft items.

- ✔ When content approval is required, you can specify whether files that are pending approval can be viewed by people with permission to read, people with permission to edit, or only the author and people with permission to approve items.

- ✔ If both Major and Minor versions are being tracked, the author must publish a Major version before the file can be submitted for approval.

- ✔ When content approval is required, people who have permission to read content but don't have permission to see draft items will see the last approved or Major version of the file.

The following steps apply only to libraries that track both Major and Minor versions and lists or libraries that require content approval.

1. **On the Settings menu, click List Settings, or click the settings for the type of library that you are opening.**

   For example, in a document library, click Document Library Settings.

2. **Under General Settings, click Versioning Settings.**

3. **In the Draft Item Security section, under Who Should See Draft Items in This List (or under Who Should See Draft Items in This Document Library), click the group of users whom you want to enable to view drafts.**

   The option for users who can approve items is available only if your library requires content approval.

4. **Click OK.**

When content approval is required, people who have permission to read content but don't have permission to see draft items will see the last approved version (or last Major version) of the file. If Major and Minor versions are being tracked, and no one has published a Major version yet, the file won't be visible to people who don't have permission to see draft items.

Chapter 17

Who's Minding the Store?

If you own a company, you have to take care of two important areas: your customers and your company itself. This chapter focuses on the latter through the use of the Company Administration applications. Company Administration helps you with several of the more mundane aspects of running a business. You can keep track of your assets with Company Assists. The Jobs and Hiring application can help you hire — and fire — employees. You can make sure new — and existing — hires receive the necessary training with the Training module. You even have access to the Employee Directory where you can log in all the important information for each employee. Finally, it's bound to happen that you'll have to pay back some of your employees for expenses they've incurred on behalf of your company; the Expenses application is up to that challenge.

You must have an Office Live Premium account to make use of Company Administration.

Administering to Your Company with Company Administration

Microsoft feels that forty bucks a month is a small price to pay a Human Resource (HR) specialist — or at least the Company Administration in the Business Applications. You might find that your headaches start as your company grows and you begin to hire more people. And, as you add more employees, you'll probably be adding equipment for them to use — and you'll want to track the whole shebang.

Follow these steps to view the Company Administration application:

1. **Click Business Applications on the Navigation bar of the Office Live Home page.**

   The Business Applications dashboard opens.

2. **Click Company Administration on the Navigation bar.**

   The Company Administration dashboard opens, as shown in Figure 17-1. The five parts of Company Administration appear in the Navigation bar:

   - Company Assets
   - Employee Directory
   - Expenses
   - Jobs and Hiring
   - Training

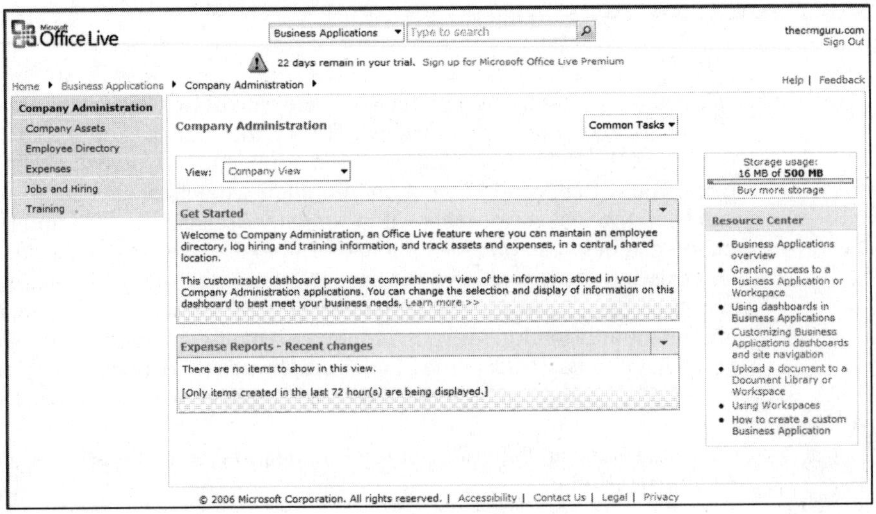

Figure 17-1: The Company Administration dashboard

Saving Your Assets

Although the Company Assets portion of the Company Administration application doesn't take the place of your accountant, it can make your life — and his or hers — a bit easier. By tracking your assets using the Company Assets module, you can build a very basic balance sheet. In addition, your employees can make formal requests for assets that they would like you to purchase in the future.

Use the Asset Requests list when one of your employees is lusting after a snazzy new laptop or shiny new delivery truck — and is hoping you'll purchase it for your company (and, ahem, *somebody's* benefit). When you've purchased it, you can add the asset to the Manage Resources list found in the Time Manager application (see Chapter 13), and your employees can check out the asset when they need it.

Listing your assets

The Company Assets page is divided into two tabs: Assets and Asset Requests. It only stands to reason that you must *own* an asset before you can *borrow* it. Follow these steps to start tracking your assets:

1. Click Business Applications on the Navigation bar of the Office Live Home page and then click Company Administration.

2. Click Company Assets in the Navigation bar.

The Assets list opens, as shown in Figure 17-2.

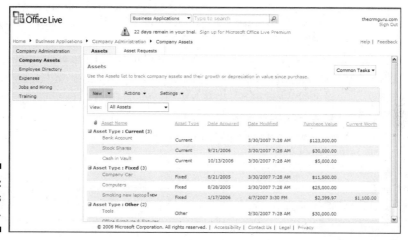

Figure 17-2:
The Assets list.

3. Click the New icon.

The Assets – New Item page opens; see Figure 17-3.

4. Fill in the information that you have about the asset.

There are a number of fields to fill in. Do your best to enter as many of them as you can.

- *Asset Name:* Give a name to the asset. This field is required.

- *Asset Type:* Choose Other, Current or Fixed. Assets are grouped according to type on the Asset List. You much choose an asset type.

- *Serial:* Enter the serial number.

- *Picture Thumbnail:* Add a link to a picture of the asset on a Web site.

- *Date Acquired:* Show the date on which you purchased the asset (required).

- *Purchase Value:* Indicate the cost of the asset when you purchased it (required).

- *Book Value:* Fill in the current value of the asset after depreciation; you might need your accountant to help you with that one. You might also need some help from your therapist because depreciated value can be quite depressing!

- *Lifespan:* Indicate the length of time you think you'll be using the asset.

- *Depreciation:* Add the yearly depreciation rate percentage.

- *Current Worth:* Show the current value. Calculate this value by taking the book value and subtracting any liabilities you might have, such as a bank note. This is a required field.

- *Location:* Here's where you indicate the physical location of the asset.

- *Assigned To:* Give the name of the lucky employee who is in possession of this asset so you'll know who to blame if the asset disappears. (Just kidding. Maybe.)

- *Intended Use:* Show what you plan to use the asset for.

- *Additional Information:* If you have any other additional information about the asset, here's the place to put it.

5. **Click OK to save your changes.**

    Your new asset is now sitting proudly among the rest of your assets on the Asset List.

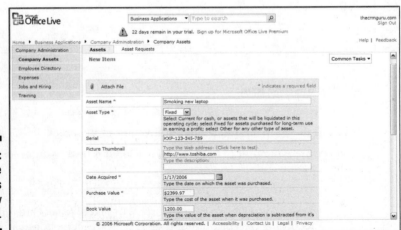

Figure 17-3:
Giving the
details
about a new
asset.

Requesting an asset

After an asset or two is added to the Asset Requests list in the Company Assets application, you can track requests for them. Alternatively you can use this list to track assets usage. For example, say one of your employees is hot to trot over a high-end laptop. You buy it, only to discover that he is the only one requesting to use it. When he suggests (a year later) that you really need to purchase a *second* laptop, you might just have a few second thoughts.

Here's how you go about putting in a request for an asset:

1. **Click Business Applications on the Navigation bar of the Office Live Home page and then click Company Administration.**

2. **Click Company Assets in the Navigation bar.**

   The Assets list opens.

3. **Click the Asset Request tab.**

   The Asset Request list opens, as shown in Figure 17-4.

Figure 17-4:
The Asset Request list.

4. **Click the New icon.**

   The Asset Request – New Item page opens; see Figure 17-5.

5. **Fill in the Request form.**

   All the fields are required except for the Description field.

   • *Asset Name:* Choose the asset from the drop-down list. You might chuckle a bit if you see items like "Bank Account" or "Cash in

Registers" because all of the company assets appear in the list. Don't worry — chances are pretty good that the boss will turn down your request to borrow the bank account for your trip to South America.

- *Assigned To:* Choose the name of the employee who is requesting to use the asset from the drop-down list.

- *Request Status:* Select a status of Not Started, Pending, In Progress, Deferred or Completed.

- *Start Date:* Enter when you'd like to start borrowing the asset.

- *Target Fulfillment Date:* Fill in when you'll return the asset.

- *Description:* Add any additional comments you might have about your request.

6. **Click OK to save your request.**

   You return to the Asset Request list. Hopefully all your wishes, er *requests*, will be granted.

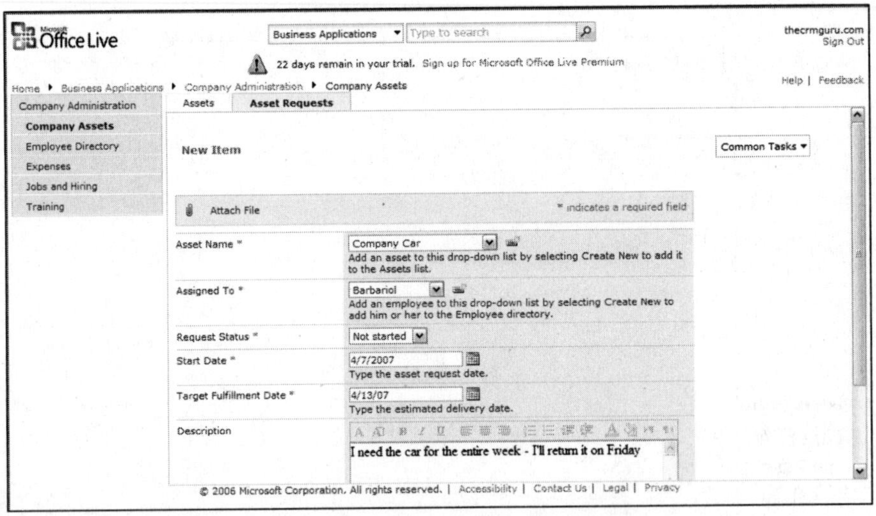

Figure 17-5:
The Asset
Request
form.

You Can't Direct Your Employees without a Directory

Company Administration includes an Employee Directory where you can add all the vital statistics about each of your employees. Or, if you share the Employee Directory with your staff, they can update their own information should it change — or access approved information about other employees.

You can assign various levels of access rights to a site. If you're not comfortable allowing your employees full access to the Employee Directory, you might assign them Reader access so they can view the information but can't change it. If you're not sure how to do that, take a gander at Chapter 3.

Here's how you can add another name to the Employee Directory:

1. **Click Business Applications on the Navigation bar of the Office Live Home page and then click Company Administration.**

2. **Click Employee Directory in the Navigation bar.**

   The Employee Directory opens.

3. **Click the New icon.**

   The Employee – New Item page opens, as shown in Figure 17-6.

4. **Fill in as many details as you have about the employee.**

   There are a lot of fields to add here; fortunately, most of them are self-explanatory. The only mandatory field is Last Name.

5. **Click OK to save your changes and return to the Employee Directory.**

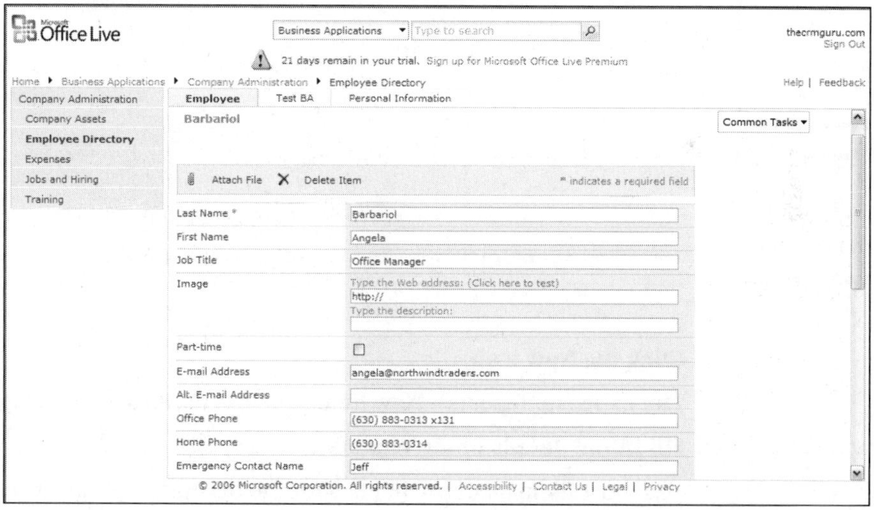

Figure 17-6: Adding an employee to the Employee Directory.

So Exactly How Much Did You Spend?

Employees should use the Expense Reports list in the Expenses application to track details about their out-of-pocket expenses. For example, one of your employees might be traveling out of town to see a client. She purchases a ticket online with her personal credit card. While there, she might wine and dine the client. On the way home, she may pay for airport parking. Rather than handing you a cocktail napkin with the total reimbursable amount scrawled on it, she can log each expense into the Expense Reports list so you *both* have an exact record of all those company-related expenses.

Adding expenses to the Expense Report is the easy part; getting the boss to reimburse you for them can sometimes be a bit more difficult:

1. **Click Business Applications on the Navigation bar of the Office Live Home page and then click Company Administration.**

2. **Click Expenses in the Navigation bar.**

   The Expense Reports tab shown in Figure 17-7 opens.

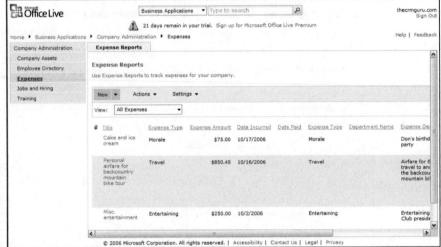

Figure 17-7:
The Expense Reports tab.

3. **Click the New icon.**

   The Expense Reports – New Item page opens, as shown in Figure 17-8.

4. **Fill in the details of the expense.**

   You must fill in all of the fields with the exception of the Date Paid, Department, Expense Description, and Comment fields.

   - *Title:* Give a brief title to the expense that identifies it. For example, you might use something like "Chicago Business Trip" or "Recent Office Supply Purchases."

   - *Expense Type:* Select Travel, Training, Entertaining, Equipment, Morale, or Other. Needless to say, Morale will probably be your favorite category; after all, those double lattes do a lot to boost your morale — and your heartbeat!

- *Status:* Choose New, Pending, Paid, or Deferred.

- *Employee:* Select the name of the employee requesting the reimbursement.

- *Department Name:* Include the department of the employee who incurred the expense.

- *Expense Amount:* Fill in the amount that you're requesting.

- *Date Incurred:* Show the date of the expense.

- *Date Paid:* The boss or bookkeeper can fill in the Date Paid when they (hopefully) pay you.

- *Expense Description:* Add an optional description of the expense.

- *Comment:* Add any additional comments you might have such as "A lot of coffee makes me work faster" or "I have a bad back, which requires that I fly only First Class."

5. **Click OK to save your changes and return to the Expense Reports list.**

    At this point it's appropriate to cross your fingers and hope that the boss won't consider a $450 dinner for two "excessive."

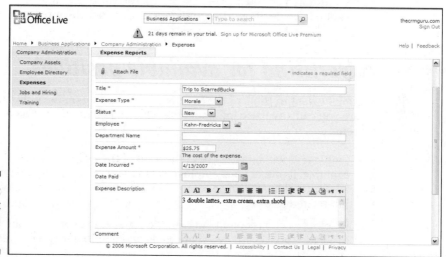

Figure 17-8:
Filling out
an Expense
Report.

Hanging Out the Help Wanted Sign

If you watch *The Apprentice*, you're familiar with the long interview process that goes into hiring a new employee. You can probably visualize The Donald going into his Office Live account, adding notes about the various candidates. In case you're wondering where he's tracking all that information, my guess is he's using the Jobs and Hiring application to guide him through the hiring process. (Well, okay, he might have other methods. But if he isn't using this application, he's missing a bet.)

You get to the Jobs and Hiring application by following these steps:

1. **Click Business Applications on the Navigation bar of the Office Live Home page.**

2. **Click Company Administration on the Business Application's Navigation bar.**

3. **Choose Jobs and Hiring from the Company Administration Navigation bar.**

    The Jobs and Hiring application opens, with the Requisition tab showing.

The Jobs and Hiring application has three tabs:

- ✔ **Requisitions:** This list shows all the available job openings.

- ✔ **Candidates:** This list displays the applicants who have applied for the various positions.

- ✔ **Candidate Feedback:** This list shows the various comments that your staff has made about the candidate throughout the interview process.

Advertising for available positions

You might want to think of the Requisitions list as an online bulletin board where you can advertise job openings. This can be helpful for a variety of reasons:

- ✔ Employees feel like they're in the loop of the hiring process. For example, if one of your employees is swamped, knowing that management is looking for an assistant will go a long way toward alleviating job-related stress.

- ✔ Employees can recommend candidates, saving expenses that would otherwise go toward newspaper ads and employment agencies.

- ✔ The company can promote in-house hiring by allowing existing employees to have the first crack at interviewing for existing positions.

- ✔ HR folks have an idea of what their workload is going to look like; for example, if the company has six positions open for seasonal help, they know they're going to be plenty busy!

You get to the Requisitions tab and post a job opening by following these steps:

1. **Click Business Applications on the Navigation bar of the Office Live Home page and then click Company Administration.**

2. **Choose Jobs and Hiring from the Company Administration Navigation bar.**

   Voilà. You're on the Requisitions tab.

3. **Click New to post a new job opening.**

   The Requisitions – New Item page opens as shown in Figure 17-9.

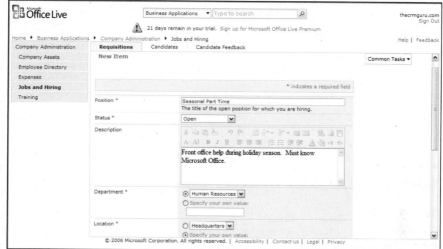

Figure 17-9:
Creating a
new job
listing.

4. **Fill in the information about the job.**

   About half the fields are mandatory; required fields have red asterisks next to them.

   - *Position:* Give a brief description of the open job.

   - *Status:* Select Open, Offer Made, Offer Accepted, Closed, or Cancelled.

   - *Description:* Add an optional description of the open position.

   - *Department:* Choose Human Resources or fill in your own department.

   - *Location:* Indicate which branch is doing the hiring.

- *Start Date:* Enter the date on which the new hire is to start.

- *Hiring Manager:* Choose the employee who is in charge of the hiring process.

- *Priority:* Select High, Medium, or Low.

- *Assigned To:* Choose the employee responsible for filling the new position.

- *Comments:* Add any additional comments you might have.

5. **Click OK to save your changes and return to the Requisitions list (see Figure 17-10).**

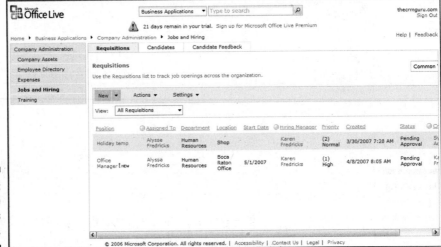

Figure 17-10:
The Requisitions list.

Not all candidates get elected

After you post your various job openings on the Requisitions list, the next step is to start interviewing candidates. The Candidates tab allows you to tie the applicant to the opening. By changing the way in which you view the Candidate list, you can see whether one candidate interviewed for several positions, or get a list of all candidates who interviewed for the same position. Should you fill one position, you might decide to place an eligible candidate in another position.

Chapter 9 shows you how to change the list view by adding columns and changing the sort and filter.

Follow these steps to look at the Candidate list:

1. **Click Business Applications on the Navigation bar of the Office Live Home page and then click Company Administration.**

2. **Choose Jobs and Hiring from the Company Administration Navigation bar.**

   The Requisitions tab opens.

3. **Click the Candidates tab.**

   The Candidates tab snaps to attention, revealing the contents of the Candidates list (see Figure 17-11).

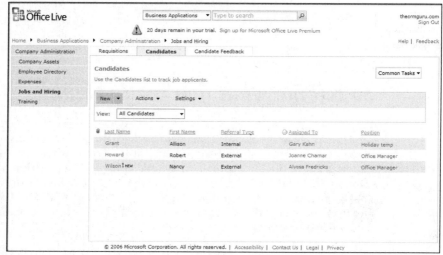

Figure 17-11: The potential job candidates list.

4. **Click the New icon.**

   Candidates – New Item page opens, as shown in Figure 17-12.

5. **Fill in as much pertinent information as you can.**

   Here the only required fields are the candidate's Last and Full Name fields, as well as the Referral Type field where you indicate how you came to find out about the candidate. Optional are the Notes field (where you can fill in any additional comments you have about the candidate) and a Position field (where you can indicate the job position that the candidate is hoping to fill). The remaining fields allow you to fill in the candidate's contact information (address, phone number and e-mail).

6. **Click OK to save your changes and to return to the Candidates list.**

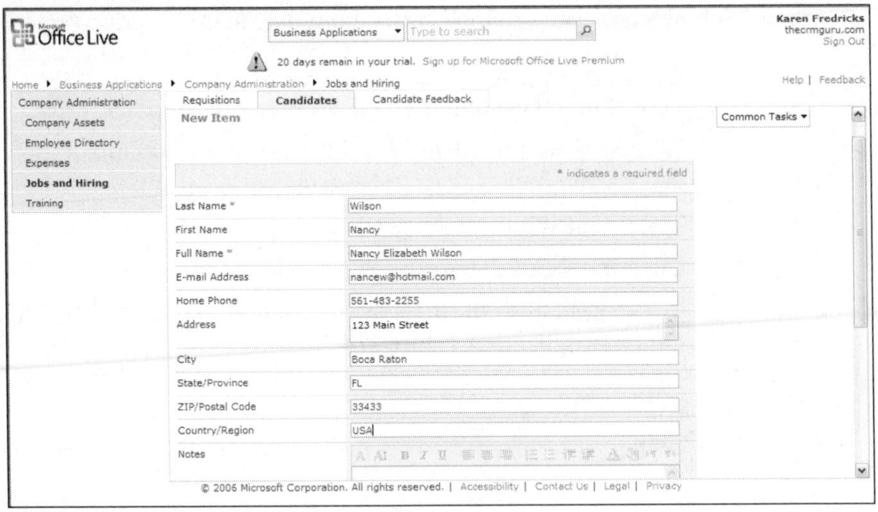

Figure 17-12:
Adding
information
about a
new job
candidate.

So tell me what you really think

The proceeding sections discussed the first two stages of the job hiring process. You use the Requisitions list to advertise open positions; your employees can refer to the Requisitions list for details when they receive inquiries about the job opening. As people apply for the position, you add them to the Candidates list so that you can match people to positions. The final stage before declaring that a candidate is "hired or fired" is to collect feedback on the candidate from the various individuals in the organization who are involved in the hiring process.

The Candidate Feedback list is the area where employees can log in their praises, comments, or trepidations about a candidate. By viewing all this feedback, the person who is ultimately responsible for hiring new applicants can make an informed decision. For example, a business owner might interview a dozen candidates for the position of Office Manager. She narrows the decision down to two candidates but doesn't have a strong feeling as to which person she should hire. However, her employees are overwhelmingly in favor of one particular candidate; she decides to hire that person because it is obvious to her that the candidate will fit in well with the rest of her employees.

Here's how you can find the Candidate Feedback list — and start entering a few opinions of your own:

1. **Click Business Applications on the Navigation bar of the Office Live Home page and then Company Administration.**

2. **Choose Jobs and Hiring from the Company Administration Navigation bar.**

   The Requisitions tab opens.

3. **Click the Candidate Feedback tab.**

   The Candidate Feedback tab opens, revealing the Candidate Feedback list.

4. **Click the New icon.**

   The Candidate Feedback – New Item page opens, as shown in Figure 17-13.

5. **Share the important details about the candidate based on your interview.**

   There are only four fields to enter here, three of them required. Ironically, the only field that is *not* required is the Title field — a field which generally *is* required in the rest of the Business Applications.

   - *Title:* Enter the title of the position the candidate is applying for; you'd think that you could choose it from your open positions but that is not the case.

   - *Candidate:* Select the candidate's name from the drop-down list.

   - *Recommendation:* You have two choices here: Hire or Do Not Hire.

   - *Notes:* This is probably the most important field because this is the spot where you can supply your feedback about the candidate.

6. **Click OK to save your feedback and return to the Candidate Feedback list.**

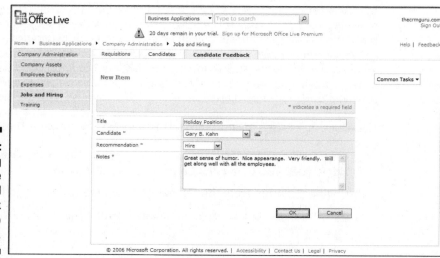

Figure 17-13:
Supplying some personal feedback on a job candidate.

Going Back to School

Congratulations! You survived the hiring process. You've posted job openings, found a bunch of interested candidates, had several of your key employees interview them — and hopefully you hired the most promising person.

Now comes the fun part. The new person arrives on his first day of work, unpacks a few pictures and other pieces of personal memorabilia, and spreads them around his office — and then sits staring blankly at the phone, wondering how to make an outgoing phone call. Or maybe you've just stocked a brand new product that you're sure is going to be a hit during the holidays. Unfortunately, your existing employees don't have a clue about how to *turn on* the hot little product — much less how to turn your customers on to the hot new product.

You might also decide to run classes for your customers and prospects. Perhaps you want to offer seminars to introduce folks to your new product line. Or maybe you own a computer shop and want to run classes on various popular software programs.

Whatever your training needs are, Office Live is up to the challenge. The Company Administration application includes a Training module designed to help you with your training needs. The Training consists of two parts: creating a course and tracking enrollments.

Setting up a training program

The Training Courses tab of the Training module helps you plan your course by making sure that you cover all bases. Before you advertise a training program, get your ducks in a row and your details in order. A very smart person once told me that when planning an event — and inviting people to attend — it's important to make sure to include information on the "who, what, where, when, and why." After all, attendees probably want to know such basics as *who* is teaching the course, *what* the course will focus on, *when* and *where* it is — and *why* they should attend.

Keeping your classes organized is surprising easy if you follow these steps:

1. **Click Business Applications on the Navigation bar of the Office Live Home page and then click Company Administration.**

2. **Choose Training from the Company Administration Navigation bar.**

   The Training Courses tab appears, as shown in Figure 17-14.

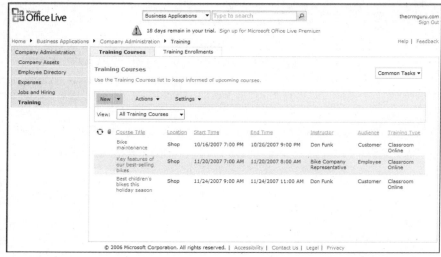

© 2006 Microsoft Corporation. All rights reserved. | Accessibility | Contact Us | Legal | Privacy

Figure 17-14:
The Training
Courses tab.

3. **Click the New icon.**

   The Training Courses – New Item page opens; see Figure 17-15.

4. **Start designing your training course.**

   Although only the Course Title and Date fields are required, I recommend that you fill in all the fields; otherwise you might find yourself teaching a class with no attendees.

   - *Course Title:* Supply a title for the training course. If the course is mandatory for your employees, you have a captive audience and the title doesn't make a whole lot of difference. If you're going to be selling the class, however, then you'll want to come up with an eye-catching name.

   - *Training Type:* Select Classroom Online, Conference Call, or Other.

   - *Instructor:* Fill in the name of the course instructor.

   - *Audience:* Select Employee, Customer, or All from the drop-down list.

   - *Location:* Show the physical location of the training course.

   - *Start Time:* Indicate the starting date and time.

   - *End Time:* Indicate the ending date and time.

   - *Description:* Here's where you can write a great description of the course — particularly if you gave it an intriguing title that might not have been absolutely clear.

- *All Day Event:* Select this check box if the event will last all day and doesn't have a specific starting or ending time.

- *Recurrence:* The frequency with which the course is offered, if it is offered more than once, such as monthly or annually.

- *Workspace:* Select this check box if you'd like to automatically create a public workspace that attendees can use to learn more about the course.

5. Click OK to save your changes and return to the Training Course list.

Your new course now appears with any other classes you've already scheduled.

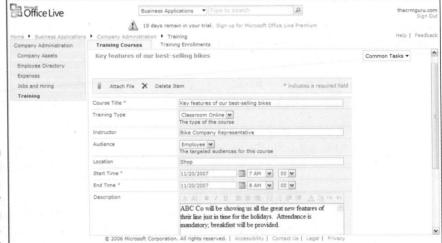

Figure 17-15:
Creating
a new
Training
Course.

Taking attendance

A popular movie contends that if you build it, they will come — but when it comes to holding training courses and seminars, I'm not sure that's the best advice to follow. If you've ever planned a seminar only to find that no one shows up, you'll know exactly what I mean.

Knowing who your attendees are in advance of a seminar is important for a number of reasons. Obviously, you don't want to run a course if no one has signed up to take it. You might also find that it isn't cost-effective to run a seminar for a small crowd. Alternatively, your offering might prove so popular that you have to limit attendance to ensure you'll have ample supplies and seats for all attendees.

Tracking enrollments can also help you plan for future courses. You might find, for example, that your Beginners course did not attract many participants — but when you relabeled the same course and called it Intermediate, its popularity increased dramatically. Along the same lines, you might find that certain instructors or topics are more popular than others.

To start tracking course enrollments, follow these steps:

1. **Click Business Applications on the Navigation bar of the Office Live Home page and then click Company Administration.**

2. **Choose Training from the Company Administration Navigation bar.**

   The Training Courses tab appears.

3. **Click the Training Enrollments tab.**

   The Training Enrollments tab opens.

4. **Click the New icon.**

   The Training Enrollments – New Item page opens, as shown in Figure 17-16.

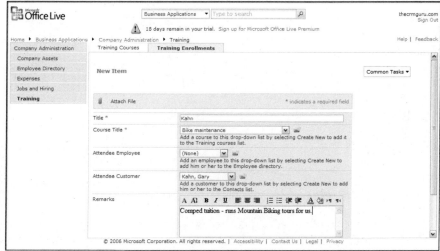

Figure 17-16:
Entering information for a new enrollment.

5. **Fill in the information you have about the enrollee.**

   Both the Title and Course Title are required fields.

   - *Title:* Fill in a title for the attendee; typically you'll use the person's name. (I'm not quite sure why this field, rather than the Attendee name field, is required.)

   - *Course Title:* Select the name of the training course from the drop-down list.

- *Attendee Employee:* Select the name from the drop-down list if the attendee is an employee.

- *Attendee Customer:* Select the name from the drop-down list if the attendee is a customer.

The Attendee fields draw list items from existing Office Live contacts. If you'd like to add a new contact to either list, click the Create New icon to the right of the appropriate drop-down list. You can add a new contact — and continue working on the Training Enrollments form.

- *Remarks:* Provide any comments that you have about the attendee. Rather than writing "nice guy" you might consider using this fields for comments like "Tuition paid in full."

6. **Click OK to save the Enrollment and return to the Training Enrollment tab.**

You might want to sort the list according to Course Title, or create separate views for each course. Not sure how that's done? Turn to Chapter 9!

Part V
The Part of Tens

The 5th Wave   By Rich Tennant

"Try putting a person in the photo with the product you're trying to sell. We generated a lot of interest in our Office Live Web site once Leo started modeling my hats and scarves."

In this part . . .

Every *For Dummies* book has a Part of Tens section — and this book is no exception. Because Office Live represents both a brand new product and a novel technology, you probably have lots of questions. This section is designed to answer a slew of them. You find out about Software as a Service, and why this technology is here to stay. You get a better understanding of the types of people who can benefit from Office Live, and finally you get a handle on some ways Office Live can help you grow your business.

Chapter 18

Ten Cool Benefits of Office Live

*T*echnology can be a double-edged sword. On the one hand, it can make your life much easier and more productive. On the other hand, it can be extremely difficult to master the current technology — much less keeping up with all the new technology that is constantly thrown at you. You've probably been lured — whether by television ads or a few of your nerdy relatives — into thinking that it's easy to master technology. You might also have a friend or two who seems to really talk the technology talk and always knows about the latest gadget or advancement.

What you might not realize is that those geeky types have spent hours of their time — and probably buckets of their money — mastering technology. Okay, the geek may sound really impressive at a cocktail party (if he ventures out of his computer room long enough to attend one), but chances are still pretty good that he hasn't mastered anywhere near as much of that arcane stuff as he's led you to believe. And that friend of yours who seems to know so much about technology might have an entire IT department at his disposal that is ready to leap in should something go awry.

Fear not, technically challenged reader: You are not alone. In fact, even Microsoft recognizes that you are actually in the vast majority of computer users; that's exactly why Microsoft developed Office Live.

Office Live is particularly well suited to the small-business community because it allows small businesses to compete against the "big boys" without having to spend an arm and two legs on an IT department. Whether your company has a handful of employees or you're the one that wears all the hats Office Live can offer you simple, low-cost solutions to your technology nightmare.

It was hard for me to limit myself to ten items — but here's my list of the ten features of Office Live that you'll particularly want to focus on to increase your bottom line.

Use a Suite Is Sweet

If you're new to the business world — or at least you entering the business arena for the first time as the owner of one — you'll definitely want to give Office Live a look. There is a plethora of software that every business needs — and scheduling, contact management, word processing, and accounting programs are at the top of that list. Unfortunately, as the list of business start-up costs gets larger and larger, the software budget gets smaller and smaller. And that's assuming you can install all the software and get it working on your own, without the help of the IT guru. And (of course) you'll want to keep your fingers crossed while you hope desperately that all the software will play nicely together once you've installed it.

Office Live comes with all the business tools necessary to run a business. Just as importantly, they all actually work together correctly. And, because Office Live is a Microsoft product you're pretty much assured that it plays nicely with your other Microsoft products including Word and Excel.

Using a suite of products has another advantage as well. In general, the cost of purchasing a suite of products is a fraction of the cost of buying each product separately.

Create an E-mage

Image is everything — at least, it is if you're trying to create the image that you are a big time operator. Depending on the nature of your business, your customers may not need to come to your office. If this is the case, you probably want to project the image that you are operating from large, imposing corporate headquarters rather than from a tree house in your backyard. Having customized e-mail addresses is one way to help you project that image.

Here are a few of the ways in which Office Live e-mail helps improve your business persona — and your bottom line:

- **Look professional:** You e-mail address might be the first contact that you have with a potential client. If you're counting pennies you might have signed up for a free e-mail account with Yahoo! or Google. You might even have an AOL account that you're using. These programs are fine if you're looking to attract customers who are also looking to pinch a few pennies. But if you're looking to attract corporate clientele, these free e-mail addresses scream "small-time operator." That potential client will view you as a little guy rather than as a sophisticated player in the corporate world.

- **Promote your Web site:** You may not realize it but some of your potential clients might use your e-mail address as a means of scouting out you — and your business. If you use a Yahoo! or AOL e-mail address your prospective customer has little else to go by when it comes to learning about your company. However, having an e-mail address such as me@mycompany.com allows that prospect to scurry over to your Web site — www.mycompany.com — and find out the latest and greatest about your company.

- **Multiple e-mail addresses:** As your company grows and you hire employees, you'll need additional e-mail addresses. You might also want to add e-mail addresses to help you route incoming messages to the correct place; for example, you might use the info@mycompany.com address to help you sort through incoming inquiries and service@mycompany.com to help you take care of customer-service issues.

- **Creative marketing:** E-mail is not just an alternative form of communication; it also offers the potential for much more imaginative marketing. You can include links to your Web site — or even to specific products and services on your site. You can use e-letterheads to enhance your image.

- **Cost-efficient advertising:** E-mail is pretty much instantaneous. You can keep your customers informed of changes to your business immediately without having to wait for the printer to print a brochure and someone to spend the time folding and stuffing your missive. E-mail is cheap — you don't have to spend money on stamps, printing, and envelopes.

Considering that even the basic version of Office Live lets you set up 25 e-mail accounts — for free — it seems silly *not* to use at least one of them.

Have a Web Site

A Web site can benefit your business in a million ways. Okay, you caught me — there might not be a million but there sure is a huge bunch of ways that a Web site can help grow your business. The Web provides all the benefits of other advertising media — with several added features:

- **Advertise and reach prospects in a cost-efficient way.** You can provide your prospective clients with up to date information about your business 24/7. Visitors can help themselves to that information; anytime, anywhere, and as often as they wish — making them more likely to do so. Best of all, the cost to you is negligible — no matter how often prospects download your information.

- **Establish your company as a global player.** Information about your company is available to prospects around the world. Compare that to the coverage you get when you take out an ad in that yellow phone book or advertise in the local paper.

- **Compete at the same level as that of the "big boys."** Your Web site is your virtual office — decorate it as you'd like to present your image. Reinforce corporate and brand identity. Look professional — even if you run your business sitting in your living room wearing your footed pajamas!

- **Interact with customers.** Include forms for customer service. Collect e-mail addresses and other information through the use of prospect forms. Conduct market research through the use of surveys on your Web site. Set up individualized portals for your clients to build customer relations.

- **Attract more business.** More and more people now buy on the Internet because of the convenience and the variety of goods that are available. For your part, these orders translate into reduced transaction costs because you don't need to have someone personally jotting down each new order. Add in the capability to integrate with your Accounting software and you can laugh all the way to the bank.

Have a Cool-Looking Web Site

If many of you consider yourselves technologically challenged, I can empathize with that — because I'm artistically challenged.

Traditionally, the best way to create a neat-looking Web site has been to hire a really good graphic artist. Once that's done, you spend a couple of hours explaining the image you'd like the artist to create for your business. Then you wait a week or two, pay a very large bill for services rendered, and decide that nope, the image isn't exactly what you wanted.

Microsoft has taken the pain out of designing a Web site by hiring a small armada of professional designers to create virtually hundreds of Web page designs. You can easily scroll through the designs and choose the one that strikes your fancy. Then, if you're still not entirely satisfied, you can personalize the design by changing the color and fonts, and by adding your own logo or graphics.

Your Web site isn't the only portion of Office Live that you can customize. You can create custom, personalized sites where your clients can access shared information.

Become an Internet Marketing Guru

Unfortunately, "if you build it, they will come" is not an adage that applies to Web sites. Once you build your really cool looking Web site you have to attract the masses to it. Office Live realizes that and has added a number of tools to send you on your e-marketing way.

Office Live provides you with some simple tips for getting your site indexed. Once indexed, Office Live provides you with the direct links for submitting your site to the major search engines. You even get hints about ways to entice other sites to link to your site.

Pay-per-click is an effective, although somewhat confusing, way to drive potential customers to your Web site. AdManager, available in all versions of Office Live, makes this somewhat complicated form of advertising bullet proof. Basically, you use adManager to create and purchase pay-per-click ads that appear on the Windows Live Search site. If you sell widgets, for example, you would determine how important it is to have your site appear at the top of the list when a prospect searches for the keyword *widgets*. You pay for that "ad" each time a prospect clicks on your link. AdManager helps you determine a monthly advertising budget and you can decide how much to pay for each keyword click. When your ad-click costs match your set budget, your ad stops appearing in the sponsored ad areas for that keyword.

Connect to Your Office Anywhere

If you are just dipping your big toe into the technology pool, Office Live is a great way to get your feet wet. Many newbie computer users "assume" that it's easy to work remotely. Then, once they realize how truly complicated it can be, they give up entirely. Enter Office Live, sporting several ways you can turn your office into a traveling road show. Microsoft has truly taken the difficulty out of these processes. The result is that you can look like a technology superstar.

Prior to Office Live you could access your office data from your home or other remote location but it wasn't an easy — or inexpensive — proposition. You could hire an IT geek to install a Virtual Private Network (VPN) or Remote Desktop Sharing. You could purchase a service such as GoToMyPC and pay a monthly service charge. With the basic version of Office Live, however, you can access your e-mail, contacts, and calendar from wherever your travels take you.

Telecommuting is the trend of the twenty-first century. Employers love the concept of spending less money on office space and furniture, and employees love the idea of spending fewer hours commuting to work each day. Prior to Office Live if several people needed to access the company data, you took out a mortgage and installed something along the lines of a terminal server — which meant that you needed to purchase an expensive new computer in addition to the services of your local IT geek. *Ka-ching!* Office Live is truly an extraordinary value when you compare its price tag to the traditional cost of sharing data. For a mere $20/month, ten of your cohorts can access your data anytime — from anywhere. Bump it up to $40/month and you have 20 people accessing your most critical data — or at least the parts of it that you're willing to share with them.

Have 24/7 Access to Your Outlook Data

Microsoft Outlook 2007 is probably the database of choice for most businesses. Companies love to interface Outlook with a variety of other Microsoft Office products. The Microsoft Office Live Essentials and Premium subscriptions enable you to access all your Microsoft Office Live Mail information through Outlook so you can manage your e-mail, contacts, calendars, and tasks, even when you're not connected to the Internet.

The Outlook Connectivity feature also enables you to do the following:

- You can access, send, and receive e-mail messages from multiple Microsoft Office Live Mail accounts in Outlook.

- You can also create multiple calendars and sets of contacts in Outlook. All of this information synchronizes with Office Live. Any changes you make in Outlook — deleting messages, adding new contacts, scheduling a meeting — are automatically synchronized and reflected in your Microsoft Office Live Mail account.

- Changes you make while working offline are synchronized to Office Live when you connect to the Internet.

- You see all that Outlook data from virtually anywhere by accessing your Office Live account.

Improve Your Communication Techniques

For many of you, creating and maintaining a Web site is a big step. Therefore, the idea of also building a private internal Web site or *intranet* might seem daunting, to say the least. Before Office Live, mostly large organizations with a full-time IT staff had intranets. Now smaller companies can enjoy the benefits of intranets by creating Workspaces in Office Live:

- ✔ Your employees can use a Workspace to find information as needed rather than being swamped with e-mails.

- ✔ You can create a company workspace to post company policies, procedures, weekly reports, and memos to keep everybody on the same page.

- ✔ You can reduce the need for meetings by allowing project information to be viewed by employees, customers, and vendors.

- ✔ Your customers can access up-to-date information about their accounts or projects.

- ✔ Your accountant can use a Workspace to view financial information created in Microsoft Office Accounting Express 2007.

Share Your Files

If you've tried to send files via e-mail lately, it's more than likely you've run into a few snags like these:

- ✔ The files are too large to send via e-mail.

- ✔ Your recipient's e-mail program prevents him or her from downloading the file.

- ✔ You have to repeat the process each and every time you make a change to the file.

If you need to share files with your customers or other members of your staff, you'll find that Office Live is a great solution. After you upload files to your Office Live site your other users can view or download them whenever — and wherever — they want. And, should your company be collaborating on shared documents, an Office Live Premium account allows you to check those files in and out so that you can keep track of the various versions of the document.

Access Your Accounting Info Online

If you are just starting a business — or using a shoebox to store your accounting information — you'll want to download Office Accounting Express 2007 if for no other reason than that it's free with all versions of Office Live. The beauty of Office Accounting Express 2007 is that you can enter basic information online and then share it with other Office products. It's an ideal way to let your remote users create quotes and invoices, track their expenses, and create timesheets. Office Accounting Express also stores your customer, vendor, and employee information in one place. You can even allow your accountant to access your books through Office Live.

Although Office Accounting Express is not a complete accounting package, it does do a few cool tricks that even higher-end accounting packages can't:

- ✓ Integrates with the ADP payroll service to help you take care of payroll.

- ✓ Lists items on eBay, tracks sales activity, and downloads and processes orders.

- ✓ E-mails invoices and allows payment via PayPal.

- ✓ Checks your customers' business credit through Equifax.

Chapter 19

Ten Types of People Who Could Benefit from Office Live

So just who should be using Office Live? Everyone! Okay, easy answer. But it's hard to imagine someone who couldn't make use of Office Live — particularly when you consider that you can use it absolutely free of charge. In this chapter, I give you a few portraits of the people I feel can benefit the most from Office Live.

The Big Cheese

You might wonder why a successful CEO or business owner might decide to switch to Office Live. Well, chances are pretty high that if you're a CEO you're the one who has to deal with the problems when the company software runs amuck. And, because your signature appears on the bottom of every company check, you're the very person who has to pay for those problems. For you, the Big Kahuna, Office Live represents a low-cost, easy way to keep your finger on the pulse of your company.

If you're a CEO, you wear a lot of hats and have lots of responsibilities. You want to know what your salespeople are doing and how your customers are being treated. You want to make sure you're retaining your current customers by providing an excellent level of customer service and developing lasting relationships. You're looking for software that can automate your business and make your employees more productive in less time. If you're in charge of a large business, you want to improve communication among your employees. If you run a small business, you have to rely on a small staff to complete a multitude of tasks. Office Live helps accomplish all these goals.

The New Business Owner

If you're a new business owner, you want to hit the ground running. You probably view technology pretty much as a necessary evil, and would prefer to focus your time — and money — on bringing cold, hard cash through the doors.

If you were creating a technology shopping list for a brand new business, you'd probably want to include these essentials:

✔ A computer with Internet access

✔ A word processor

✔ An e-mail address

✔ Accounting software

✔ Contact-management software

✔ A Web site

Although Office Live won't provide you with a computer, and you'll have to purchase a word processor, it provides you with all the other tools you need to start your business. You will find the cost of Office Live Basic — free — to be extremely appealing. And, as the business grows, Office Live can grow right along with you. You can upgrade to Office Live Essentials when the need for a better system of contact management arises. Then you can move up to Office Live Premium when you have a few new employees into the mix. And, if you're working on a tight budget, you'll love the fact that you only have to pay for services you actually use.

Anyone on the Go

If you're a road warrior, you're easy to identify. You know where to locate the best cup of coffee in the airports of all the major cities. Your car is starting to resemble your office; in fact, you often search through your car to locate critical pieces of information. You have a cell phone permanently embedded in your hand — and a silver gizmo stuck to your ear. You know that you are the ultimate road warrior if a little old lady throws you a dollar and mumbles something about deaf lunatics.

Office Live is intended for people like you because:

✔ You can synch Office Live to your smart phone or PDA.

✔ You can access your Office Live data as long as you have Internet access.

✔ You can synchronize your Office Live data to your Outlook data.

The Real Brains behind the Operation

Whether your boss calls you a Secretary or an Administrative Assistant, no one doubts that you are the glue that keeps the business together, the bright blue sports drink that keeps the business up and running. You are the underpaid and overworked individual who is responsible for:

- ✔ Knowing, organizing and scheduling everyone's activities
- ✔ Knowing the contact information of every employee, customer, prospect, and vendor that has ever come into contact with the business
- ✔ Finding files and documents that no one else seems to be able to put their hands on
- ✔ Remembering the birthday of the boss's significant other

In general, you're lucky just to find all of this pertinent information, much less have the time to enter it into multiple computers. Office Live provides you with a great tool to keep yourself — and everyone else — organized.

The Sales Star

If you're a salesperson, your goal is make money. Your boss measures your success in dollars and not in how much information you manage to enter into a database. In fact, if you're tied to your computer, you're probably *not* focusing on the task at hand.

With Office Live, you can run around the planet making sales — and access contact information when and where you need it. For example, you can access a list of your products from any computer, rather than having to carry around all that pricing information in your briefcase — or in your head. You can enter in new contact information, or even generate a quote, while sitting in the airport if necessary. In the meantime, the home office knows exactly what you're up to without your having to send a mountain of e-mail or make a ton of phone calls.

The Disorganized Person

You can spot a disorganized person walking down the street — the ones with sticky notes stuck to their foreheads and papers trailing out of their briefcases. If that sounds like you, I'll hazard a guess that your address book — if you have one — is hardly legible because a half-inch film of white-out covers many of the phone numbers. Your calendar isn't in much better condition — if you can find it.

Because you're disorganized you often mumble to yourself, trying to remember some tidbit of information that escapes you just now. This adds to your stress level, makes people look at you strangely, and scares young children. While Office Live won't miraculously transform you into Mr. Clean or Ms. Super Exec, it does give you a place to keep your "stuff." It'll keep your addresses and schedule in one neat place — and you won't even have to find a place in some messy closet to store the software box!

The Efficient (or Lazy?) Person

There's nothing wrong with being lazy. In fact, there is a very thin line between being efficient and being lazy. Think it through: Lazy people know it's more fun to play than to work. Therefore the goal of all lazy people should be to do more work in less time so they have more time left over to play. So don't think of yourself as *lazy* — you're *efficient*! Provided you can make it work.

So just how can Office Live help you to become that lazy, er, *efficient* individual? Well for one thing you'll have all the pertinent information that you need, right at your fingertips. You'll never miss a meeting, and you'll have a clear list of all the tasks at hand. And, if you're assigned to work on a major project, you'll be able to perform my favorite trick — delegate the job to someone else!

The One-Person Business with Champagne Tastes and a Beer Budget

Office Live was truly created for the little guy who wants to compete with the Big Guys — but doesn't necessarily have the budget to do so.

Big Guys — or, in this case, large corporations — generally have the following things in common:

✔ Big, fancy Web sites that they spend a lot of money to host and update

✔ Multiple e-mail addresses for their various employees and departments that their IT department maintains

✔ Expensive contact-management and accounting software and a full time staff install and update it

✔ Remote hosting solutions so they can access their information online

✔ An outside vendor for their e-marketing needs — offering everything from Web site optimization and pay-per-click to mass e-mailing

✔ IT departments that create private "portals" for their best customers

You'll notice that all these features have two things in common: They give the business a professional appearance and cost a whole lot of money. Coincidentally, Office Live offers you those same exact services for just pennies. Hmm, you might just think Microsoft knows a thing or two about running a large, professional organization — and the size of the pockets of smaller businesses.

The Techno-Phobic

If you find yourself nodding *yes* as you read the following list, you just might suffer from technophobia:

✔ The thought of *having* a Web site for your company is way beyond your realm of expectation.

✔ The thought of *creating* a Web site is enough to send cold chills down your spine.

✔ If your customers want more information, you're more than happy to stuff your latest price sheet into an envelope and send it to them — as soon as you pick up your new brochures from the printer.

✔ Telephones were invented long before computers. By golly, if your customers want to get in touch with you, they can pick up the phone.

✔ Your marketing campaign consists of an ad in a big yellow book.

✔ Your IT needs are handled by the high school kid who lives down the street — the one who seems to "know a lot" about computers.

If you're a bit of a technophobe, your head probably spins any time someone starts to rhapsodize about the latest technological advances. You might even feel threatened by technology; after all, you've been running your business using your trusty abacus with no problems so far.

Well, worry not, my friend: This software has your name written all over it. Office Live simplifies some very complicated tasks. You set up just about every feature through a wizard. There are lots of online instructions. The interface is very intuitive and easy to navigate. And you don't have to dive into the whole thing head first. Start by utilizing the features that are most important to you — and build from there.

The Leader of the Pack

So far, much of this book has been devoted to the entrepreneurial spirit who runs — or is thinking of starting — a business. However, I just can't miss the opportunity to share some of the neat ways that Office Live can benefit your personal life as well as your business life. I wouldn't be surprised if you feel the way I do about that: There is absolutely no reason that a club or organization should not be taking advantage of a free Office Live Basic account.

Does this scenario sound familiar to you? You race home from work, pick up the kids from soccer practice, throw some dinner on the table, and then sit down to call the first five members of the soccer team to remind them that it's their duty to provide the refreshments for Saturday's game. You hunt around for the team roster, which you find wadded up in the glove compartment of your car. You get involved in a long conversation with the third person on your list, who just has to catch up on the latest gossip. In the meantime the first person you called is already calling you to tell you that her kid won't be at the game on Saturday. By that time you're too tired to call the next people on your list, and go to bed frustrated.

With Office Live you could set up a game schedule that is accessible to all members of your team. They could also see any schedule changes any time they occur. The schedule could include other team responsibilities as well — saving the need to print instructions and/or make a ton of phone calls.

Contact information could be kept online, again eliminating the need for photocopying and telephoning. Team members could actually update their contact information should it change or be incorrect. What a concept!

You'd probably find a team Web site unnecessary — unless, of course, you'd want to post pictures of the team and include a few words about the various people who have contributed to the success of the team.

If you're the Official Team Mom and/or Coach, you'd probably love to have a team e-mail address — particularly if your boss frowns at the thought of your receiving personal e-mail at work.

Chapter 20

Ten Questions You Might Have about Software as a Service (SaaS)

*I*t's one thing to learn about all the great features in Office Live. It's quite another to understand the underlying technology that goes into a product like Office Live. In this chapter, you discover everything you've always wanted to know about Software as a Service (SaaS) — but were afraid to ask!

Am I Going Where No Man Has Gone Before?

Your dad might have encouraged you not to be the first on your block to buy the newest version of a snazzy sports car. Dad's advice still holds true — especially with software. If you've ever had the misfortune of purchasing the latest and greatest software product the moment it hit the shelves — and being among the first to tussle with the inevitable bugs — you know exactly what I mean. Therefore you might be a bit hesitant to rely on SaaS to run your business. Don't be.

Probably the best-known example of SaaS is Salesforce.com. This company has been in business for over five years, and has nearly a half million users. NetSuite, an on-demand service that provides e-commerce, accounting, and contact-management capabilities, has been in business eight years.

Is This Just Another Fad?

I can think of two reasons why Office Live is here to stay:

✔ Microsoft doesn't venture into new territory without doing some home-work. Traditionally, even the Microsoft products that experienced grow-ing pains were tweaked relatively quickly.

✔ In general, computer users are cheap. They want a lot of bang for their bucks — whether it comes in hardware or software. As businesses real-ize what Office Live can do for them — and get a look at the small price tag — don't be surprised if they turn to products like Office Live in droves.

As long as the quality and reliability of SaaS solutions continues to improve, the appeal of SaaS isn't going to go away.

Will SaaS Make an ASP Out of Me?

Technology is confusing. Acronyms are confusing. When you combine the two, it's no wonder if your eyes start to spin faster than a Las Vegas slot machine. If you do any research on SaaS you might come across the term *application service provider* (ASP). SaaS and ASP are fairly similar approaches; it's easy to get them confused. But here's the difference . . .

ASPs became popular in the 1980s and 1990s. These companies hosted third-party, client-server applications. Basically, ASPs transferred a customer's applications and data into mini-data centers. Unfortunately, most ASPs didn't have much — if any — knowledge of the applications they were hosting so customers still had to have in-house expertise to make sure the applications were working properly correctly. The high cost of building and maintaining data centers and running customer specific applications caused many ASPs to shut down. That didn't exactly bode well for prospective customers.

Rather than just hosting a customer's application and data, the SaaS approach (of which Office Live is a prime example) offers applications specifically designed to be hosted over the Internet. Although each customer has his or her specific data, all customers are basically using the same software. In addition, the customer doesn't have to buy the software and then pay for a provider to host it. The customers can decide which people have access to specific fea-tures, and can tweak the software via a Web interface to fit the needs of their companies. An SaaS can generally be up and running very quickly — which makes it a great alternative to both shrink-wrapped software and ASPs.

Is SaaS Too Sassy for Me?

Has this ever happened to you?

- ✔ You purchase a brand new piece of software, wrestle the shrink wrap off the package, fish out the installation instructions — and realize you're stuck at the bottom of yet another "learning curve."

- ✔ You start to install the software, and watch as the completion indicator slowly makes its way across the screen, pauses . . . and then grinds to a complete stop.

- ✔ Once the new software is installed, you click one of the icons and wait for something to happen. When nothing does, you call Tech Support, get routed to an overseas call center, and are told that you'll have to download and install a "bug fix."

- ✔ You call for help with your software and find that it's out of date and no longer supported — meaning you're going to have to shell out big bucks for the latest version to replace the version that was already working well for you.

- ✔ Your existing software is not "compatible" with software you're already using on a daily basis.

- ✔ You purchase a new computer and need to install your existing software on it — but you can't find the installation CD. Or the license number. Or both!

- ✔ You purchase a new version of your existing software, install it, and find that a few items have been "overwritten" — like your accounting information for the last five years.

These problems don't exist for users of SaaS software. There is no software to install — if you can access the Internet, you can use the service. Any bug fixes appear automatically the next time you log on to the software. There is no cost when you upgrade; new features are added automatically. You don't have to reinstall the service on a new computer, or buy a new version of the software to use it with a new operating system.

Will SaaS Save Me Money?

SaaS is a very economical solution, particularly when compared with the cost of traditional software. Among the areas of savings are these:

- ✔ Because the manufacturers of SaaS save money on everything from packaging to shipping costs, the savings get passed along to you.

- ✔ Many business applications charge a yearly licensing fee. So far this has not been the case with SaaS.

- Basically, the only thing you need to run SaaS is Internet connectivity and a Web browser. That means you're not going to have to call in extra IT staff — or spend hours wrangling with new software yourself.

- Most SaaS applications charge by the number of users, the features you use, and the size of your data. Because it is so easy to change your usage you only pay for what you're using. Most upgrades — and downgrades — can be carried out immediately.

What's the Catch?

While there is no such thing as a free lunch, Microsoft is coming fairly close to giving you a Blue Plate Special. Although there is no "catch" to the Office Live pricing plans, Office Live does translate into some benefits for Microsoft:

- Microsoft is entering fairly late into the SaaS arena, and has some catch-up work to do. Consequently the pricing for Office Live is very competitive.

- Microsoft is offering the Basic service to users for free, funding it with the advertising that's included on Basic sites. Microsoft is, in effect, betting that their advertising revenues will be sufficient that they can keep offering the Basic service at no cost.

- Microsoft is hoping that although many consumers and small business start with the free Basic subscription, they will soon upgrade to a paying subscription. After all, $20 a month is a small price to pay for additional functionality — and an escape from advertisements!

- Microsoft is counting on the fact that Office Live will entice users to stick with Microsoft products. They're targeting small to mid-size businesses. These businesses represent a growing portion of the business community — one that has often been overlooked in the past. By offering small businesses the same functionality and services used by larger corporations — for a fraction of the cost — they're banking on getting these companies to stick with Microsoft as they grow.

- Office Live offers Microsoft additional sources of revenue. As your business — and Web site — expand, you might need to pay more for bandwidth or additional users. Or you might be enticed to try adManager, which comes with an additional price tag.

- Unlike traditional software, there are no packaging and shipping costs tied to a SaaS.

Are There Hidden Costs?

Theoretically, Microsoft could raise — or lower — the pricing at any time. Because the subscriptions are charged monthly rather than annually, however, you can bail immediately if a price increase occurs. However, Microsoft is hoping that if you start with the Basic subscription you will soon outgrow it and want to add additional services. Fortunately, expanded service comes with a very small price tag.

Here are some areas that might start costing you a bit extra each month:

- **Upgrading:** If you're yearning for a few extra features, they're available — but keep in mind that you'll have to pay for them.

- **Space:** Office Live comes with ample storage space. If you build a Web site with dozens of pages, graphics, and files, however, you might need to purchase additional storage space.

- **Bandwidth:** Bandwidth becomes a factor if tons of users all hit your Web site at the same time. If you start experiencing a lot of visitors, Office Live politely informs you that Microsoft is going to start charging you for additional bandwidth.

- **Additional users:** If your business grows beyond twenty users, you're hit with an additional charge.

- **Additional mailboxes:** Need more mailboxes? Office Live is happy to supply you with them — for an additional charge.

- **adManager:** Pay-per-click is available with all levels of Office Live. There is an additional cost for this service, although you can determine your advertising budget in advance.

What if I Don't Need All the Features?

Office Live tries to address nearly every business-application need. The feature structure is pretty simple. All versions allow you to set up multiple e-mail accounts, create a Web site, use Office Accounting Express 2007, and share your information with multiple users. Office Live Essentials throws Business Contact Manager into the mix, along with some extra storage space. The Premium version includes Project Manager, Sales Manager, Document Manager, Time Manager, and Company Administration.

Typically, larger corporations have more use for the team-oriented collaboration tools in the Essentials and Premium versions of Office Live. If you're running a small company and organization, and want to make use of only one of the Premium features (such as the Document Manager), you have to pay the same price as someone making use of *all* the Premium features.

Can the Really Big Guys Use SaaS?

Companies of all sizes can take advantage of Office Live. Office Live is extremely scalable — you can increase your usage of the program as the need arises. If you need more than twenty users, you can add more (in groups of five at a time) for a mere $12 per group. Best of all, your users can log on to Office Live immediately without having to wait for software delivery and/or the company IT person.

Salesforce.com was one of the first SaaS vendors. To date they have attracted a number of clients including AOL Time Warner and United Way. Considering that the basic edition of Salesforce.com starts at $90 a month — and only allows for five users — the exodus to Office Live should happen rather quickly.

Can the Little Guys Use SaaS?

Office Live is aimed at small and midsize businesses and the home user. And if you think that Office Live is too complicated, think again. Many of these users have already used AOL, or have automatically updated their McAfee or Symantec antivirus software online. They have a handle on what to expect.

SaaS works pretty much the same way as other online services. All software upgrades and bug fixes are free, with no installation required. You access new features and enhancements instantly when you log on to the service. You always have the latest version of the software. And you'll never have to call the IT guru to help you!

Index

• Q •

• R •

registering domain name, 21, 24
rejecting Pending document, 276
Reminder area (calendar), 120, 125–126
removing
 alert, 154
 contact, 62
 data in datasheet, 162
 e-mail account, 46–47
 image from Web site, 83
 information, 13–14
 item from workspace, 186
 keyword, 112
 Office Live account in Outlook, 191–192
 page from workspace, 176–178
 project item, 236
 record from Business Contact
  Manager, 158
 workspace, 172–173
renaming page
 in Web site, 76–77
 in workspace, 178–179
renewal fee, 26
Reply or Forward window, 53–54
replying to message, 53–54
requesting asset, 285–286
Requisitions tab (Jobs and Hiring), 290–292
Requisitions–New Item page, 291
Reset Account Password page, 48
resetting e-mail password, 47–49
resource
 adding, 230–231
 scheduling, 229–230
Resource Center (Home page), 33
Resources tab (Time Manager), 224,
  229–231
Resources–New Resource page, 231
Restore Completed message, 199
Restore Your Site page, 198
restoring
 backup copy of data, 198–199
 from Recycle Bin, 200–201
review file, transferring to accountant,
  203–204
road warrior, benefits to, 312
role, assigning to user, 36

• S •

SaaS (Software as a Service) technology
 appeal of, 318
 ASP compared to, 318
 benefits of, to Microsoft, 320
 cost of, 321
 description of, 9–10
 ease of using, 319
 as economical, 319–320
 examples of, 317
 scalability of, 322
Sales applications
 accessing, 247
 Competition Tracker, 258–264
 Customer Support, 252–258
 description of, 213
 Estimates, 248–252
sales staff, benefits to, 313
Salesforce.com, 317, 322
saving
 document, 268
 Web site design, 70
Schedule Activity page, 119–120
Schedule and Reservations tab (Time
  Manager), 224, 225–228
scheduler, 11
scheduling
 meeting, 118–122
 recurring event, 227
 resource, 229–230
Screen Resolutions report, 102
scrollitis, 73
search box (Home page), 33
search engine
 choosing keywords, 95–96
 overview of, 93
 submitting keywords, 97–98
 verifying site is indexed, 94–95
Search Engine Optimization tab, 95–96
Security Development Lifecycle, 12–13
security issues
 credit card information, submitting, 25–26
 versioning, 273
 workspace, 168

BUSINESS, CAREERS & PERSONAL FINANCE

Fundraising For Dummies
0-7645-9847-3

Investing For Dummies
0-7645-2431-3

Also available:

- Business Plans Kit For Dummies
  0-7645-9794-9
- Economics For Dummies
  0-7645-5726-2
- Grant Writing For Dummies
  0-7645-8416-2
- Home Buying For Dummies
  0-7645-5331-3
- Managing For Dummies
  0-7645-1771-6
- Marketing For Dummies
  0-7645-5600-2

- Personal Finance For Dummies
  0-7645-2590-5*
- Resumes For Dummies
  0-7645-5471-9
- Selling For Dummies
  0-7645-5363-1
- Six Sigma For Dummies
  0-7645-6798-5
- Small Business Kit For Dummies
  0-7645-5984-2
- Starting an eBay Business For Dummies
  0-7645-6924-4
- Your Dream Career For Dummies
  0-7645-9795-7

HOME & BUSINESS COMPUTER BASICS

Laptops For Dummies
0-470-05432-8

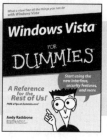

Windows Vista For Dummies
0-471-75421-8

Also available:

- Cleaning Windows Vista For Dummies
  0-471-78293-9
- Excel 2007 For Dummies
  0-470-03737-7
- Mac OS X Tiger For Dummies
  0-7645-7675-5
- MacBook For Dummies
  0-470-04859-X
- Macs For Dummies
  0-470-04849-2
- Office 2007 For Dummies
  0-470-00923-3

- Outlook 2007 For Dummies
  0-470-03830-6
- PCs For Dummies
  0-7645-8958-X
- Salesforce.com For Dummies
  0-470-04893-X
- Upgrading & Fixing Laptops For Dummies
  0-7645-8959-8
- Word 2007 For Dummies
  0-470-03658-3
- Quicken 2007 For Dummies
  0-470-04600-7

FOOD, HOME, GARDEN, HOBBIES, MUSIC & PETS

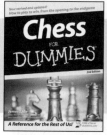

Chess For Dummies
0-7645-8404-9

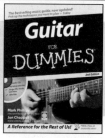

Guitar For Dummies
0-7645-9904-6

Also available:

- Candy Making For Dummies
  0-7645-9734-5
- Card Games For Dummies
  0-7645-9910-0
- Crocheting For Dummies
  0-7645-4151-X
- Dog Training For Dummies
  0-7645-8418-9
- Healthy Carb Cookbook For Dummies
  0-7645-8476-6
- Home Maintenance For Dummies
  0-7645-5215-5

- Horses For Dummies
  0-7645-9797-3
- Jewelry Making & Beading For Dummies
  0-7645-2571-9
- Orchids For Dummies
  0-7645-6759-4
- Puppies For Dummies
  0-7645-5255-4
- Rock Guitar For Dummies
  0-7645-5356-9
- Sewing For Dummies
  0-7645-6847-7
- Singing For Dummies
  0-7645-2475-5

INTERNET & DIGITAL MEDIA

eBay For Dummies
0-470-04529-9

iPod & iTunes For Dummies
0-470-04894-8

Also available:

- Blogging For Dummies
  0-471-77084-1
- Digital Photography For Dummies
  0-7645-9802-3
- Digital Photography All-in-One Desk Reference For Dummies
  0-470-03743-1
- Digital SLR Cameras and Photography For Dummies
  0-7645-9803-1
- eBay Business All-in-One Desk Reference For Dummies
  0-7645-8438-3
- HDTV For Dummies
  0-470-09673-X

- Home Entertainment PCs For Dummies
  0-470-05523-5
- MySpace For Dummies
  0-470-09529-6
- Search Engine Optimization For Dummies
  0-471-97998-8
- Skype For Dummies
  0-470-04891-3
- The Internet For Dummies
  0-7645-8996-2
- Wiring Your Digital Home For Dummies
  0-471-91830-X

* Separate Canadian edition also available
† Separate U.K. edition also available

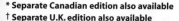

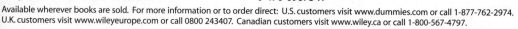

Available wherever books are sold. For more information or to order direct: U.S. customers visit www.dummies.com or call 1-877-762-2974.
U.K. customers visit www.wileyeurope.com or call 0800 243407. Canadian customers visit www.wiley.ca or call 1-800-567-4797.

WILEY

SPORTS, FITNESS, PARENTING, RELIGION & SPIRITUALITY

0-471-76871-5

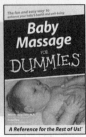
0-7645-7841-3

Also available:
- ✔Catholicism For Dummies
  0-7645-5391-7
- ✔Exercise Balls For Dummies
  0-7645-5623-1
- ✔Fitness For Dummies
  0-7645-7851-0
- ✔Football For Dummies
  0-7645-3936-1
- ✔Judaism For Dummies
  0-7645-5299-6
- ✔Potty Training For Dummies
  0-7645-5417-4
- ✔Buddhism For Dummies
  0-7645-5359-3

- ✔Pregnancy For Dummies
  0-7645-4483-7 †
- ✔Ten Minute Tone-Ups For Dummies
  0-7645-7207-5
- ✔NASCAR For Dummies
  0-7645-7681-X
- ✔Religion For Dummies
  0-7645-5264-3
- ✔Soccer For Dummies
  0-7645-5229-5
- ✔Women in the Bible For Dummies
  0-7645-8475-8

TRAVEL

0-7645-7749-2

0-7645-6945-7

Also available:
- ✔Alaska For Dummies
  0-7645-7746-8
- ✔Cruise Vacations For Dummies
  0-7645-6941-4
- ✔England For Dummies
  0-7645-4276-1
- ✔Europe For Dummies
  0-7645-7529-5
- ✔Germany For Dummies
  0-7645-7823-5
- ✔Hawaii For Dummies
  0-7645-7402-7

- ✔Italy For Dummies
  0-7645-7386-1
- ✔Las Vegas For Dummies
  0-7645-7382-9
- ✔London For Dummies
  0-7645-4277-X
- ✔Paris For Dummies
  0-7645-7630-5
- ✔RV Vacations For Dummies
  0-7645-4442-X
- ✔Walt Disney World & Orlando
  For Dummies
  0-7645-9660-8

GRAPHICS, DESIGN & WEB DEVELOPMENT

0-7645-8815-X

0-7645-9571-7

Also available:
- ✔3D Game Animation For Dummies
  0-7645-8789-7
- ✔AutoCAD 2006 For Dummies
  0-7645-8925-3
- ✔Building a Web Site For Dummies
  0-7645-7144-3
- ✔Creating Web Pages For Dummies
  0-470-08030-2
- ✔Creating Web Pages All-in-One Desk
  Reference For Dummies
  0-7645-4345-8
- ✔Dreamweaver 8 For Dummies
  0-7645-9649-7

- ✔InDesign CS2 For Dummies
  0-7645-9572-5
- ✔Macromedia Flash 8 For Dummies
  0-7645-9691-8
- ✔Photoshop CS2 and Digital
  Photography For Dummies
  0-7645-9580-6
- ✔Photoshop Elements 4 For Dummies
  0-471-77483-9
- ✔Syndicating Web Sites with RSS Feeds
  For Dummies
  0-7645-8848-6
- ✔Yahoo! SiteBuilder For Dummies
  0-7645-9800-7

NETWORKING, SECURITY, PROGRAMMING & DATABASES

0-7645-7728-X

0-471-74940-0

Also available:
- ✔Access 2007 For Dummies
  0-470-04612-0
- ✔ASP.NET 2 For Dummies
  0-7645-7907-X
- ✔C# 2005 For Dummies
  0-7645-9704-3
- ✔Hacking For Dummies
  0-470-05235-X
- ✔Hacking Wireless Networks
  For Dummies
  0-7645-9730-2
- ✔Java For Dummies
  0-470-08716-1

- ✔Microsoft SQL Server 2005 For Dummies
  0-7645-7755-7
- ✔Networking All-in-One Desk Reference
  For Dummies
  0-7645-9939-9
- ✔Preventing Identity Theft For Dummies
  0-7645-7336-5
- ✔Telecom For Dummies
  0-471-77085-X
- ✔Visual Studio 2005 All-in-One Desk
  Reference For Dummies
  0-7645-9775-2
- ✔XML For Dummies
  0-7645-8845-1

HEALTH & SELF-HELP

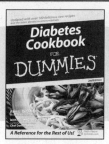

0-7645-8450-2

0-7645-4149-8

Also available:

- Bipolar Disorder For Dummies
  0-7645-8451-0
- Chemotherapy and Radiation
  For Dummies
  0-7645-7832-4
- Controlling Cholesterol For Dummies
  0-7645-5440-9
- Diabetes For Dummies
  0-7645-6820-5* †
- Divorce For Dummies
  0-7645-8417-0 †

- Fibromyalgia For Dummies
  0-7645-5441-7
- Low-Calorie Dieting For Dummies
  0-7645-9905-4
- Meditation For Dummies
  0-471-77774-9
- Osteoporosis For Dummies
  0-7645-7621-6
- Overcoming Anxiety For Dummies
  0-7645-5447-6
- Reiki For Dummies
  0-7645-9907-0
- Stress Management For Dummies
  0-7645-5144-2

EDUCATION, HISTORY, REFERENCE & TEST PREPARATION

0-7645-8381-6

0-7645-9554-7

Also available:

- The ACT For Dummies
  0-7645-9652-7
- Algebra For Dummies
  0-7645-5325-9
- Algebra Workbook For Dummies
  0-7645-8467-7
- Astronomy For Dummies
  0-7645-8465-0
- Calculus For Dummies
  0-7645-2498-4
- Chemistry For Dummies
  0-7645-5430-1
- Forensics For Dummies
  0-7645-5580-4

- Freemasons For Dummies
  0-7645-9796-5
- French For Dummies
  0-7645-5193-0
- Geometry For Dummies
  0-7645-5324-0
- Organic Chemistry I For Dummies
  0-7645-6902-3
- The SAT I For Dummies
  0-7645-7193-1
- Spanish For Dummies
  0-7645-5194-9
- Statistics For Dummies
  0-7645-5423-9

Get smart @ dummies.com®

- **Find a full list of Dummies titles**
- **Look into loads of FREE on-site articles**
- **Sign up for FREE eTips e-mailed to you weekly**
- **See what other products carry the Dummies name**
- **Shop directly from the Dummies bookstore**
- **Enter to win new prizes every month!**

* Separate Canadian edition also available

† Separate U.K. edition also available

Available wherever books are sold. For more information or to order direct: U.S. customers visit www.dummies.com or call 1-877-762-2974.
U.K. customers visit www.wileyeurope.com or call 0800 243407. Canadian customers visit www.wiley.ca or call 1-800-567-4797.